Reinventing Dance in the 1960s

Everything Was Possible

Edited by

Sally Banes

with the assistance of Andrea Harris

with a Foreword by

Mikhail Baryshnikov

THE UNIVERSITY OF WISCONSIN PRESS

The University of Wisconsin Press
1930 Monroe Street
Madison, Wisconsin 53711

www.wisc.edu/wisconsinpress/

3 Henrietta Street
London WC2E 8LU, England

1   3   5   4   2

Printed in the United States of America

Library of Congress Cataloging-in-Publication Data

Reinventing dance in the 1960s: everything was possible / edited by
Sally Banes; with a foreword by Mikhail Baryshnikov.
p. cm.
Includes bibliographical references and index.
ISBN 0-299-18010-7 (hardcover: alk. paper)
ISBN 0-299-18014-X (pbk.: alk. paper)
1. Modern dance—History. 2. Dance—Anthropological aspects. I. Banes, Sally.
II. Baryshnikov, Mikhail, 1948–

GV1783 .R44 2003
792.8—dc21
2002152195

Contents

Illustrations

Foreword

People who write about experimental dance in the 1960s often stress its conceptual nature, its ideas, but what I liked so much about the choreographers of Judson Dance Theater, and the reason I wanted to do a show with them—the show that became PAST*Forward*—was something completely different, and that was the human immediacy of their work. In Russia dancers are trained as theater artists, almost as dancing actors. I was always interested in this side of performance. In *Giselle*, for example, dancing the role of Albrecht, you are telling a very old story, a vulgar story, even. This is what sitcoms are made of, and life too: people betraying each other, because they want it both ways— safety and romance, Bathilde and Giselle. So in theory it should be easy to make this story compelling, and I have seen a few people succeed. Even though the role was not created with them in mind, they managed to put themselves inside it in a personal way. Still it was them, in a role, in a metaphor. With the Judson dancers, on the other hand, what you saw was not a metaphor. It was *them,* and when it worked, it was you too. Watching them, I was carried across the orchestra pit, so to speak, and deposited at their feet. I was inside their story, whether I wanted to be or not.

But with the Judson artists, it was more than their connection with me. It was their connection with the world, the "street." Really, this is the essence of any dance form. Movement should communicate. It should be inclusive, not distancing, and even the best, most artistic choreographers can come across as distancing, so that spectators say to themselves, "What's that? It's beautiful, but I'm afraid to think that it might be about me." With the Judson dancers, people might say, "Maybe I don't actually like that, but it's about me."

Even apart from their effect on the audience, the Judson choreographers were admirable for their heroic simplicity. As Sally Banes says in her essay in this book, simple actions such as walking became symbolically charged for them, and they made those actions speak. The dances of Yvonne Rainer and Steve Paxton and Trisha Brown captured the stoic quality of the ordinary person, in ordinary times and situations. This is true also of Lucinda Childs's *Carnation*. It may have had a lot of equipment, but the focus was entirely on the ordinary. Such austerity is something we should prize right now, because it is rare. The choreographers of the generation after Judson, however much they were influenced by their predecessors, have turned away from such spareness just as Judson turned away from the theatrical grandeur of Graham, and so, in the last twenty years, simplicity has been in short supply. Once again we have had theatricality: bright lights, makeup, *presentation*. These are starting to wear thin now, and the modesty of the Judson group is once again very appealing.

Then there was their moral courage. I remember, in the early 1980s, seeing David Gordon and Valda Setterfield do their monologues with chairs and frames. This was before I knew them, but by seeing those pieces I felt I knew them already. David's performances, with his sometimes hesitant or even awkward mixing of different roles—he was choreographer, writer, and performer—was fascinating to me. Such a revealing of the self, with all the ambivalences, was utterly arresting to watch.

You see this again, in a different, almost preconscious way, in the improvisers Simone Forti and Deborah Hay. Actually, Deborah says that she is not improvising. As she describes it, she is engaged in a "performative exercise," one that changes every time. She goes onstage and feels what is there—the lights, the sounds, the audience, how close it is, or how far away—and she waits until this triggers something in her and makes her move. But she's not so much interested in the movement as in the motor behind it. The movement might come out beautiful, or strange, or even embarrassing, uncomfortable. But in my opinion it is always interesting. I would say profound as well. To watch it is like standing behind a painter as she paints, when she has stopped making willed decisions, when the imagination has taken over.

So yes, it is true that the Judson people had ideas, sophisticated ideas, but their ideas were not so much a rejection or rebellion, as is generally said about them, as they were a digging into themselves, and into reality. In PAST*Forward*, Yvonne Rainer's *Trio A* was performed several times in succession, differently each time, but finally it was done by seven dancers together, to the Chambers Brothers' "In the Midnight Hour." And here it was fascinating, and also moving, to see how, while doing a fully choreographed dance, each made different choices of space and timing and emphasis. One of them on the right would one minute be in unison with someone on the left, and then slip out of unison, and then slip back again. This cumulative effect of samenesses and differences, as the dancers adjusted to each other, sometimes leading the way, sometimes yielding and waiting, was difficult but satisfying. I felt as though I were looking at the very skin of art, or of theatrical art: the cooperation and the independence, the pride and deference. Of course, what we were seeing there was also very American. It was about pluralism and democracy, or our hope for those things, a hope that's as strong today as it was in the 1960s.

Mikhail Baryshnikov

Introduction

The 1960s was a decade of ferment in the arts, society, and politics. So many things that had been viewed complacently, in a world that seemed always to be the same as it ever was, were suddenly cast in a new light. And this led to a desire to cast off the old ways, to break all the rules, to find new directions and new freedoms. There were no limits, nothing that could not be tried, from rising up to protest injustices like racism, sexism, and the Vietnam War to ingesting mind-expanding drugs to sexual experimentation.

The arts both reflected and participated in pushing the envelope beyond recognition. Artists razed the boundaries among art forms and scaled the barriers between art and life. On the one hand, they invented entirely new genres of art, such as Happenings and Fluxus, and on the other, they created alternative forms of existing arts, such as painting, film, drama, and dance. From Fluxus to Pop Art to underground film to downtown dance, artists of the 1960s celebrated the everyday, and this took on political meaning, serving as a metaphor for radical democratization. In this volume's first essay, "Gulliver's Hamburger: Defamiliarization and the Ordinary in the 1960s Avant-Garde," I analyze various techniques this generation of artists used to defamiliarize and refamiliarize the ordinary in their work, raising questions not only about the political status quo but also about the identity of art.

One example of defamiliarization, or "making things strange," may be seen in the work of Anna Halprin, documented by Janice Ross in "Anna Halprin and the 1960s: Acting in the Gap between the Personal, the Public, and the Political." During that decade, the California-based

Halprin was involved in ritualizing daily life through dance. A progenitor of the Judson generation but a radical experimentalist in her own right, Halprin was, as Ross shows, an active part of West Coast counterculture.

If Halprin was a mother to the Judson Dance Theater, James War-ing, working in New York, was a father. As Leslie Satin observes in "James Waring and the Judson Dance Theater: Influences, Intersec-tions, and Divergences," Waring's eclecticism gave rise (in his protégés) to a postmodern sensibility, but it arose partly from his own involvement in recontextualizing popular entertainment—estranging it, while loving it—in high art dances by using collage methods. In his reframing of popular forms, Waring's work was also related to the emerging Pop Art movement.

The work of Halprin and Waring, along with the more widely recog-nized influence of Merce Cunningham, John Cage, Robert Dunn, and others, gave rise to the explosion of dance innovation by the Judson Dance Theater. A collective that included choreographers with training as visual artists and musicians as well as dancers, the group formed in 1962 and showed work regularly at the Judson Memorial Church, a pro-gressive Protestant congregation in Greenwich Village that also spon-sored the Judson Poets' Theater, Pop Art exhibitions, experimental film screenings, Happenings, and other events.

In "The Philosophy of Art History, Dance, and the 1960s," Noël Carroll discusses the theoretical issues addressed by the Judson Dance Theater, situating them in the broad sweep of art history in general and dance history in particular. He aligns the project of the Judson dancers to install the ordinary in their dances with Andy Warhol's use of the everyday in visual art, showing how these radical acts brought the histo-ries of the two art forms to a climax. Jill Johnston's autobiographical "Dance Quote Unquote" chronicles the upheavals in the arts and culture during the 1960s. The dance critic for the *Village Voice*, New York's most important alternative newspaper, and a champion of avant-garde dance, especially of the Judson dancers, Johnston had graduate training in dance and also wrote visual art criticism. Her reminiscence reani-mates her bold, boundary-breaking actions that turned commentary into performance (and vice versa) and launched a new mode of criticism in the arts.

Of course, not all dance experiments during the 1960s took place at the Judson Dance Theater, though the ones at the Judson were at times the most notorious. Gus Solomons jr's vivid memoir of the period, "Dancing in New York: The 1960s," yields a picture of a variegated dance world in a complex social milieu. From this informal reminiscence we can see that innovation was not hermetically sealed off in Greenwich Village but was brewing at multiple sites around New York and around the country. At that time, Solomons's work engaged incredibly diverse strata of the dance world: in Martha Graham's modern dance company uptown, with Merce Cunningham and the experimentalists downtown, and on the Broadway stage in midtown. Solomons's and other dancers' ability to move among these dance subcultures is connected to the appropriation of popular culture by other avant-garde choreographers, such as Waring, David Gordon, and Yvonne Rainer. Solomons's essay itself defamiliarizes our historical preconceptions about experimental dance in the sixties, including notions that it led a hothouse existence separate from other dance forms and that it was an all-white enterprise.

In "Monk and King: The Sixties Kids," Deborah Jowitt examines the work of Meredith Monk and Kenneth King, often called second-generation Judson choreographers. She considers their connections to contemporaneous developments in art and film as well as their use of alternative performing spaces. She argues that they expanded on certain ideas and methods inherited from the earlier Judson artists, founding a new form of dance theater, and that they carried on the Judson spirit of a collaborative community working in an atmosphere of artistic freedom. Wendy Perron, a "third-generation" postmodern choreographer as well as a historian of the Judson Dance Theater, writes in "One Route from Ballet to Postmodern" about her own experiences of moving from ballet to modern dance to postmodern, post-Judson dance in the 1960s and 1970s.

Stephanie Jordan's "Radical Discoveries: Pioneering Postmodern Dance in Britain" considers parallel developments in British dance. Influenced in part by American innovations but also reacting against mainstream British dance institutions and enlivened by developments in the other arts in Britain, what Jordan calls postmodern countermovements blossomed even under the very auspices of such major modern dance institutions as the London School of Contemporary Dance from the late 1960s to the mid-1970s. Jordan's article calls to our attention the fact that the United States was not the only place where experimental dance evolved in the 1960s.

The volume continues with an interview Joan Acocella and I conducted with Arlene Croce about the founding and early life of the dance journal *Ballet Review*. Our interview with Croce is meant to recall the famous group interview, led by Croce and published in *Ballet Review*, that gave many of us our first entry into the history of the Judson Dance Theater. The title *Ballet Review* hardly gives one a sense of how heterodox and wide-ranging the journal was in its early years. Run on a shoestring, for only a small circle of subscribers at first, *Ballet Review* covered the entire dance field, from the New York City Ballet and visits by the Royal and Bolshoi Ballets to modern dance to Fred Astaire films to the downtown dance avant-garde; its writers experimented with styles and formats of writing about dance. Thus Croce's interview, like Solomons's memoir, provides a view of the artistic diversity of the dance world of the 1960s as well as a partial history of dance criticism of the era.

Finally, this book comes full circle with the final section, which reproduces the choreographers' statements from the recent White Oak PAST*Forward* project. Organized by Mikhail Baryshnikov (the virtuoso ballet dancer who in 1990 cofounded, with Mark Morris, the White Oak Dance Project, a modern dance repertory company) together with choreographer David Gordon, PAST*Forward* presents reconstructions of dances from the 1960s and new works by several choreographers—Trisha Brown, Lucinda Childs, Simone Forti, David Gordon, Deborah Hay, Steve Paxton, and Yvonne Rainer, several of whom were members of the Judson Dance Theater. Ironically, as Rainer points out in her statement, through PAST*Forward*'s touring program many more people will now see these dances—which have had such an impact on the history of contemporary dance—than ever saw them in the 1960s.

The present volume, like the early *Ballet Review*, experiments with different formats and styles of writing. It is not meant to be comprehensive. Rather, it offers glimpses of the myriad activities and authors of a richly inventive period, showing both how the dance experiments of the 1960s were linked to earlier avant-gardes and how, by constantly changing over the course of the decade, they seemed (and seem) endlessly to make things new.

Sally Banes

Reinventing Dance
in the 1960s

1

Gulliver's Hamburger

Defamiliarization and the Ordinary in the 1960s Avant-Garde

Sally Banes

In 1979, the choreographer/filmmaker Yvonne Rainer recalled that in the 1960s, "people said of me, 'She walks as though she's in the street!'" Dance audiences found her casual pace unnerving, Rainer explained, because at that time, "if you walked as a dancer, you walked as though you were a queen, an aristocrat, a character—someone who was *more* than ordinary, more than human."[1]

One of the most shocking aspects of avant-garde art in the 1960s was its conspicuous use of ordinary gestures, actions, rhythms, and objects. Artists combed their hair, shaved, played cards, shook hands, jogged, folded newspapers, coughed, took showers, and got dressed; they created telephones, sandwiches, ice cream bars, Brillo boxes, and soup cans, or they incorporated household objects in their paintings and performances—and they called it art. To critics of the avant-garde, this radical blurring of the boundaries between art and everyday life, this arrant celebration of the banal, signaled a vulgar lack of taste and the utter disintegration of art, perhaps even its disappearance.

To us in the new millennium, scrutinizing the ordinary might seem like a boring proposition. But in its time this fascination with the mundane was often shocking. It was also central to the avant-garde project of this period. Although different artists had diverse reasons for emphasizing the prosaic, ranging from the political to the spiritual to the aesthetic, that they shared this focus was a striking, unifying factor. Still, it is helpful to keep this variety in mind while analyzing the 1960s avant-garde emphasis on the ordinary, for not every use of the commonplace had the same function, meaning, or effect.

The Concept of Defamiliarization

In thinking about the appreciation of, or perhaps obsession with, the mundane in 1960s avant-garde dance and the other arts—the urge to deflate the pomposity of recent high art and at the same time to renew art by training its sights on what had in the past been considered unimportant or inappropriate material and subject matter—I have found useful an expanded notion of the Russian Formalist concept of defamiliarization (or "making things strange"), as outlined by Victor Shklovsky in his essay "Art as Technique."[2]

Although Shklovsky's essay, originally written in 1917, did not appear in English until 1965, his influence had long been felt in the West, and in many indirect ways his ideas were tied to the arts of the 1960s. In the 1920s in Europe, his ideas about defamiliarization had been applied to montage in film by his friend Sergei Eisenstein and to the epic theater, especially in the idea of the *Verfremdungseffekt* (alienation effect), by his acquaintance Bertolt Brecht, both of whose theories and artworks were well known to (and extremely potent for) American artists and critics in the sixties. Avant-garde artists and critics in the sixties may not have been directly familiar with Shklovsky's writings, even after 1965, but his ideas had already entered the vocabulary of the avant-garde and were widely available in the intellectual milieu of the American sixties. Shklovsky's ideas (indeed, his actual rhetoric) resonate not only with much of John Cage's thought but also with that of filmmaker Stan Brakhage, as well as with Susan Sontag's notions of literary criticism. Certainly Sontag, who wrote about many of these artworks in terms of defamiliarization, was familiar both with Brecht's *Verfremdungseffekt* and with French Structuralism, a movement closely related to (indeed, descended from) Russian Formalism.

According to Shklovsky, defamiliarization (*ostranenie*) is a strategy writers have long used for reinvigorating perception. In everyday life we become automatized, inured not only to the qualities of the objects around us but even our to own actions. The problem is that "after we see an object several times, we begin to recognize it. The object is in front of us and we know about it, but we do not see it." And this numbing automatism has a political as well as a moral effect on people. "Life is reckoned as nothing. Habitualization devours works, clothes, furniture, one's wife, and the fear of war." For Shklovsky the purpose of art is to smash that "algebrization"; to infuse life with consciousness; to "recover the sensation of life . . . [to] feel things, to make the stone *stony*." Shklovsky analyzes how by using various devices—retardation, euphemism, recontextualization, giganticization, episodic structure, all sorts of formal difficulties, and what he calls "baring the device"—the artist prolongs perception and restores sight, which had been dimmed by knowledge.[3]

It seems to me that, expanding on Shklovsky, the term "defamiliarization" can encompass two sides of a single coin: making familiar things strange and making strange things familiar.[4] Further, although Shklovsky was vague on this point, I argue that these operations either may be contained within the experience of the artwork itself or may be intended to carry over into other experiences in everyday life as well. So, in my view, there are at least four categories involved in an analysis of defamiliarization techniques in the avant-garde art of the 1960s: making familiar things strange *inside* the work; making familiar things strange *outside* the work; making strange things familiar *inside* the work; and making strange things familiar *outside* the work. Let us explore each of these cases in turn.

Making Familiar Things Strange

Robert Whitman's Happenings, such as *Water*, seem to be involved in making the familiar strange *inside* the work.[5] Like the surrealists, Whitman juxtaposed objects, textures, and actions that by themselves might seem mundane but which in combination (in the process of recontextualization) took on mysterious, sensuous properties. *Water*, a multimedia performance that took place in a temporary structure on a driveway in Los Angeles, involved a great deal of water and many washing activities. Taking a shower and shaving are the most daily events; hoses, inner tubes, and buckets are the most ordinary objects. Yet in the ways they were put together, in particular their rhythms and rhymes, they became unfamiliar: strangely evocative, poetic, and dreamlike, mixing human bodies and objects in a surrealistic manner.[6]

Similarly, in Judith Dunn's dance *Acapulco*—a collage of common-place activities including a woman ironing a dress, two women playing cards, and a woman combing another woman's hair—the use of slow motion in parts of the piece transformed these banal events into dance movement. Here the device of retardation served to "make things strange."[7] In both *Water* and *Acapulco*, the defamiliarization process aestheticizes the ordinary. That is, the everyday is removed from its standard context and is framed and reworked by the artist in order that the audience comes to appreciate not only certain usually overlooked surface qualities of the ordinary (the sounds of water, the movement in the act of combing the hair) but also its latent significance (as she approaches the seated woman in slow motion, the woman with the comb suddenly seems threatening, and her comb seems to become a weapon).

In much the same way, two dances—Carolee Schneemann's *Newspaper Event* and Elaine Summers's *The Daily Wake* —"discovered" the potential of that mundane object, the newspaper, through recontextualization. Schneemann's event began with the dancers carrying in cartons of newspapers, which they unfolded, threw in thick cascades, and also used to build sculpture or costumes, while Summers's dance used images from newspaper photos (the twist, swimming, an umpire, soldiers, a handshake, Rockefeller, a bride, graduation, and a Pantino advertisement) as well as a floor pattern based on a newspaper layout.[8]

Steve Paxton's *Flat* used an episodic structure to defamiliarize the everyday action of getting undressed. In this dance, Paxton repeatedly walked in a circle, removed his shoes, jacket, shirt, and pants, and hung his clothing on hooks taped to his body. All these actions were interrupted by freezes, as well as by Paxton's assuming emblematic masculine poses taken from sports and classical sculpture. The dance is organized by segment rather than by rhythmic phrase. Moreover, Paxton introduced another method of defamiliarization when he juxtaposed iconic gestures from everyday life against iconic gestures from earlier art conventions.[9]

Different from these uses of the ordinary but still involved in the operation of making the familiar strange was the giganticization of objects favored by Claes Oldenburg. In his sculptures, Oldenburg took a decidedly comic/erotic turn not only by changing the scale of objects but also by changing their texture. For instance, his *Giant Hamburger*, made of colorful painted sailcloth and stuffed with foam, measures fifty-two inches high and eighty-four inches wide. It is not only huge, but its wrinkles and swollen parts are surprisingly anthropomorphic. The red meat protruding from the bun is reminiscent of a tongue lolling between two lips, and it hints at other body parts as well. As Sidra Stich points out, "[Oldenburg's] imagery goes beyond the sensually appetizing to the sexually provocative."[10] Oldenburg's oversized, sometimes shiny objects bulged and sagged, and they were often soft and stiff at the same time. They seemed to make not only themselves but also the human body they so uncannily resembled grotesquely alien, very much in the manner of Swift's story of Gulliver's encounter with the Brobdingnagians, the giants whose bodies Gulliver has an opportunity to examine in microscopic detail.[11]

In another variation of this category, Stan Brakhage's film *Dog Star Man* is not comic but rather cosmic. Brakhage turns the simple act of a man (himself, in fact) climbing a hill with his dog and chopping down a tree into an act of epic magnitude. Through the use of various visual obstacles and elaborations, or what Shklovsky calls "formal difficulties"—not only the repetitions and juxtapositions of montage but also superimpositions, shots using filters and distorting lenses, slow and fast motion, and various means of distressing the film itself (with paint or scratches)—Brakhage transmutes the image of a bearded filmmaker tramping through the Colorado woods into a figure of a titan enacting a cosmogonic battle with nature itself.[12]

George Segal's sculptures are shockingly realistic life-sized images of ordinary people engaged in daily tasks, at work and at home. They seem to represent the most common people in the most banal places. In fact, at first glance they are so lifelike that they barely seem to be representations at all—except that the figures are a ghostly white. In *Cinema* (1963), a man reaches up to put plastic lettering on a back-lit movie marquee. *Gas Station* (1964), a twenty-four-foot-long portrait of two mechanics, is complete with Coke machine, Bulova clock, tires, and cans of motor oil behind plate-glass windows. The people are, as well, made of the most mundane materials—chicken wire and plaster—and cast from life. And the sculptures incorporate real objects as part of the figures' environment. The defamiliarization is located in the contrast between the reality of the objects, in living color, and the ghostly plaster of the figures.

Commenting on *The Butcher Shop* (1965), a piece made in memory of his father, a kosher butcher, Segal noted that the laws of kashruth permeated the everyday life of all Orthodox Jews with ritual: "The Jews are famous for drenching most acts of daily life with inordinate weight."[13] This suggests an early source for his own fascination with dailiness. But Segal's pieces are very much of their time in the particular way he explores the commonplace. For his realism, unlike that of the socialist realist–influenced generation of the 1930s, not only copies life but also incorporates actual fragments of it. That is, he combined techniques formerly associated with abstraction (the cubist and dadaist collages were anything but realistic) with an almost obsessive sense of verisimilitude. And further, he portrayed his subjects with a clinical eye, not suffusing them with the aura of nobility one finds, for instance, in the workers in Works Progress Administration murals.

Like Brakhage, Segal peopled his artworks with his family and friends. He was his own model for the first piece he made that used bandages for live casting, *Man at a Table* (1961).[14] And while his technique of surrounding the ghostly impression of a human body with real objects was clearly an act of making familiar things strange, at the same time he relates that he saw, in the process of casting his quite commonplace models, something extraordinary: a new and surprising notion of beauty and grace, which, I would argue, was itself a product of defamiliarization. "When I started casting people," Segal writes, "I discovered that ordinary human beings with no great pretensions of being handsome were somehow singing and beautiful in their rhythms. . . . I discovered that I had to totally respect the entity of a specific human being, and it's a whole other set of insights, a whole other set of attitudes. It's a different idea of beauty and it has to do with the gift of life, the gift of consciousness, the gift of a mental life."[15]

To return to a dance example, in Yvonne Rainer's *We Shall Run*, one of the most mundane human movements, a prosaic, low-key, steady jog, assumed a quiet heroism. This sense of heroism arose not because the movements themselves were virtuosic, for they were deliberately mundane, in fact anti-virtuosic. Rather, this feeling accumulated partly through an image of collective human endurance the dance created as the group of twelve men and women, both dancers and nondancers, dressed in street clothing, maintained its inexorable pace. Breaking up into smaller groups and recoalescing into the whole over the course of seven minutes, the group shifted leaders as it shifted directions to follow various floor patterns. It seemed to project an ideal democracy based in shared daily work, repetitive but pure and human. And this modest grace was underscored by the musical accompaniment, the "Tuba Mirum" section of Berlioz's *Requiem.* Rainer had hoped the repetitive movement would create "an ironic interplay with the virtuosity and the flamboyance of the music."[16] The irony the dance produced was the defamiliarization of human movement normally taken for granted and its transformation into a "heroism of ordinary people."[17]

While Andy Warhol's Brillo boxes also contain the banal within the experience of the artwork, their defamiliarization has a different effect from that of the works discussed above.[18] That is, we are not meant to go back to the supermarket with a refreshed sense of the boxes there as artworks but rather to notice how a Brillo box, or the replica of one, has become an artwork in the gallery itself. Philosopher Arthur Danto has pointed out that "Warhol's [objects] were chosen for their absolute familiarity and semiotic potency. It was not merely that Brillo pads were part of every household, as the Campbell's Soup can was part of every kitchen . . . but beyond that, the cardboard container was ubiquitous, disposable, and part of Americans' itinerant mode of life. . . . It was what everyone threw away."[19]

In this respect, Warhol availed himself of the very simple technique of defamiliarization that Shklovsky also attributes to Pushkin and to the Soviet "peasant poets" of the 1920s: the utter difficulty in reception caused when prosaic (or vernacular) diction replaces poetic language— what Shklovsky calls "roughened form." In this case, poetry (and visual art) is paradoxically made more difficult through transgressing artistic convention by means of utter simplicity.

Simone Forti operated similarly in her early dances, such as *See-Saw* and *Rollers,* created from actions derived from children's play and games, specifically by presenting them at a visual art venue, the Reuben Gallery. Her "5 dance constructions + some other things" (including *Slant Board* and *Huddle*), performed in a lower Manhattan loft, also created the atmosphere of an art gallery, for the spectators walked around the ongoing "dance constructions" rather than viewing them as a seated audience in a theatrical setting.[20] Not only did Forti make "familiar things strange" by reframing children's play as art objects, much as Warhol reframed the soup can, she likewise appropriated it for the gallery.

Perhaps the most striking example of making the familiar strange

was Lucinda Childs's *Street Dance,* created for an audience inside a
building that looked out the window to see Childs and another performer at times pointing out architectural details of buildings on the street
and at times blending in with activity on the street, while a tape instructed the viewers where to look and described the signs and orna-
ments in more detail.[21] Through recontextualization—the act of reframing vision—Childs called attention to what is usually ignored but also
suggested that the environment is part of the dance.

Art Reinvigorates Life

Danto's insistence that Warhol's work must be seen in the context
of art history as well as cultural history locates the defamiliarization of
the mundane object in the gallery—that is, in the art experience itself.
Yet Warhol himself suggested that his own attitude toward Pop Art was
that it trained one to return to life itself with a new appreciation for the
familiar. This is category number two of our four operations: making
the familiar strange *outside* the artwork, in daily life. Describing his
trip to California with Gerard Malanga, Wynn Chamberlain, and Taylor
Mead in the fall of 1963, for an opening of Warhol's Liz and Elvis paintings at the Ferus Gallery in Los Angeles, Warhol remembered: "The
farther West we drove, the more Pop everything looked on the high-
ways. Suddenly we all felt like insiders because even though Pop was
everywhere—that was the thing about it, most people still took it for
granted, whereas we were dazzled by it—to us, it was the new Art. Once
you 'got' Pop, you could never see a sign the same way again. And once
you thought Pop, you could never see America the same way again."[22]

It was on this trip to the West Coast that Warhol also saw the Marcel
Duchamp retrospective in Pasadena. So perhaps it is not surprising that
in his fantasy that Pop Art has appropriated all of life, Warhol seems to
echo composer John Cage's observation about Duchamp: "Therefore,
everything seen—every object, that is, plus the process of looking at
it—is a Duchamp. . . . Say it's not a Duchamp. Turn it over and it is."[23]

Children of Cage, the Happenings makers such as Al Hansen and
some members of Fluxus concerned not only to make room in
art for sounds and actions previously overlooked and discriminated
against but also to return their spectators and themselves to life itself
with ears, eyes, and consciousness newly attuned to humble details. "We

get as much as we are tuned up to receive," Hansen explained. "Perhaps in my happenings I am trying to tune people up."

Many things happen in real life that are quite like a happening. The events and traumas of the average shipping room during the rush season often present the quality of happenings. A leftist student meeting in Union Square, any transportation terminal—air, sea, rail or bus—all have this happening feeling. Many people have told me that, after leaving a happening in my loft, the happening seemed to follow them home. An altercation between two cab drivers, a person knocking a jug of wine that had been on the windowsill out into the street, a woman screaming for her children, a bum standing talking to the moon on a street corner, fire engines going by . . .[24]

This new consciousness, Hansen claimed, came not only from integrating segments of ordinary life, unaltered, into Happenings but also from noticing how life was structured much like a Happening.[25]

Fluxus performances gave ample opportunities for any spectators who desired it to "take the performance home with them." For one thing, you didn't have to be a trained musician or dancer to perform them properly. For another, the material for many of the pieces could be found in any household. For instance, George Brecht wrote the following instructions for his *Three Aqueous Events:*

- ice
- water
- steam[26]

This is a score open to multiple interpretations for "correct" performance. It opens up the imagination, making the performer as much a creator as the author. But more importantly, it requires very little in the way of materials; ice, water, and steam, the three basic variations on a single common element, are cheap and easy to come by. Moreover, *Three Aqueous Events* can not only be performed by anyone, it can be done as easily (if not more easily) in a kitchen as on a stage. And by simply naming these three forms of water without specifying how the states should be achieved, what agent should perform them, or how long the events should take, Brecht left open the possibility that natural processes and even the passing of the seasons could qualify as a correct performance of the score. He seemed to appropriate and reframe all of nature as an artwork.

Ray Johnson's mail art pieces—collages or instructions for performances sent to friends and strangers through the U.S. Post Office—
were perhaps the epitome of reinserting the defamiliarized quotidian
act back into everyday life. Open a letter, but you haven't received a
letter; you've received an artwork.

Perhaps Steve Paxton's dance *Afternoon* worked in much the same
way. Although the dance phrases involved technical—rather than pedestrian—movements, they were performed outdoors in a glade in a
New Jersey forest (spectators were transported there from New York
City by bus). Several trees as well as the five adult dancers and one
performing child were costumed.[27] The use of the natural setting was
an even further break from the usual proscenium theater that had already been challenged by the Judson Dance Theater's use of a church
sanctuary and a roller-skating rink. Dance critic Jill Johnston wrote that
she enjoyed "the unexpected entrances, the nonchalant disappearances,
and not knowing or caring too much where to look when something was
going on in more distant places."[28] Transplanting dance to a natural setting is another aspect of recontextualization that carries over into life
itself, this time by reinvigorating the ordinary, familiar landscape by in-
fusing it with art.

Making Strange Things Familiar

Using the mundane in artworks is already the first step toward making it strange (that is, making it art automatically removes it from the
realm of the commonplace); later steps might or might not include devices, referred to above, such as giganticization, retardation, episodic
structure, and so on. Other artworks, however, seem to have been involved in an entirely opposite operation, the *re*familiarization aspect of
defamiliarization: making the strange familiar, either in the work itself
or extending outside the work back into life. In other words, by "baring
the devices," or showing their own seams and process of construction,
these works showed how the aura of culture could be dissipated—how
art could be secularized, so to speak, brought down to earth and made
part of daily life.

Referring to the audience's participation in his Happening/environ-
ment *Words,* Allan Kaprow explained that the activities—in which the
spectators composed their own poems, stapling pieces of paper with

verbal fragments on the walls of the Smolin Gallery from floor to ceiling, and listened to records they were invited to play on portable record players—were "analogous to some in which we might normally engage—doodling, playing anagrams or scrabble, searching for just the right word to express a thought, climbing a ladder to hang a picture on the wall, listening to music, leaving a note for someone."[29] Here we can see how Kaprow—in the days when he still allowed for the presence of an audience—hoped to demystify his artwork by showing the audience how much like daily life it actually was, despite its location in a gallery.

Similarly, when Ruth Emerson used banal actions in her dance *Cerebris and 2*—among the movements included in a gamut to be ordered by spontaneous determination were "yawn, slap ass, scratch, fluff hair, laugh, talk, cough"—she was not only making ordinary actions such as scratching unfamiliar; she was also bringing something unfamiliar (choreography) down to earth, showing how it can be composed not only of abstract or esoteric movements but also of the most familiar bodily events.[30] That is, she demystified choreography by baring the device.

Yvonne Rainer titled a solo *Ordinary Dance*. She included in it not only a spoken, poetic autobiography but also movement images based on fairy tales and "fragments of observed behavior. . . . —a ballerina demonstrating classical movements, a woman hallucinating on the subway."[31] Rainer laid bare her devices when she interrupted her story to speak directly to the audience about the difficulty of dancing and talking simultaneously: "1941–42. The story gets denser around here. 1-2-3-4-5. MacDonald, Barrett, Myers, King, Myers, McCarthy, Kermoian, Pepina. 5-6-7-8-9. I'm not going to be able to talk for awhile." Her frank admission during the performance that talking while dancing is difficult was another way of demystifying art.[32]

Three other important dances from this period show, in different ways, the interest choreographers took in baring the device. David Gordon's *Random Breakfast* parodied "the Judson Church Dance Factory Gold Rush in which choreography ran rampant," as well as "other show business manifestations," including an elegant, witty striptease by Valda Setterfield, an imitation of Milton Berle doing a Spanish dance in drag, and a salute to Judy Garland. "Prefabricated Dance," the commentary on Gordon's own choreographer-colleagues, involved improvised instructions on how to make a successful modern dance.[33] In her solo *Break*, Meredith Monk left the stage and stood in the auditorium, looking at the empty space her exit had created and thus calling attention to its making.[34]

Art, however, is not the only element in the category of "the strange." In his homespun puppet show spectacles, Peter Schumann of the Bread and Puppet Theater wanted to show not only theater itself as something simple and direct but also how a sense of the holy inheres in life's smallest, most commonplace things. In his *Christmas Story*, for instance, the story of the Nativity was shown with puppets of different sizes, a tin drum, hand-clapping, and a paper-scroll "cranky" (a low-technology filmstrip) about the birth of Christ.[35] But even in the Bread and Puppet works that were not directly illustrations of biblical stories—such as *One Story about Everybody, Starting with Breakfast*, or *The Story of the World*—there was a sacral element rooted in the use of the mundane. As Stefan Brecht put it, "This theatre presents with simple gestures the simple gestures of simple people. . . . The simple & innocent individual images the innocence & simplicity of the sacred: 'Whosoever shall not receive the kingdom of God as a little child, he shall not enter therein' (Mark 10:15). . . . The ideals of Schumann's theatre are plain living (moderation & voluntary poverty) & resistance. They are stylistic & operating principles as well as themes & message."[36] In these examples, art and God are demystified, made comprehensible—domesticated, so to speak—within the artwork itself.

Life Domesticates Art

There were also artists who sought a broader function of this side of defamiliarization, who wanted to make the strange familiar *outside* the artwork, as part of life itself. Into this category would fall the insistence—by Stan Brakhage and Jonas Mekas, especially—that filmmaking can move from the world of art into everyday life. With the spread of 8-millimeter home movie equipment, film technology was for the first time inexpensive and lightweight enough that almost anyone could afford the mechanical means to become a filmmaker. Furthermore, potential audiences would, it seemed, be able to buy 8-millimeter films for home viewing the way they did records for home listening (and the way they buy videotapes in more recent decades).

Brakhage had been documenting his domestic life, including films of the births of his first and third children, since his marriage in 1958. In 1964, after his film equipment was stolen, he began working in the 8-millimeter format himself. According to P. Adams Sitney, this switch had to do not only with the theft and with the prospect of cheaper laboratory costs but also with the hope that his films would reach home distribution and would serve as a model to younger filmmakers who couldn't afford 16-millimeter technology.[37] For Mekas, the use of 8-millimeter film extended even further than a vast, inexpensive distribution system for avant-garde film: it could lead to the folklorization of filmmaking itself. Mekas foresaw the day "when the 8 mm. home-movie footage will be collected and appreciated as beautiful folk art, like songs and the lyric poetry that was created by the people."[38]

In dance, Yvonne Rainer similarly conceived of her *Trio A* as a popular or folk art form. A four-and-a-half-minute series of movements, the piece flattened dance phrasing to an even level of energy, listed discrete movements instead of repeating or varying them, and deliberately obstructed eye contact between performer and spectator. It was the manipulation of energy, Rainer felt, that pumped performers up to superhuman scale. In *Trio A* she sought "an alternative context that allows for a more matter-of-fact, more concrete, more banal quality of physical being in performance, a context wherein people are engaged in actions and movements making a less spectacular demand on the body and in which skill is hard to locate."[39] Thus the piece could be accessible to all, and rather than looking heroic, dancers looked like ordinary people.

Rainer thought the piece was something anyone could take home with them. She writes: "When I first began teaching *Trio A* to anyone who wanted to learn it—skilled, unskilled, professional, fat, old, sick, amateur—and gave tacit permission to anyone who wanted to teach it to teach it, I envisioned myself as a post-modern dance evangelist bringing movement to the masses, watching with Will Rogers–like benignity the slow, inevitable evisceration of my elitist creation." But, she ruefully recalls, "I finally met a *Trio A* I didn't like. It was 5th generation and I couldn't believe my eyes."[40] Nevertheless, even after she stopped choreographing and performing, Rainer continued to practice the piece herself as a home warmup, and she continued, at times, to teach it and to allow others to teach it.

Making the Familiar Familiar: The Disappearance of Art

The transformation of art into something no longer sanctified, com-
modified, or, indeed, in any way separate from the rest of life was a
utopian goal toward which several artists of the 1960s aimed, including
George Maciunas and Allan Kaprow. Maciunas's interest in the ordinary
was politically motivated, but from a different standpoint than that of
many of the other artists of the decade. Maciunas, the founder of Fluxus,
and composer and fellow Fluxus artist Henry Flynt subscribed to an
early Soviet-inspired belief, in tune both with the short-lived Proletcult
organization and with some notions of constructivism, that art as a spe-
cialized activity and the role of the artist as a separate profession were
bourgeois notions; that in a proletarian, socialist society art is an everyday, commonplace activity in that all people can make art and in that
it is not separate from daily life. In a sense, Maciunas's attitude creates
a fifth category for defamiliarization that extends my fourth category,
above: rather than making the familiar strange or the strange familiar,
Maciunas wished to do away with art altogether, that is, to make the
familiar familiar, so to speak. That is, the familiar in the sense of life
becomes even more familiar by being reframed, not as art, but as a
deautomatized part of life itself.

In fact, much of Fluxus art tends in that nearly indiscernible direction, as if already enacting the idea that once the senses were fully awak-
ened to the familiar in life itself—once defamiliarization actually suc-
ceeded as an ongoing process that circulates completely between art
and life—the defamiliarization stage could be eliminated. This notion
calls to mind John Cage's often repeated maxim that "Before studying
Zen men are men and mountains are mountains. While studying Zen,
things get confused. After studying Zen men are men and mountains
are mountains. No difference except that one is no longer attached."[41]

Kaprow early on did away with audiences, aiming for an art experience that could only be perceived through active participation. More
recently, he has written that his concept of "un-art" liberates the artist
from conventional modernism: "The experimental artist of today is the
un-artist. Not the antiartist but the artist emptied of art. . . . The un-
artist makes no real art but does what I've called lifelike art, art that
reminds us mainly of the rest of our lives." Like Maciunas, Kaprow looks

forward to a time when art as such is no longer a separate category of experience: "As un-art takes a lifelike form and setting, as it begins to function in the world as if it were life, we can speculate that art and all its resonances may one day become unnecessary."[42]

Both Deborah Hay's Circle Dances, created in the late 1960s, and the Contact Improvisation movement, begun by Steve Paxton in the early 1970s, brought aspects of choreographed dance into everyday life. They seem to exist on a blurry border between my fourth and fifth categories. Hay published instructions for how to conduct and do her dances in her book *Moving through the Universe in Bare Feet: Ten Circle Dances for Everybody.*[43] The dances, set to readily available popular music, alternate meditative and exuberant body states, using movements based on principles of tai chi chuan (an ancient Chinese Taoist form of nonviolent martial art). Incorporating only the simplest pedestrian movements, and done in a large group without an audience, the Circle Dances demystify choreography by creating group dance experiences more akin to folk dancing than concert dance. Hay advises her readers to "Bring the dances with you to the lab and the A&P. / Bring 'em on the bus, into the garden, and upstairs. / Take them out walking and take them to bed."[44] Thus even choreographed dancing can reinvigorate every aspect of automatized daily life by taking the form of vernacular dancing.

Contact Improvisation is a duet dance form that draws its movement vocabulary from any number of one-on-one physical experiences, including social dancing, wrestling, lovemaking, and martial arts (especially the Japanese form of aikido). Since 1972, when Paxton developed the form with students at various colleges, Contact Improvisation has entered the daily lives of hundreds of practitioners in the United States, Canada, and Europe. A form of dance that owes its heritage to 1960s and early 1970s values of democracy and participation, it can be performed in theatrical settings, but more often it is done, without spectators, in an informal "jam" situation (as when jazz musicians "jam"). Although Paxton originated the "rules" of the form, it has taken on a life and developed an artistic-social network of its own.[45] Even more than is the case with Hay's Circle Dances, the improvisatory nature of this dance form allows for a demystification of choreography and the transformation of dance from an art form to a practice of everyday life.

Conclusion

The reasons for the 1960s avant-garde's fascination with the prosaic as both subject matter and method are complex and varied, and they were never fully articulated by the artists or critics of the period. Rainer and several of her peers in the Judson Dance Theater and in other arts movements of the early 1960s were interested in expanding the possibilities of artmaking. But many of them had political as well as artistic motivations; they were interested in finding ways of moving (and other human actions and expressions) that would have meaning for the democratic majority, valuing the ordinary lives of ordinary people. This determination stemmed from egalitarian political principles. Thus for Yvonne Rainer, Steve Paxton, and several other choreographers of the time, simple actions such as walking became symbolically charged, revolutionary acts.

The avant-garde artists of the period certainly did not share a single homogeneous ideological stance; some were anarchists, some were socialists, some were communists, some were pacifists, some were liberals. And many were entirely apolitical, both in their art and their lives. But a respect for the commonplace spoke powerfully to a number of different political convictions and fit, as well, with the progressive liberal politics of the Kennedy New Frontier.

Besides political convictions, other ideas and beliefs led to the new emphasis on the everyday. Influenced by John Cage, many artists in this generation were interested in Zen Buddhism, whose precepts included a deep appreciation of the simple, even banal aspects of daily life. (While some of the artists who embraced Zen did so in retreat from political engagement, Zen was often coupled with a political philosophy, such as anarchism, as in the case of both Cage and poet Jackson Mac Low.) Other spiritual or religious commitments, including Quakerism and other forms of Protestantism, as well as some forms of Judaism, also stressed simplicity and the sanctity of everyday actions.

Of course, the criticism in the 1960s that art now imitated life all too closely was nothing new. This reproach had been leveled at modern literature, visual arts, and theater at least since the realist movement of the late nineteenth century, and in certain ways the 1960s generation of artists was involved in rediscovering a latter-day realism for a new technological age of mass culture and mass consumption. But the avant-gardists of the 1960s took the breaking of boundaries between art and life, and between the humble and the elite, to unprecedented, postmodern heights of uncertainty.

In the early 1960s, the avant-garde arts created models and dreams that, however flawed, limited, or ultimately unrealized, joined with radical political forces to help mobilize a mass countercultural movement by the end of the decade. But the utopian, often politically motivated desire to make dance more accessible by installing the ordinary and by demystifying choreographic structure never appealed to mass audiences. It was not postmodern dance but ballet that reaped the largest mass audiences—both live and through film and television—during the dance boom of the 1970s and 1980s. Ironically, it seems that in order to savor the prosaic in art, spectators must already be trained in artistic conventions and other aspects of connoisseurship.

Notes

1. *Beyond the Mainstream,* narr. Alan Titus, prod. Merrill Brockway and Carl Charlson, dir. Merrill Brockway, *Dance in America.* WNET-TV, New York, 21 May 1980.

2. Viktor Shklovskii, "Iskusstvo kak priem," *O teorii prozy* (Moscow, 1929). I have used the English translation from "Art as Technique," in Lee T. Lemon and Marion J. Reis, *Russian Formalist Criticism: Four Essays* (Lincoln: University of Nebraska Press, 1965), 3–24. For a more recent English translation, see Viktor Shklovsky, "Art as Device," in *Theory of Prose,* trans. Benjamin Sher, intro. Gerald L. Bruns (Elmwood Park, Ill.: Dalkey Archive Press, 1990).

3. Shklovsky, "Art as Technique," 12–13. It should be noted that Shklovsky did not refer only to modernist works in analyzing the technique of defamiliarization. Many of his examples come from Tolstoy's novels.

4. Shklovsky took pains to show how his notion of defamiliarization proposed a different function for literature than the theory of the earlier Russian literary critic Alexander Potebnya, for whom art translated the unfamiliar into the realm of the familiar. For Potebnya, art's function was to make the strange familiar. Yet if one sets art and everyday life—poetry and the prosaic, as it were—into opposition, then in his concept of baring the device Shklovsky also seems to suggest that art can be engaged in what one might call "*re*familiarization"—that is, making strange things (like poems or novels, or artworks in general) familiar. Certainly as that concept was translated into theater by the Soviet director Vsevolod Meyerhold and by Brecht, baring the device became a way of demystifying the theater, bringing its hitherto magical techniques down to earth and the spectator's level, for the purpose of making art intelligible, intelligent, accessible, and politically engaged.

5. Because the art of the early 1960s cleared a space for so much of the rich experimentation of the entire decade, most of my examples come from these formative years. And because interdisciplinary ferment was one of the hallmarks of this time, my examples come not only from dance but also from Happenings, Fluxus, Pop Art, and underground film.

6. *Water* was performed on 20 and 21 September 1963 in Westwood, California. It is described in detail, with documentary photographs, in Michael Kirby, *Happenings* (New York: Dutton, 1966), 172–83.

7. *Acapulco* was first performed as part of the Judson Dance Theater Concert #9, Gramercy Arts Theater, 30 July 1963. It is described in Jill Johnston, "The New American Modern Dance," in *The New American Arts*, ed. Richard Kostelanetz (New York: Collier Books, 1967), 184, and in Jill Johnston, "Motorcycle," *Village Voice*, 19 December 1963, 11. It was also described to me by Judith Dunn in my interview with her, Burlington, Vermont, 8 July 1980, and by Beverly Schmidt Blossom in my interview with her, New York City, 6 April 1980.

8. *Newspaper Event* was first performed as part of Judson Dance Theater Concert #3, Judson Memorial Church, 29 January 1963, by Arlene Rothlein, Ruth Emerson, Deborah Hay, Yvonne Rainer, Carol Summers, Elaine Summers, John Worden, and Carolee Schneemann. It is documented in Carolee Schneemann, *More Than Meat Joy* (New Paltz, N.Y.: Documentext, 1979); Jill Johnston, "Judson Concerts #3, #4," *Village Voice*, 28 February 1963; and Allen Hughes, "Dancers Explore Wild New Ideas," *New York Times*, Western Edition, n.d. *The Daily Wake* was first performed as part of Judson Dance Theater Concert #1, Judson Memorial Church, 6 July 1962. According to the program, the performers were Ruth Emerson, Sally Gross, John Herbert McDowell, Rudy Perez, and Carol Scothorn. The music was by Robert Dunn, John Herbert McDowell, Elaine Summers, and Arthur Williams. Elaine Summers described it to me in an interview in New York City, 5 April 1980.

9. *Flat* was first performed in Concert for New Paltz (an event organized by members of the Judson Dance Theater at the State University of New York at New Paltz) on 30 January 1964. I saw Paxton perform a reconstruction of the dance at Bennington College on 18 April 1980. A videotape of that reconstruction is in the archives of the Dance Collection of the New York Public Library for the Performing Arts. I analyze *Flat* in depth in "Vital Signs: Steve Paxton's *Flat* in Perspective," in *A Spectrum of World Dance: Tradition, Transition, and Innovation,* ed. Lynn Ager Wallen and Joan Acocella, CORD Dance Research Annual 16 (New York: CORD, 1987). The essay is reprinted in my *Writing Dancing in the Age of Postmodernism* (Middletown, Conn.: Wesleyan University Press, 1994), 227–39.

10. Sidra Stich, *Made in U.S.A.: An Americanization in Modern Art, the '50s and '60s* (Berkeley: University of California Press, 1987), 79.

11. Fredric Jameson uses the example of Gulliver in *The Prison-House of Language: A Critical Account of Structuralism and Russian Formalism* (Princeton, N.J.: Princeton University Press, 1972), 55–56.

12. See P. Adams Sitney, *Visionary Film: The American Avant-Garde,* 2nd ed. (New York: Oxford University Press, 1979), 173–99.

13. George Segal, "Commentaries on Six Sculptures," in *George Segal: Sculptures* (Minneapolis: Walker Art Center, 1978), 41.

14. "The Silent People," *Newsweek,* 25 October 1965, 107.

15. Barbaralee Diamonstein, "George Segal," in *Inside New York's Art World* (New York: Rizzoli, 1979), 366.

16. Yvonne Rainer, "Rreeppeettiittiioonn iinn mmyy Wwoorrkk," unpublished essay, May 1965, 1.

17. See Jill Johnston, "Judson Concerts #3, #4," *Village Voice*, 28 February 1963, 9.

18. The Brillo boxes were first exhibited at the Stable Gallery, 21 April–9 May 1964.

19. Arthur C. Danto, "Art: Andy Warhol," *Nation*, 3 April 1989, 459. See also Danto, *The Transfiguration of the Commonplace: A Philosophy of Art* (Cambridge: Harvard University Press, 1981), and Danto, *The Philosophical Disenfranchisement of Art* (New York: Columbia University Press, 1986). For an overview of Danto's ideas, see Noël Carroll, "Essence, Expression, and History," in *Danto and His Critics*, ed. Mark Rollins (Oxford: Blackwell, 1994), and for an application of Danto's ideas about Warhol to the Judson Dance Theater, see Carroll's essay in this volume (chapter 4).

20. *See-Saw* and *Rollers* were first performed at the Reuben Gallery in December 1960, sharing the program with Happenings by Jim Dine and Claes Oldenburg. "5 dance constructions + some other things" took place at Yoko Ono's loft at 112 Chambers Street on 26 and 27 May 1961. See Simone Forti, *Handbook in Motion* (Halifax and New York: The Press of the Nova Scotia College of Art and Design and New York University Press, 1974).

21. *Street Dance* was first performed as part of Robert Dunn's composition class, at Dunn's loft on East Broadway, in 1964. He describes it in his unpublished Notes, 30 March 1980, 6–7, which I quote in *Democracy's Body: Judson Dance Theater 1962– 1964* (1980, 1983; reprint, Durham, N.C.: Duke University Press, 1993), 208–9. The piece is documented in Lucinda Childs, "Lucinda Childs: A Portfolio," *Artforum* 11 (February 1973): 52. I discuss the piece in *Terpsichore in Sneakers: Post-Modern Dance*, rev. ed. (Middletown, Conn.: Wesleyan University Press, 1987), 135–36; in that book (146–47) the score for a 1965 performance at Robert Rauschenberg's loft is reprinted from the *Artforum* article.

22. Andy Warhol and Pat Hackett, *POPism: The Warhol '60s* (New York: Harcourt, Brace, Jovanovich, 1980), 39–40.

23. John Cage, "Twenty-six Statements re Duchamp," *A Year from Monday* (Middletown, Conn.: Wesleyan University Press, 1969), 70, 72.

24. Al Hansen, *A Primer of Happenings and Time/Space Art* (New York: Something Else Press, 1965), 87, 34.

25. By the mid-1960s, Happenings maker Allan Kaprow came to believe that there should be no audience for his events, only participants. In this way, he wrote, "by willingly participating in a work . . . people become a real and necessary part of the work." With the presence of an audience, Happenings are nothing more than ordinary theater. But, banishing the passive spectator, "Happenings are an active art, requiring that creation and realization, artwork and appreciator, artwork and life be inseparable" (Kaprow, "Happenings Are Dead: Long Live the Happenings!" *Artforum* 4 [June 1966]: 39. Reprinted in Allan Kaprow, *Essays on the Blurring of Art and Life*, ed. Jeff Kelley [Berkeley: University of California Press, 1993], 64.)

26. Written in the summer of 1961, published in *Water Yam*, a Fluxus edition, 1963, and in Hans Sohm, *Happening and Fluxus* (Cologne: Kölnischer Kunstverein, 1970), n.p. *Three Aqueous Events* was performed on a program of Happenings, Events, and Advanced Musics presented by Al Hansen and the New York Audio-Visual Group for Research and Experimentation in the Fine Arts on 6 April 1963 at Douglass College, Rutgers University, New Brunswick, New Jersey. It was also performed at subsequent

Fluxus and Fluxus-related events, including the Yam Festival's Yamday at the Hardware Poet's Playhouse, 11–12 May 1963.

27. *Afternoon* was performed on 6 October 1963 at 101 Appletree Row, Berkeley Heights, New Jersey, on the grounds of Billy Klüver's house. Klüver, an engineer for Bell Telephone Labs, was an active collaborator with avant-garde artists, including Jean Tinguely, Claes Oldenburg, and Robert Rauschenberg, as well as an organizer of exhibitions and the founder of Experiments in Art and Technology (EAT). More recently, he has written on the history of the French avant-garde of the 1920s.

28. Jill Johnston, "Fall Colors," *Village Voice*, 31 October 1963, 7.

29. Dorothy Gees Seckler, "The Artist in America: The Audience Is His Medium!" *Art in America* 51 (April 1963): 66. *Words* was shown at the Smolin Gallery on 11 and 12 September 1962.

30. Ruth Emerson, Score, *Cerebris and 2*. The dance was originally performed on Judson Dance Theater Concert #6, Judson Memorial Church, 23 June 1963. According to the program, the dancers were Lucinda Childs, Deborah Hay, Arlene Rothlein, Ruth Emerson, and Yvonne Rainer; music was by Malcolm Goldstein.

31. Interview with Yvonne Rainer, New York City, 24 June 1980; Yvonne Rainer, *Work, 1961–73* (Halifax and New York: Press of the Nova Scotia College of Art and Design and New York University Press, 1974), 288–89; Rainer, unpublished notebook. *Ordinary Dance* was first choreographed during the time of Robert Dunn's composition class, 1960–62, and was first performed as part of the Judson Dance Theater Concert #1. On Dunn's composition class, see my *Democracy's Body*, 1–33.

32. Rainer, *Work*, 288.

33. David Gordon, "It's about Time," *Drama Review* 19, no. 1 (1975; T65): 45–46; Christina Svane, interview with David Gordon, New York City, 28 February 1980, Bennington College Judson Project.

34. See Banes, *Terpsichore in Sneakers*, 151. A reconstruction of *Break* was performed as part of the Megadance program, part of the Serious Fun! Festival at Lincoln Center, New York, 29–30 July 1992.

35. According to Stefan Brecht, in *The Bread and Puppet Theater*, vol. 1 (New York: Methuen, 1988), 107, 433–40, *The Christmas Story* was first performed in 1962 at the Putney School in Vermont and then at the Living Theater (20 and 21 December). *The Christmas Story* was repeated at various locations, including the Judson Memorial Church, Washington Square Methodist Church, the Pocket Theater, the Bridge Theater, the Astor Library, P.S. 122, and other locales, throughout the 1960s, until perhaps 1973. The description given here is taken from Robert Nichols, "Christmas Story, 1962," *Drama Review* 14, no. 3 (1970; T47): 91 (Brecht believes that this is probably a description of the 1963 performance at Spencer Church), and from a description by the Reverend William Glenesk, "Puppets Tell the Christmas Story," *Face to Face*, December 1969, quoted in Brecht, *Bread and Puppet Theater*, 439–40.

36. Stefan Brecht, "Peter Schumann's Bread and Puppet Theatre: Sacral Theatre," *Drama Review* 14, no. 3 (1970; T47): 78, 81.

37. Sitney, *Visionary Film*, 200.

38. Jonas Mekas, "8 mm. Cinema as Folk Art," *Village Voice*, 18 April 1963. Reprinted in Mekas, *Movie Journal: The Rise of the New American Cinema, 1959–1971* (New York: Macmillan, 1972), 83.

39. Yvonne Rainer, "A Quasi Survey of Some 'Minimalist' Tendencies in the Quantitatively Minimal Dance Activity Midst the Plethora, or an Analysis of Trio A," in *Minimal*

Art, ed. Gregory Battcock (New York: Dutton, 1968), 267. Reprinted in Rainer, *Work*, 65.

40. Rainer, *Work*, 77.

41. This statement appears in several places, including "Lecture on Something," in John Cage, *Silence*, 2nd ed. (1961; Cambridge: MIT Press, 1966), 143.

42. Allan Kaprow, "The Meaning of Life," *Artforum* 28 (Summer 1990): 144. Reprinted in Kaprow, *Essays*, 229–30.

43. Deborah Hay and Donna Jean Rogers, *Moving through the Universe in Bare Feet: Ten Circle Dances for Everybody* (1974; reprint, Chicago: Swallow Press, 1975). I analyze the Circle Dances in *Terpsichore in Sneakers*, 119–25.

44. Hay and Rogers, *Moving through the Universe*, 231.

45. See Cynthia Novack, *Sharing the Dance: Contact Improvisation and American Culture* (Madison: University of Wisconsin Press, 1990), and my *Terpsichore in Sneakers*, 64–69, as well as the periodical *Contact Quarterly*.

2

Anna Halprin and the 1960s

Acting in the Gap between the Personal, the Public, and the Political

Janice Ross

In May 1969, *Esquire* magazine published a special section on "The Final Decline and Total Collapse of the American Avant-Garde." The centerpiece of this acerbic look at experimental performance was a two-page photomontage of twelve avant-garde leaders in theater, music, and dance, set against a picture of the main building of the Black Mountain College campus. It was captioned "Xanadu (Class of '52) Revisited."[1] Only two choreographers were included in this lineup of "the twelve who gave their all to free your shackles and blow your mind."[2] The two were Merce Cunningham, who really did spend the summer of 1952 (also 1948 and 1953) teaching at Black Mountain,[3] and Anna Halprin, who never set foot in the place.

Black Mountain College has been called a Shangri-la in the hills of North Carolina. Founded in 1933, the same year Adolph Hitler was appointed chancellor of Germany, the college was to exist for the next twenty-four years as an oasis of creative experimentation and idealism both for artists fleeing Nazism and for the subsequent generation of young Americans who would study with them. This liberal arts college was home to a who's who of the European and American avant-garde: composers, choreographers, painters, architects, designers, and writers, individuals who collectively shaped an entire era of modern art in America.

Two things are interesting about the *Esquire* article, which was written by Eleanore Lester. First, Halprin is the only artist based outside

New York. Second, it is in large part because of this fact that she fits so comfortably in this imaginary "graduating class" of artists who were some of the key generals in the cultural uprisings of the 1960s.

Unlike Cunningham, who by his own admission was rebelling against many of the tenets of Martha Graham's expressionist dance, in which "every movement had a meaning," Halprin initiated her artistic divergence from the New York dance establishment through a geographical separation that eventually grew into an aesthetic one. Working alone in the Bay Area, she found that discovering her own style became a more pressing (and likely more tangible as well) need and was preferable to continuing as a long-distance disciple of her mentor, Doris Humphrey.

By the late 1960s, Halprin was on her way to becoming one of the household names of the American avant-garde. She had, however, been living in the Bay Area since 1945, experimenting in isolation. This separateness may have been a precondition for her radicalness. Partly because she was isolated from mainstream dance issues, which emerged for the most part in New York, she created freely in a way that wedded her work instead to 1960s social issues. This too reflected a certain influence of living in the West, particularly the private, liberal Marin County pocket of the San Francisco Bay Area, where Halprin has resided and worked all of her adult life.

The national notoriety to which the *Esquire* article alluded stemmed in large part from Halprin's use of nudity in one piece, the 1965 *Parades and Changes*. Part of what made this work so shocking for dance (as well as theater) audiences was the way each of the performers was neutral, yet personal and precisely his or her real self rather than a character onstage. For the simple tasks the unisex costumed dancers performed in the dance's various sections—stomping; unrolling sheets of plastic down the aisles, exploring these lengths of plastic with flashlights, and then dragging them up onstage to drape over a scaffold and play as if they were an instrument; talking out loud in the audience; dressing up in layers of clothes from rows laid out for each dancer in a line on the floor; and tearing paper—the emphasis was always on the dancers as ordinary, unglamorized people just doing jobs onstage. They were neither bigger nor grander than life, but life-size, real people whose actions onstage, such as undressing and dressing, rang with the simple honesty of someone unashamedly and untheatrically doing something real. Halprin's dancers removed their clothes with the same matter-of-factness

Paper-tearing section of *Parades and Changes*. Author's private collection.

they would exhibit if undressing at home. This wasn't "danced" undressing but rather undressing presented as dance. In the realm of theater, slicing art this close to life can be very unnerving, and so it was for many observers in America in the 1960s.[4]

On one level, *Parades and Changes* was a simple artistic statement about one's freedom to display one's nude body as a form of honesty rather than sexual allure. But in the era of the Vietnam War, it was also possible to read the dance as a statement of staking a claim to one's body, one's freedom to choose not to risk one's life in a war many did not want to fight. Already in the late 1950s the body was on its way to becoming an important battleground for West Coast artists fighting what they saw as the stifling conservatism of the middle class. Allen Ginsberg's sexually graphic and erotic poem "Howl," published in the collection *Howl and Other Poems* by City Lights in October 1956, was seized by U.S. Customs agents in San Francisco in early 1957, and the publisher, Lawrence Ferlinghetti, and the manager of City Lights Bookstore, Shigeyoshi Murao, were tried, but not convicted, for obscenity.[5] Three years later, comic Lenny Bruce's frank accounts of his body as the locus of sex acts resulted in his 1961, 1962, and 1964 arrests for using obscenities in his San Francisco nightclub act. Both of these events were important cultural backdrops for *Parades and Changes,* and their influence is both complex and recondite. On its culturally most political level, *Parades and Changes* represented a rendering of the artist's right to use her body as an expressive medium. At the same time, on a social level, it asked for a recognition of this body as sentient, knowing, and capable of a special honesty. Long-standing taboos about not speaking of the sexualized body and not questioning society's control over sexual practices were being addressed and challenged in many of the most important West Coast Beat writings of the time.

Parades and Changes was a work that could only have been made in California in the 1960s, because its aesthetic so clearly developed out of this revolutionary West Coast Beat aesthetic. But rather than revealing an understanding of Halprin's unique aesthetic, the *Esquire* article simply refers obliquely to *Parades and Changes,* without identifying it by name; a teasing quote on the article's opening page reads, "Used to be, reader, if a man took off his pants in public you called the police. Now you applaud."[6] Indeed, Halprin and California in the 1960s were cultural models for what many in the political New Left were both applauding and seeking.

In particular, the college town of Berkeley, just across the bay from Halprin's Marin County home and studio, became a symbol, on many fronts, of the social turbulence of the time. From the free speech movement on the University of California at Berkeley campus, to the struggles of the black community and the emergence of the Black Panthers, to the anti–Vietnam War demonstrations at Oakland's Induction Center, to women's consciousness groups and the flowering of hippie culture, the Bay Area in the 1960s showcased the intersecting concerns of politics and life, the New Left, and the new counterculture.

California had long been a land where direct experience was seen as counting more heavily than talk or theory. Along with Halprin, several other artists, such as poet Michael McClure, painter/filmmaker Bruce Conner, and the agitprop San Francisco Mime Troupe, found their goals for a newly democratic art neatly in step with New Left political objectives. Tom Hayden's call in the *Port Huron Statement* for "a reassertion of the personal" is a theme that also comfortably fits within the aesthetic of Halprin's work of this time.[7]

Both cultural and political leaders in the state were concerned with charting a new direction for modern society. While the New Left was aggressively seeking massive social change (the withdrawal of the American armed forces from Vietnam and an end to the draft), cultural activists like Halprin dreamed of effecting more modest cultural changes in the frontiers of the performing arts rather than in American society at large.

Ironically, in some ways it was this wing of the 1960s revolts that was the most enduring, for changing oneself in the context of an art statement turned out to be far easier than changing the war, the draft, and U.S. counterintelligence practices. "The game is no longer to explore and conquer your physical environment, nor to build empires on the face of the earth, but to explore and expand yourself, your institutions and all of human possibilities," *Look* magazine prophetically proclaimed of this era in a special issue in 1966 that was devoted to California.[8] While the tone may have been derisive, the list of where change was meant to happen was quite accurate.

Halprin continued to explore ways of effecting change, oftentimes on what seemed a prosaically personal level, in a variety of settings over the next few years. Indeed, mainstream media of the time didn't know whether to classify her as a prankster or a visionary. The 28 June 1966 issue of *Look*, subtitled "California," featured a photo document of one of Halprin's explorations by depicting three performers from her Dancers' Workshop in a huge cargo net. Halprin's dancers had used this net like a vertical stage in *Exposizione*, a piece commissioned in 1963 for the XXVI Festival Internazionale di Musica Contemporanea at the Venice Opera House in Italy. The caption accompanying the photo reads: "A cargo net in the woods on a damp morning is not an obstacle for Ann Halprin's Dancers' Workshop but a situation to call out feelings. Says Mrs. Halprin, 'Things like this don't need words.'"[9] Halprin shares this page, headlined "The Turned-on People," with Sister Mary Corita, a pacifist printmaking nun from Los Angeles, and Charles Dederich, the founder of Synanon, an aggressive drug addiction treatment center. Clearly, practices like these did need words as far as the editors of *Look* were concerned, and they suggested that a venting of raw emotion was the point and goal of Halprin's dance.

The links among this trio of celebrities are strange; their strongest bond seems to be their iconoclasm and their boldness in defining new, offbeat terrain in their respective arenas: a nun who deals with pro-peace pop art images; a drug rehab director who makes comprehensive changes in people's lives; and Halprin, a "Mrs." whose hippie-attired dance company practices in the woods by scaling a grid of soft ropes.

Yet they all also chip away at the institutions that frame them—a posture typical of the 1960s. For Halprin it was the modern dance establishment and all its rules of representation, theatricality, and illusion that stood for the status quo she had escaped. Meredith Monk and Yvonne Rainer, both of whom traveled west to take Halprin's 1960 summer workshop, remember most the intensity and dynamism of the working atmosphere Halprin generated. It was this climate of permissibility, the notion, as Rainer once said, that "there was ground to be broken and we were standing on it," that both of them took away from the workshop.[10]

Halprin neatly represented the dance equivalent of these sentiments. A native of Winnetka, Illinois, schooled in the Midwest, she was emboldened by being in California, and particularly the Bay Area. In an article in *Dance Magazine* in April 1963, Halprin told Jack Anderson that she happened upon a whole new way of working one day while outside in her California garden: "It happened that I was looking at sunlight on a tree. For no reason at all, and without apparent preparation I became intensely aware of a foghorn in the bay, a red berry at my side, and passing birds overhead. I saw each thing first as a separate element and then as independent elements related in unpredictable ways."[11]

On this very same deck where Halprin made her discovery of the natural order and harmony among independent elements, Merce Cunningham, contemporary dance's master of chance composition, had also performed. In the summer of 1957, Cunningham, on a visit west from New York, had given a lecture-demonstration on Halprin's dance deck in which he outlined his incorporation of independent elements and his use of chance for ordering dance movement.[12] He was to spend the next five decades of his career pursuing the possibilities his outlooks generated, particularly in regard to composition in dance. The point is not so much that influence was running from Cunningham to Halprin but rather that, culturally, boundaries of personal control in both the creative and performing domains of dance were being tested by artists on both sides of the continent. A perception of oneself as a small part of a much larger natural order was starting to emerge in the arts just as it was in politics.

The notion of allowing disparate elements to coexist was to become the model for Halprin's way of collaborating with other artists, composers, visual artists, lighting designers, costumers, and, especially, performers. Like a kinetic equivalent of the snapped lyric line in Bob Dylan's tunes, offering fractured visual and sensory associations, Halprin's dances posited movement situations as patchwork quilt pieces, fragments each with their own little histories sewn together in the context of a performance. Cultural historian Todd Gitlin links this artistic representation with Dylan's firsthand familiarity with being stoned: "So Dylan's cascading lyrics matched the marijuana experience of snapping the normal links, breaking the usual associations, quilting together patterns from rags . . . the everyday had been converted to the extraordinary."[13]

Although she was a generation older than those who came of age in the 1960s, Halprin was in synch with the hippies' drive to "get out of their minds and into their senses."[14] She had in fact come of age as an *artist* in this period. For an artist like Halprin, whose medium is the human body, the translation she was seeking was more complex than simply sitting still and seeing psychedelic images in one's mind. The human body, which customarily had to be made extraordinary in order to become an art medium in dance, was now being made noteworthy by virtue of its physical ordinariness doing task procedure movements. For Halprin the push was rephrased slightly, to "get out of your mind and *into* your *body.*" This reflected her quest to find a new candor in her art, one defined in the balance between the human body as an art medium and the performer as a medium with a personal history, dispositions, and responses.

"I felt totally connected to that spirit of searching and looking," Halprin said, confirming that, like other cultural provocateurs of the time, she shared a drive to find new models for acting in the gap between art and life. Dance, with the human body as its medium, offered the ideal means for doing this. "I think we were looking for ways a new set of values could be established in our culture, values that had to do with how you care about people," Halprin said. "I was concerned with overcoming the stylization of movement which kept me separate from the reality of myself as an artist. For me the concern was always how to get rid of this armor."[15] This sensation of being straitjacketed by conventions, whether they be dance techniques, conservative clothing, or short haircuts and obedient behavior, was another link between artists and political activists of the 1960s. Halprin wanted not only a more personal movement vocabulary (rather than one codified by Martha Graham or Doris Humphrey) but also a less guarded performer, someone willing to move into the risky territory of personal revelation onstage.

For Halprin the starting point of her ideals had been her exposure in the early 1940s to the ideas of Walter Gropius at Harvard. Anna sat in on Gropius's famous series of lectures about his theories of design. The lectures were later collected and published under the title *Total Architecture*. A recent émigré from Nazi Germany, trained as an architect, Gropius was the former director of the internationally renowned art center for experimental design in Weimar, Germany, the Staaliches Bauhaus Weimar, or Bauhaus. Halprin's husband, the pioneering landscape architect Lawrence Halprin, studied architecture under Gropius at Harvard during 1941 and 1942. Anna, although not part of the program, shared her husband's fascination with Gropius's ideas.

Gropius had founded the Bauhaus movement in 1919, inaugurating what turned into one of the most influential artistic and architectural movements of the century. Originating in the socialist thinking of the early Arts and Crafts movement in Europe, the Bauhaus tried to forge an alliance between the practical products of industrial production and craft design. In other words, the emphasis was on negotiating a new relationship between the beautiful and the practical, the aesthetic and the real.

A credo of the Bauhaus movement was "art and technology, a new unity." Gropius readily adapted these ideals to an educational environment, recasting teachers and students as members of a working community who had to become vital participants of the modern world through a well-managed use of a blend of art and technology. Yet he was also adamant that it not be a didactic process but rather a path of personal discovery. "The stimulation received from the teacher was only to help the student find his own bearings."[16] Here was not only a model of teacher-pupil interaction but also an educational sensibility and ideas of community building that Halprin would embrace as the foundation of her own art, her Dancers' Workshop. This sensibility meshed well with the most profound pedagogical method Halprin encountered in her life—that of the Wisconsin dance educator Margaret H'Doubler.

In the four years immediately preceding her introduction to Gropius, Halprin had been the protégée of H'Doubler, the founder and head of the dance program at the University of Wisconsin at Madison. H'Doubler's philosophy of dance was based on having each student discover the simple truths of his or her body, through exercises that might be called structured improvisations today. Instead of repeating set phrases of movement, students were given an anatomical "problem," such as "what happens to the spine in a rollover on the floor?" The "found" dance material generated by the problem then became the basis for a dance.

In this way, Halprin discovered and translated into vital terms for herself some of the same Bauhaus ideals that Cunningham may have encountered during his summers at Black Mountain, where another famous Bauhaus émigré, Josef Albers, was also teaching. The Bauhaus and its focus on the balance between spirit and mind, form and content, informed much of the art experimentation at Black Mountain College in all media. If, as Lester's essay in *Esquire* suggests, this Bauhaus influence was the bedrock of the avant-garde in America, then Halprin indeed shared some of the same aesthetic roots as the Black Mountain crowd.

The Bauhaus credo "form follows function" also had particular appeal for Halprin and the dancers who would follow her. Halprin interpreted this Bauhaus ideal of functionalism quite literally. It suggested a new sensitivity to the inherent nature of an artist's medium, whether it be fabricated steel, plastic, or the human body. In Halprin's work this would come to be interpreted as a new candor about the performer's relationship to the choreography, or as Halprin preferred to call it, the "score" he or she was performing. For Halprin here was a liberating simplicity and practicality that would help lay the groundwork for her own practice and satisfactions. More broadly it would do the same for American postmodernism.

Interestingly, while this Bauhaus influence helped lead Halprin into social activism in the 1960s, it, blended with John Cage's interest in Zen Buddhism, had the opposite effect on Cunningham, who instead developed an aesthetic posture that suggested a cool retreat from personal disclosure and political engagement. But Cunningham and Halprin, each in his or her own way, explored ideas in terms of an efficient focus on movement for its own sake, movement free from concerns of narrative and meaning. Halprin, too, allowed for the controlled use of chance in her work, shaping and editing her dancers' rehearsal discoveries as they played within the parameters of movement invention so that this material was molded into more or less finished work for the stage. For Halprin and Cunningham, chance was a work procedure to be utilized in the *process* of making material and less often as a variable in live performance.

Unlike Cunningham, however, Halprin did allow for inventing one's own movement phrases in performance within the given parameters of her score, or general plan, for each dance. It is this outlook in particular that has resonance for some of the exuberance of New Left politics of the time. "Thrilled by the prospect of change, young people plunged across the frontiers of experience, boldly exploring altered states of consciousness, new types of bodily pleasure, nonhierarchical forms of community," James Miller writes in his history of the American New Left in the 1960s, in a passage that seems equally descriptive of the spirit of Halprin and her dancers. "Like Marx and Nietzsche before them, they dreamed of creating new men and new women, undivided without shame, each one in tune with a unique constellation of animal instincts and creative ideas."[17]

In a dance like Halprin's *Birds of America or Museum without Walls,* in which the only rules governing one section were that a big body and a small body were to explore the dynamics of working together, one senses a coming together of Gropius's outlook on the role of teachers and the New Left's emphasis on individuals' exercise of personal power. In *Parades and Changes* the rehearsal score described the dancers' general tasks in functional terms like "tear paper making long and short sounds," but the precise physical actions to accomplish this were left up to the performer.

On a deeper level in *Parades and Changes,* Halprin, in eschewing tradition, was slicing into the emotions and internal motivations that underlay movement choices. She opened these internal motivations up to the audience, making them as much the focus of a performance as the movement phrases they generated. At times the result was a dance that was more interesting to look at as a process than as a product. The film of an early workshop for *Ceremony of Us,* for example, quickly becomes tedious if viewed strictly as performance, because so little outward performing is going on. Rather, the participants are moving through a series of getting-to-know-oneself-and-each-other exercises, physically supporting each other as, one by one, they fall backward or describe in minute detail the exact look of their partner's skin, hair, and facial features. In some regards the most interesting viewing perspective to take is that of a voyeur, because then one can simply eavesdrop, without any expectation of "content" or "meaning," on the participants interacting with one another.

Although Halprin wasn't at Black Mountain College, she was indeed one of the midwives to the birth of its ideals: of fostering individual voice and an economy of emotion and means in American culture in the 1960s. In fact, had Halprin been at Black Mountain College, Cunningham's model might have eclipsed, or at least significantly influenced, her own, because it wasn't until the mid-1960s that Halprin began creating her fullest realizations of works based on the constellation of animal instincts and creative energies that Gropius's Bauhaus ideals extolled. As it was, Halprin was creating herself as a twentieth-century artist against the geographical background of the West at the same time she was defining herself as a woman, a mother, and a wife. Doing so during the same decade the durability of America's democracy was being tested in the streets and the New Left was aggressively seeking new models of social, sexual, and political interaction provided a fertile backdrop for her own search.

It is only a slight exaggeration to say that if Anna Halprin had not existed as a radical dance-maker in the 1960s, someone would have invented her. But what they wouldn't have known was that the appositeness of Halprin's theater style with its countercultural objectives worked because it evolved out of her own art concerns rather than in response to New Left political agendas. Halprin responded honestly to the same shifting social order to which the New Left activists were responding. Personally, she was also seeking a more just social order, and while this posture chronologically complemented that of the New Left activists, Halprin, who was forty-six in 1966, was a generation older than most 1960s radicals.[18]

Although some of her childhood friends were Red diaper babies,[19] Halprin grew up as a second-generation American in a family of Ukrainian and Lithuanian Jewish émigrés, people who aggressively sought middle-class, bourgeois assimilation rather than socialist politics and the fringe social status that such politics would have granted in America between the two world wars.

The compelling correspondences between the social and political concerns of America in the 1960s—particularly those of California—and Halprin's aesthetic ideals and experimental dance events reveal an artist who was not so much politically as stylistically in tune with her times. Halprin worked on the boundaries of dance as interpersonal exploration, dance as healing, dance as non-elitist entertainment, and dance as education at a time when none of these were mainstream yet all were nascent areas of concern. The resulting hybrid Halprin founded was a form of contemporary ritual for a new democracy. Here the ordinary, "otherness," radicalism, and the educative force of dance were celebrated within the structure of movement as art.

Just as Gitlin observed that rock music of the 1960s showed its distrust of language with its use of nonsense lyrics, Halprin's work in the same decade also rudely snapped narrative continuity. "We can invent a new vocabulary, we can coin our own,"[20] Gitlin interprets rock musicians as saying. With her use of nonsequential situations, Halprin was trying to make a new vocabulary for the body and for performance. As Gitlin notes, the use of the name "The Movement" for 1960s politics reflected its emphasis on direct action.[21] This, too, was precisely the fresh emphasis on action, on gesture not governed by choreographic design, that Halprin was seeking in her dance theater works.

For Halprin, this creation of the new meant a public undoing of the old temporal logic of dance. Her signature works of the 1960s—*Birds of America or Museum without Walls* (1960), *The Four-Legged Stool* (1962), *Parades and Changes* (1965–67), *Apartment 6* (1965), and *Ceremony of Us* (1969)—all involved a challenge to traditional notions about narrative logic and dramatic sequence in performance. While plot is not wholly refuted here (it never is in her work), actions in these dances are discontinuous, and the order starts and stops in a hybridization between the waking dream of surrealism, theater of the absurd, and the fractured logic of Beat literature. In *Parades and Changes*, for example, the dance is composed of seven or eight short movement situations where the dance is almost a by-product of the dancers' fulfilling a designated task—like shredding huge lengths of brown paper and stuffing it into the trapdoor on the floor of the stage. The result is what writer Kenneth Rexroth lauded in *The Five-Legged Stool* as "anti-dance in impeccable taste." He called Halprin an exceptionally good "apostle of alienation," on the order of Beckett or Genet.[22]

As we look back, it is clear that even in the midst of that decade of rebellion and redefinition Halprin stood out as a figurehead, one of a handful of avant-gardists forging new rules for a society in the midst of unrest. In part because of her almost naive focus on her own work, as well as her relative innocence in the face of current politics, Halprin came to be looked to by those *inside* The Movement in the West as one of the most authentic expositors of its issues in *movement*.[23] In fact, had she pointedly tried to be political, her art probably would not have been as affecting. Halprin was a master at incorporating ideas and issues of the moment and using them as performance materials. The ideas and issues didn't necessarily have to be her own.

Norma Leistiko, who performed with Halprin throughout the 1960s, said, "I don't think Anna ever had the slightest sense that Vietnam was even going on. She's the most naive person I ever met. But she was brilliant as a pure art animal. Here we, her dancers and students, were marching and sitting in, trying to ban the bomb, and I don't think she was aware of any of it. We did our own thing and she did hers, but the odd thing was we felt so akin to all these political events through her work. It's almost as if she's so neutral she never creates; she just draws it out of people."[24] Halprin seems not so much apolitical as deeply committed to fashioning art that comes from real moments of personal introspection. To start from a political statement was simply antithetical to her notions of how meaningful art is generated.

In fact, Halprin did create three consciously activist works in the late 1960s and early 1970s, *The Bust* (1969), *Blank Placard Dance* (1970), and *Kadosh* (1970), dances she regards as commentaries on the Vietnam War and its accompanying climate of protest. *The Bust* was actually a film made spontaneously by photographer Paul Ryan of Halprin and her dancers undergoing a real arrest by the San Francisco Tactical Squad. The officers saw Halprin and her dancers, several of whom were dressed in flesh-colored leotards and tights, performing an outdoor dance in what Halprin recalls as "a very agitated manner" on the street outside Halprin's Divisadero Street studio. "The police decided we must be freaking out on drugs and arrested us," Halprin said.

A more stylized protest, created in 1970 and referred to simply as *Blank Placard Dance,* was a response to the arrest filmed in *The Bust.* This danced response featured each performer marching with a huge placard that was completely blank. They did so while staying the requisite ten feet apart so as not to constitute a demonstration. In speaking about this work, Halprin commented, "My idea was that there were so many protests going on and this way each person watching us could just imagine whatever protest slogan they wanted on the placards." Halprin's dance thus became another layer of commentary, a performed comment on those who were commenting on society and government through public demonstrations.

In *Kadosh,* staged at Beth Sinai Temple in Oakland, Halprin and a group of dancers she assembled for the event staged a Friday-night Shabbat candlelight vigil in this Oakland synagogue. Here the performers "confronted" Rabbi Samuel Broude in a rehearsed encounter as they tore their garments and asked the eternal question about the Holocaust, rephrased for the current war: How can there be a God if he allows all the suffering of the Vietnam War to continue?

For Halprin, topicality in dance never meant merely layering a contemporary visual arts decor or sound score or current theme onto generic modern dance movement. Rather, she conceived her events in functionalist terms, where the primary goal was to foster a climate of community and personal reflection among performers as well as with the audience. Hers was a cultural challenge that called for exposing and questioning the assumptions behind accepted ideas about art and about life. In this way, Halprin questioned dance gestures that weren't generated by the performers themselves. This is, in part, a way of making work that Halprin developed collaboratively with her husband, Lawrence. This approach allowed for a general mapping of the intellectual territory in which one worked. The Halprins dubbed this the "RSVP cycle," a process of creating consensus among participants as to the form and efficacy of a public event. This can range from the fashioning of a city park to a dance for a group of African American community actors from Watts. Lawrence Halprin too has long made the designing of his landscape plans for a city a participatory process, incorporating into his designs suggestions from the people who will use the space.

This process of gaining consensus is what gave many of Anna Halprin's signature pieces of the 1960s their appeal and resonance for contemporary youthful audiences. *The Four-Legged Stool, Parades and Changes,* and *Apartment 6* all publicly probed the underpinnings of relationships. In *Apartment 6,* Halprin, John Graham, and A. A. Leath enacted a skewed domestic scene with Halprin as an anxious housewife frantically trying to cook the perfect pancake for her indifferent, newspaper-reading husband, played by Graham. Meanwhile, Leath was going through a self-contained solo. Dressed in baggy pants, shirtless, and walking like a crumpled-over eccentric, he recited poetry to himself and generally remained on the outskirts or backstage, at times doing slow backward falls across the room as Halprin and Graham's banter continued.

Most of the movement here was in the service of a new kind of coarse theatrical reality. Halprin was inventing a choreographic theater of the ordinary, a drama of the prosaic. If it was not just the elected officials but suddenly the man or woman in the street who could ask government to be responsive to his or her needs, then why couldn't art also speak with a new candor stripped of artifice? In Halprin's hands, mundane domestic material and prosaic actions became reduced to task performance, the functional physical gestures one usually performs as part of day-to-day life. The plot in *Apartment 6,* for example, is described by Halprin as being about "of-the-minute relationships." As such it demonstrates how to make onstage choices, to be "authentically in the moment" and to engage in interactions that are in keeping with one's character for that performance.

In 1968 Halprin was invited to perform for the national meeting of the Associated Council of the Arts at the Hilton Hotel in San Francisco. She responded with a work that could have been scripted by Abbie Hoffman or The Diggers, two radical organizers of New Left guerrilla theater. In the center of the hotel banquet room, where the delegates were being served lunch, was a raised platform supporting a table set with white tablecloth, napkins, silver, and dishes, all identical to those on the delegates' lunch tables around the room.

Arranged around this spotlighted and raised table, however, were Halprin's dancers, each posed in a frozen attitude of vacant concentration. Norma Leistiko crouched on top of the table and stared down at the food like a half-wild, half-domesticated animal ruled by hunger and unsure of the proper social decorum in such an environment. Beneath the surface of docility, this was performance with an edge. The table had become a stage, and the commencement of lunch triggered the beginning of the performance.

As the delegates ate, the dancers echoed their actions in excruciatingly slow motion. "It was like watching living sculptures," wrote William Glatkin in his review for the *Sacramento Bee*.[25] Underneath this surface of naive simplicity, *Lunch* resonated with social satire. It was marked by Halprin's slightly acid commentary on the conventions of business luncheons as overdone social rituals, contrasted with people's simple need to take in midday nourishment. Leistiko remembers that the form of the event came about in typical Halprin fashion—Halprin simply analyzed just what the physical act of having lunch involved. She decided this could be reduced to sitting down, picking up a fork, moving it to your mouth, and so forth. "Anna then did variations on this theme, playing with tempi and spacing, and the result was a work that brought the audience to a cheering ovation at its conclusion," Leistiko said.[26]

The establishment, even if it was the arts-administration establishment, was accustomed to being the butt of public jokes by this time, so it was likely in this spirit that they applauded Halprin, fully aware that they were the objects of her satire. Additionally, Halprin's method of working was seemingly innocent of social agendas, allowing her to focus on formal experimentation in her work. She trusted that one's values radiate through one's work and that being overtly political, as in true guerrilla theater of this time, resulted too often in statements that were as weak artistically as they were strong politically.

A few months earlier, in the fall of 1967, two of the most flamboyant antiwar activists, Jerry Rubin and Abbie Hoffman, in a purely political gesture, had created a public event that shared the same spirit of confrontation cloaked in humor that Halprin's *Lunch* demonstrated. Under the guise of responding to an announcement by the Washington, D.C., police that they were ready to use a new stinging, temporarily blinding spray called Mace, Hoffman and Rubin responded by announcing a new drug of their own, Lace.[27] Lace, they said, when squirted onto the skin or clothes, quickly penetrates to the bloodstream, causing the subject to disrobe and get sexually aroused. As Gitlin describes it, "Before bemused reporters, two couples sprayed each other with water pistols full of a fluid actually called, *Schwartz Disappear-O!* imported from Taiwan, which made purple stains and then disappeared. The couples proceeded to tear off their clothes and make love."[28]

Here, as in Halprin's *Lunch*, the object was to illuminate reality by satirizing a business-as-usual practice and holding it up for public scrutiny. In *Lunch* this had meant exposing the hypocrisy of the business lunch, where consuming food is the least significant part of this corporate ritual. Likewise, in Hoffman and Rubin's demonstration, the notion of a new weapon in the chemical warfare of the streets that would cause individuals to make love not war neatly turned the tables on the escalating aggression of the moment. What if we performed art three times a day instead of just eating a meal? What if police sprayed affection instead of discomfort over the crowds of disenfranchised students? A revolution could start here.

It was during the 1960s that Halprin devised a performance structure in which, just as Gitlin noted was true of The Movement, "The counterculture thus devised institutions in which hip collectivity and the cultivation of individual experience could co-habit."[29] In *Birds of America, Parades and Changes, Esposizione, Apartment 6,* and *Ceremony of Us,* each performer was allowed to first find his or her individual voice and manner of dealing with the general instructions Halprin gave, and then to lose him- or herself to the bigger goal of the stage picture. The lighting designer, costumer, and composer then all joined with Halprin in collectively shaping the stage image. In these works one performed oneself, oftentimes in speech as well as movement, rather than subordinating one's identity to a silent choreographic persona devised by Halprin.

Halprin accomplished this by reworking the actual physical vocabulary of her dancers' movements, making them less like dance and more like life. Then, taking another step back, she probed how movement itself was generated by individuals. If one were completely invested in the reality of the moment of performing, what kind of newly honest movement portraits would emerge? This questioning meshed neatly with 1960s political notions of nonviolent direct action and a social emphasis on grassroots democracy that leaned toward spirituality. The answers to the pressing issues of the day, both Halprin and the New Left leaders seemed to be saying, lay in intuiting what was fundamental to social behavior.

In *Ceremony of Us,* a work created in the aftermath of the Watts riots, Halprin used a group of black performers from Studio Watts in the Watts neighborhood of Los Angeles as well as her own white San

Dancers' Workshop and Studio Watts in *Ceremony of Us*. Photo by Bera.

Francisco Dancers' Workshop members. The focus was on building a community among the performers in rehearsal as a metaphor for social rebuilding. To hammer the point home, Halprin made the instructions explicit but not the specific movements of the various sections of the dance. The premiere of *Ceremony of Us* was held at the Mark Taper Forum in Los Angeles, a venue the Watts performers had secured in part because of Halprin's participation and because this event was emblematic of an art-in-the-community, non-elitist spirit the administration of Los Angeles's new performing arts center wanted to promote.

On 2 February 1969, opening night at the Mark Taper, Halprin aggressively confronted the audience, forcing each ticket-buyer who wanted to enter the theater to get to his or her seat by walking through a corridor of either black or white performers. The intention was that each viewer would publicly register consciousness of his or her skin color, his or her social community. Anonymous spectatorship was out. One was forced, at least fleetingly, to regard oneself as a perceiver with a history, a cultural identity, and ethnic origins.

The performance then unfolded as a series of encounters between the two groups of performers. The dancers in a line skittered forward in deep second-position squats like a lurching human centipede and then later paired off, one black and one white, and ritually bathed one another's legs, face, and arms. The whole piece was a physical metaphor for the process of getting to know one another and for the discovery that encountering other people as individuals makes them far less threatening than when one thinks of them only as a part of an intimidating and monolithic social or ethnic group.[30]

A work Halprin did in early 1960, *Birds of America or Museum without Walls*, had marked the beginning of what she referred to as her period of trying to shake loose from habits and trying to find new values. The only section of the dance that now exists on film shows John Graham, a gangly man, six feet, six inches tall, partnering Halprin's slim, preadolescent daughter, Daria, in a chaste yet sensuous duet on Halprin's celebrated outdoor dance deck. Repeatedly, Graham tugs the reclining Daria to standing, pulling her arms as her head hangs limply backward. It is a posture of relaxation so complete that it borders on erotic surrender, an interpretation Halprin at the time seemed unaware of, but one that is impossible to escape when viewing it four decades later. Daria looks like a large doll in Graham's arms, and he manipulates her with a gentle but persistent forcefulness. Remarkable in its single-minded investigation of what a big and little person can do together, both on and off balance, this section of *Birds* is also memorable for its absolute naïveté. There is no deliberate eroticism here, only frank physical facts about performers' sizes and the physical reality of the adjustments one body has to make to lift another.

Halprin's daughter, who currently directs Halprin's Tamalpa Institute (a nonprofit movement center in Kentfield, California), observed the following about her mother: "The sixties were a perfect time for her. That's when her art really blossomed. It wasn't that she was following the sixties—she *was* the sixties! She's always *been* the sixties and she always will be."[31] For the younger Halprin, the correlation she saw between her mother's aesthetic and that decade was the sense of innocence and trust Halprin evidenced in revealing her perception of the human condition onstage. Like the New Left activities in the streets, Halprin's work depended on an inherent faith in less governance, whether in life or in art.

This period was an instance of one of those felicitous correspondences between a moment in society and the arrival of an artist who speaks directly through her work to the social, political, and aesthetic concerns of the time. Halprin's works of the 1960s were in many regards the kinetic equivalent of popular rhetoric played back to an America in a decade of revolt. A work like *Parades and Changes* celebrated the peeling away of layers of social control and pretense. It offered undressed performers and loosely structured moments of encounter between prop-carting dancers as evidence of the real reframed for the viewer as timely art. The individual mattered here far more than the institution.

It hardly mattered that, as Gitlin noted, no one at the time even thought to anticipate how history might soon regard this whole decade. "One can see the late Sixties as a long unraveling, a fresh start, a tragicomic *kulturkampf,* the overdue demolition of a fraudulent consensus, a failed upheaval, an unkept promise, a valiant effort at reforms camouflaged as revolution—and it was all of those."[32] The fact that it would soon be looked at nostalgically as a valiant effort at reforms camouflaged as revolution wasn't part of anyone's raised consciousness. "The Whole World Is Watching" might have been the bravado chant on the street in moments of encounter between protesters and police, but it was the world of the moment, not the world of history, that the New Left, and also Halprin, saw as their true audience.

In terms of her background, Halprin had many similarities with the leaders and activists of the New Left in the early 1960s. Her family profile neatly matches that of New Left leaders like Jerry Rubin and Abbie Hoffman. As cultural historian Barbara Epstein writes: "The activists of the sixties confronted different issues from those that had dominated the thirties, and they brought a different sensibility to political activity. Though many of them were the children of the second-generation immigrants who had been swept up in the movements of the thirties and supported the New Deal, most had grown up thoroughly middle-class, secure in the American identity that had been so problematic for their parents and grandparents."[33]

This profile closely matched that of Halprin. She was, like Rubin and Hoffman, a child of liberal Jewish immigrants, people who had supported the New Deal. Also, as Gitlin notes, young middle-class Jews were behind The Movement because "the fact of affluence and the terror of destruction" were especially important for this group. "There were some, or many, for whom the Holocaust meant that nothing—neither private satisfactions nor the nation's greater glory—could ever supplant the need for public morality."[34] Halprin, in fact, often talks of feeling sick and helpless when, as a girl growing up in Winnetka, she heard reports of Nazi atrocities. This was when her determination to include in her work those without political voices—the young, the minority, the aged, and, most recently, the HIV-positive—began.

The eclectic, improvisational style of Halprin's dance theater was in synch with the quest of moving past established culture. Her art seemed to make manifest many people's view that the enemy was established culture, or civilization itself. "I think the most important thing for me about the sixties was that we were fighting to have a new set of values heard," Halprin said. "We felt human relations were important, they weren't something to be hidden. They were part of nature and it was important that they be up front and honest. Theater should take place in one's life in every way."[35] For Halprin, using improvisation as a means of generating honest interaction in rehearsal was a way to elicit real emotions and thus make difficult interactions the bedrock of her dance theater. Eventually she would bring in therapists like Frederick (Fritz) Perls, Paul Baum, and John Rinn to aid her and her dancers in reaching new emotional reserves in rehearsal.

Ironically, those in The Movement at times seemed to have seen more clearly than Halprin herself, or certainly better than the dance world, the strong links between artistic aspirations like Halprin's and New Left political ideals. Jerry Rubin and Abbie Hoffman's performance of their magical aphrodisiac spray-on chemical that caused couples to disrobe and make love came less than six months after the celebrated April 1967 American premiere of Halprin's *Parades and Changes,* with its infamous introduction of theatrical nudity, at Hunter College in New York.

Halprin's period of rebellion against the established New York dance scene, which she felt in 1960 was still dominated by the expressionist aesthetic of Martha Graham, had really come a decade earlier when she walked out on what she called performances of the "modern dance clones," students of Graham, Humphrey, and Holm.[36]

From that 1955 visit on, Halprin found herself increasingly under the influence of the aesthetic qualities of nature in the West, of the Bay Area's closeness to nature, and of a social atmosphere that celebrated individual differences. By the early 1960s, she wasn't so much reacting against dominant trends in American dance (as some of the Judson Church rebels were doing) as she was in step with those who were re-defining for themselves how to engage the dancer that existed in every-one—performer and viewer alike.

Yvonne Rainer has recalled that when she traveled to California to take a workshop from Halprin in the summer of 1960, she was surprised how up-to-date Halprin was on current developments in the New York performance world, despite the fact that by 1960 Halprin had been working outside the dance center of New York for fifteen years.[37] Since the 1950s her deck in the woods had become a stopping-off point for the avant-garde touring the West. Merce Cunningham and John Cage visited and showed work, while a larger circle of artists, including sculp-tor George Segal, painter and filmmaker Bruce Conner, and musicians La Monte Young, Terry Riley, and Morton Subotnik, among others, were frequent guests for informal salons at the Halprin home.

Halprin also ventured into cultural hot spots in the Bay Area. In 1967 she was billed as a "kinetic catalyst" when she visited the rock ballroom known as the Straight Theatre as a guest choreographer with her dancers and the ad hoc performers. Once, at the invitation of Bill Graham, she also performed with her dancers at his Filmore Audito-rium, where she tried to orchestrate the loose gyrations of the crowd while people moved to the beat of the Charlatans, the Congress of Won-ders, Janis Joplin, and the Grateful Dead.[38] Using her dancers as cata-lysts, Halprin staged an entrance over the auditorium's top balcony so that her dancers literally descended on the dance floor. Illuminated by a pulsating light show, they balanced on one another's shoulders and offered more varied examples of spontaneous physical partnering to the delighted crowd. "I liked working with these large groups of people," Halprin said. "I'd have the men hold women on their shoulders and we'd work toward configurations that formed a sense of community because everyone seemed so isolated and into themselves."

Halprin's statement echoes concerns identical to those of the political activists of the time who were also seeking to build a sense of community and encourage egalitarian values in the disenfranchised. The idea in both arenas seemed to be that if you learned it in your body first, the personal would ultimately expand into the political. For antiwar protesters, the reality of fleeing the Chicago police batons at the 1968 Democratic Convention translated into an understanding of how meaningless the individual's voice had become in the machinery of the state.

For Halprin this would prove to be the artistic territory she would plumb in the future, as her workshops and classes repeatedly stressed focusing on oneself and one's movement proclivities as a first step to being able to interact with others on a meaningful level. In 1969, *Ceremony of Us* marked the beginning of this kind of art by consensus. The idea for Halprin was that if not just the performance but the actual structure of an evening-length work were the project of group decision and interaction, then it stood the best chance of speaking most meaningfully to the performers as well as the audience. This was particularly true of the racial tensions *Ceremony of Us* explored.

While she didn't actively participate in many 1960s political demonstrations, Halprin did at times appear as a guest artist at New Left political events in much the same spirit that she served as a "kinetic catalyst" at rock concerts. One of the most visible of these occasions was in 1966, when Halprin and her Dancers' Workshop dancers were part of a "Whatever It Is" event at San Francisco State University organized by Stewart Brand (who would later found the Whole Earth Catalogue). For this occasion, Halprin brought a thirty-foot-high scaffold, her trademark prop since the 1964 *Procession*. Framed by the pulsing rock music of Jefferson Airplane and the Grateful Dead during this lunchtime gathering, Halprin's dancers hung off the bars of the scaffold, piled atop one another, and freely collided with each other as they scrambled over the scaffold's metal pipes. They performed in the functionalist, tasklike manner that Halprin encouraged to generate movement from props and domestic situations.

A film of *Procession* made several months earlier, during a performance at UCLA, shows the dancers performing a slow, stately, continuous walk, all the while adding flotsam of clothing, hats, lengths of fabric, poles, and props to themselves until they become slow-moving assemblages, ambulatory heaps of rags. "We're not so much dancers as visual artists working with color and form," Halprin said of the work. "The task in *Procession* is to keep moving forward. The way the performer responds to this determines whatever meaningfulness is brought into play."[39]

Just how deeply Halprin embraced 1960s aesthetic, moral, and political values as her own was made apparent by her evolution into a member of the "human potential" movement in the subsequent decades. She was to become a regular workshop leader at the Esalen Institute, a teaching center for Perls's self-actualization techniques, in Big Sur, California. In the end, the major cultural legacy of the 1960s may well have been this impulse to transform society into more than a world governed by political and economic structures and to achieve it by integrating moral values with social ones. As Barbara Epstein has noted, "The attraction to Cultural Revolution, and the idea that culture is a substitute for strategy, has been an important current in the movements of the 1960s and beyond; it has become dominant among left and feminist intellectuals."[40]

In the 1970s, as Halprin became more involved with the human potential movement, so too did many 1960s activists. Rennie Davis discovered the guru Maharaj-Ji, and Students for a Democratic Society (SDS) activist Sharon Jeffrey, from Cleveland, ended up studying self-actualization at Esalen.[41] It's not that these New Leftists had the same plan or even the same goals as Halprin but rather that they shared similar ideals—Halprin as an artist interested in social reform, and the New Left activists as social reformers with theatrical sensibilities. Across the board, loyalty to organizations like SDS was being supplanted by a new loyalty to oneself, one's own goals, and one's immediate community.

One aspect of the 1960s revolt was the redefinition of adulthood and the responsibilities of that role. For Halprin this meant creating a new place for the socially responsive adult in her dance. The great personal hope for Halprin as well as the New Left idealists was that one would be able to live a life of ongoing self-examination, and for Halprin there was no better vehicle than a movement form that demanded physical candor and emotional and mental openness. As New Left historian Richard Flacks observed of this same impulse among the political activists of the time, "What the New Left wants most from life is love . . . to be whole and free, to find peace through overcoming the conflict between ourselves and others."[42]

The 1960s changed Halprin, and she in turn changed the decade by contributing to its cultural identity. From the 1960s Halprin learned how to look at all life as material for art, from the rudimentary task performances of daily life to the individual's search for fulfilling relationships, spiritual meaning, and new social systems. While her work was appropriate for the time, it also was flexible and catholic enough in the topics it embraced to serve as a template through which she would keep pace with social changes through the 1990s. She had evolved a method for making work that promised effective theater if one were honestly invested emotionally, physically, and spiritually—whether the cause be equal rights or AIDS. Anna Halprin couldn't have found any period in contemporary life outside of the 1960s more supportive of her early experiments at shaving the boundary between art and life. She had come of age through the preceding three decades when new relationships among the personal, the public, and the political were being forged in society. It was in part because Halprin's choreographic methods required such intense participation from the real person inside each dancer that there was often a sharp sense of topicality and emotional intensity associated with her works. In political activism this investment—and at the same time revelation—of the self is expected. However, it has always been rarer in the arts, because here the custom is to put on a mask in order to strip away illusion. Halprin showed that the mask too could be stripped away and the gap between the personal and the public could thus be made even narrower.

Notes

1. Eleanore Lester, "The Final Decline and Total Collapse of the American Avant-Garde," *Esquire*, May 1969, 142–51.

2. The other ten were John Cage, Jackson Mac Low, Judith Malina, Julian Beck,

Richard Schechner, Ellen Stewart, Allan Kaprow, Saul Gottlieb, Tom O'Horgan, and Dick Williams.

3. Mary Emma Harris, *The Arts at Black Mountain College* (Cambridge: MIT Press, 1987).

4. Todd Gitlin, *The Sixties: Years of Hope, Days of Rage* (Toronto: Bantam, 1987).

5. L. Phillips, ed., *Beat Culture and the New America, 1950–1965* (New York: Whitney Museum of American Art, 1996).

6. The six minutes of performing this simple task of dressing and undressing so outraged authorities that the New York police were ready to arrest Halprin at the American premiere at Hunter College.

7. James Miller, *Democracy Is in the Streets* (Cambridge: Harvard University Press, 1994).

8. George Leonard, "California: A New Game with New Rules," *Look*, 28 June 1966, 28.

9. The photo was taken with the net stretched between two trees on the Halprins' Kentfield property.

10. Yvonne Rainer and Meredith Monk, interview by Stephen Cobbett Steinberg, November 1991. Unused footage from KQED-TV documentary on Anna and Lawrence Halprin.

11. Jack Anderson, "Manifold Implications," *Dance Magazine*, April 1963, 44.

12. Untitled 1957 document from the personal archives of A. A. Leath, Madison, Wisconsin.

13. Gitlin, *The Sixties*, 203.

14. Ibid., 206.

15. Janice Ross, interview with Anna Halprin, 5 September 1991, Kentfield, California. Unless otherwise noted, all following quotations from Anna Halprin were taken from this interview.

16. Arthur Wensinger, ed., *Theatre of the Bauhaus* (Middletown, Conn.: Wesleyan University Press, 1961), 7.

17. Miller, *Democracy Is in the Streets*, 3.

18. Richard Flacks, *Making History: The Radical Tradition in American Life* (New York: Columbia University Press, 1988).

19. The term "Red diaper baby" referred to children of Americans who were active members of the Communist party in the 1920s and 1930s.

20. Gitlin, *The Sixties*, 41.

21. Ibid., 84.

22. Kenneth Rexroth, "San Francisco Dancers' Workshop," in *San Francisco Dancers' Workshop*, 21. Unpublished manuscript, Anna Halprin Archives.

23. The Movement, as sociologist Todd Gitlin defines it, is "the youth movement, principally the white student part of it, and its self-conscious core, the New Left, which borrowed from the black movement the habit of calling itself 'the movement'" (*The Sixties*, 4).

24. Norma Leistiko, interview by the author, 21 June 1992, Kentfield, California.

25. William Glatkin, "The Art of Eating," *Sacramento Bee*, 16 June 1968.

26. Leistiko interview.

27. Gitlin, *The Sixties*, 234.

28. Ibid.

29. Ibid., 206.

30. Daria Halprin, interview by the author, May 1991, Kentfield, California.

31. Daria Halprin, interview by Janice Ross, 1991, audiotape, Marin, California.

32. Gitlin, *The Sixties*, 26.

33. Barbara Epstein, *Political Protest and Cultural Revolution: Nonviolent Direct Action in the 1970's and 1980's* (Berkeley: University of California Press, 1991).

34. Gitlin, *The Sixties*, 26.

35. Anna Halprin, interview by the author, 5 September 1991, Kentfield, California.

36. In 1955 Halprin was chosen by Martha Graham and the Baroness de Rothschild to be presented in New York at the American Dance Festival, a series of performances by young choreographers at the ANTA Theatre. Anna Halprin, interview by the author, 11 September 1989, Kentfield, California.

37. Yvonne Rainer, interview by Stephen Cobbett Steinberg, November 1990. Unused footage from KQED-TV documentary on Anna and Lawrence Halprin.

38. From a 1967 poster for a concert at the Straight Theatre, Anna Halprin Archives.

39. Anna Halprin in conversation with Alma Hawkins, *Procession*, U.C. Media Center (1964). Directed and produced by Mark McCarty.

40. Epstein, *Political Protest and Cultural Revolution*, 18.

41. Miller, *Democracy Is in the Streets*, 318–19.

42. Flacks, *Making History*, 38.

3

James Waring and the Judson Dance Theater
Influences, Intersections, and Divergences

Leslie Satin

The only dance by Doris Humphrey I ever really liked was *The Life
of the Bee*, and I suspect the reason I liked it was that it reminded me
a little of Radio City Music Hall.

James Waring

"Judson Dance Theater," announced Jimmy Waring to Judith Dunn
with characteristic hyperbole, "is the world!"[1] Waring was given to making such grand pronouncements, and his slyly ambiguous declaration
probably drew a laugh or a roll of the eyes from Dunn at the time.
Now, looking back at that rich period of arts experimentation exemplified by the Judson Dance Theater, the line also suggests Waring's complicated personal and artistic relationship to the Judson: his admiration
and enthusiasm, his aloofness, his roles as teacher and mentor, the aesthetic concerns and choreographic strategies he shared with the group
and those he explored alone—the "influences, intersections, and divergences" of this chapter's title.[2]

Waring had begun making dances in the late 1940s and was deeply
involved in the span of arts experimentation in the 1950s and 1960s,
but he was never actually a member of the Judson. Older than most of
its members by at least ten years, he had already been working in the

51

dance avant-garde for over a decade when the workshops began. He was a noted teacher, and his ballet and composition classes as well as his dances drew many Judson dancers: Yvonne Rainer, David Gordon, Valda Setterfield, Deborah Hay, Lucinda Childs, Freddy Herko, Arlene Rothlein, Sally Gross, Toby Armour, Gretchen MacLane, and Meredith Monk, among others; some of these dancers were also provided an early opportunity to perform their own work in his concerts.[3]

The relative elusiveness of Waring's work and his position in dance history might be understood in terms of the difficulty of "placing" it: it was never secure either in the mainstream or in the "official" avant-garde of his time. In part, this had to do with Waring's own fluidity of style: he felt no compulsion to choose any particular camp or genre or to ally himself with any single movement or moment of the avant-garde. So, while the expressionist modern dance born in the 1930s and 1940s reigned in the United States, Waring made dances that resembled Happenings or recalled seventeenth-century commedia dell'arte. And when dancers such as Yvonne Rainer and Steve Paxton were running or talking or eating apples onstage, Waring dressed his ballerinas in lavender tulle and set them to spinning.[4]

During certain periods, Waring's choreography tended toward formalism and abstraction, in line with the modern dance classicism of Merce Cunningham and the neoclassicist ballets of George Balanchine, choreographers whom Waring admired and by whom he was influenced. More often, his focus was on the blatantly theatrical and romantic pieces with which he is most strongly identified. His work was closely entwined with the experimental theater, dance, visual arts, and literature of his time, but he was strongly influenced by his feelings for the past; earlier styles of dance, vaudeville and variety performance, silent and musical films, and other arts were pervasive inspirations for Waring's choreography.

Exactly *how* Waring employed this early work is a compelling question: Did he "simply" reconstruct it, in the manner of pastiche? Or did he rework it in a more postmodern vein, restating the rules of past models along the non-denigrating lines of what Linda Hutcheon calls parody, in which the new work is seen as an updating of the original object, a re-placement of the original in history?[5] Waring's use of past material and his collagelike combinations of historical as well as structural and aesthetic elements, including the mixture of "high" and "low"

James Waring. Photo by Theresa King.

art and his expression of a sensibility that was understood by his admirers and detractors as, respectively, poetic or camp, were in line with concepts of postmodernism in other fields, but they distanced his work from many of the explorations of the Judson. Like that of the Judson dancers, Waring's work was generally at odds with the modern dance sensibilities prevalent through the 1950s and exemplified by the choreography of Martha Graham and Doris Humphrey; however, he gravitated toward the spectacular, the fantastic, the whimsical, and the beautiful rather than the formal and objective material with which the Judson Dance Theater is primarily identified.

In 1976, Yvonne Rainer considered the Waring/Judson interplay in connection with her own work:

Judson started in '62 and I was dancing with Jimmy through 64, maybe I even did something in '65. I felt, and this is not an objective view at all . . . [that] these activities were very separate. My memories of the situation with Jimmy is—the rehearsals are clearer to me than the work. I always felt—I was some-what critical . . . there was quite a difference in temperament. I'd come from the art world, a kind of macho abstract expressionist ambience, if you want to call it that, and the camp sensibility, which to me Jimmy was the prime mover and exponent of, was somewhat alien to me. And even though, in retrospect, some of my own wackiness and sense of humor certainly converged with his sense of humor, and he certainly helped me through his support to exploit this area of my talent, so to speak. But I felt very strongly that the experiments or investigations at the Judson were of a quite different order, and most of the people there . . . at the beginning were not directly related to Jimmy's company.[6]

Rainer's remark recalls the three categories cited by Sally Banes in the introduction to *Democracy's Body,* her history of the group. Banes sees the Judson's work as divided into the "analytic, reductive," the "the-atrical, often humorous, baroque," and the "multi-media," and she de-fines the first category as the one that "proposed and tested theories of dance as art."[7] Certainly, Rainer belonged to the first category, and what we now experience as the legacy of the Judson most clearly fits into that area: work that tested the definitions of dance through a range of formal-ist strategies that called attention to themselves, to the historical dance traditions they refuted or rebelled against, and to the interchange of performance and perception. Those dances of the second and third cate-gories, less "hard-edged" in addressing choreographic concerns, had the most obvious correspondence with Waring's dances; some dancers, too, experimented with different styles and performance modes in their ap-proaches. Works that challenged preexisting attitudes about dance did so in more or less overt ways, or were blatantly humorous, chaotic, and cluttered, or slipped back and forth across the categories suggested by Banes.

Waring's early training had taken place primarily at the Oakland, California, studio of Raoul Pausé, who taught both ballet and plastique, a style and form in which movements flowed together seamlessly. Waring noted that Pausé's classes influenced his own early work, which even then displayed his openness to the use of seemingly unrelated choreographic elements: "[My] own first ideas and feelings about choreography, due in part to my training, and in part to my own natural instincts, were toward not necessarily a synthesis of styles but at least a kind of accommodation in which I felt at liberty to work with whatever materials seemed right at the moment."[8]

In San Francisco, Waring studied Graham technique with Gertrude Schurr, improvisation with Anna Halprin, and plastique with Welland Lathrop (who shared a studio with Halprin), and he trained in ballet with the Christensen brothers at the San Francisco Ballet School. Later, he noted that during those years (the mid-1940s), most ballet dancers and modern dancers "held themselves rigidly aloof from each other,"[9] and he claimed to be the only dancer in the area studying the two forms "with equal seriousness."[10] It was with that same "equal seriousness" that he later combined those forms in his choreography, through modes of collage and counterpoint as well as unification, and in his composition classes, whose materials were drawn from a vast array of aesthetic and philosophic disciplines.

Waring came to New York City in the late 1940s. In New York he began to make dances, and he studied at the School of American Ballet and with Antony Tudor, Merce Cunningham, and Louis Horst. For the duration of his career, Waring was extremely attached to ballet as a technique and a dance form, and his dances grew increasingly balletic over the years. David Vaughan suggests that it was Waring's extremely detailed knowledge of dance history, his "lov[ing] those steps for what they were," that added to the often elementary level of the ballet steps he used in his dances and infused them with a "poetic flavor."[11]

Not everyone, though, was fond of that "poetic flavor"; both critics and colleagues were apt to be put off by Waring's dances, which anticipated more recent unorthodox approaches to ballet. By the late 1970s, many choreographers, such as David Gordon, Twyla Tharp, Mark Morris, Laura Dean, and Karole Armitage, would begin to move back and forth between ballet and postmodern dance without arousing such critical ire.[12] The years since then have formed a very different framework

in which to make dance, one of increasingly permeable boundaries between styles and genres.[13] While some of Waring's more balletic works
were suitable for a traditional ballet company, others were too idiosyncratic, too eccentric. Waring felt free to depart from the canon, to use
or ignore "ballet proper" or to include any material at all: nondance
movement and movement drawn from diverse dance genres, humor and
quirks and choreographic non sequitur. And his choreographic methods
often depended less on the lexicon and schematics of classical ballet
(and the resources of a company of technically superior, classically
trained dancers) than on intuition and circumstance.

Waring was intrigued by ballet's layered history and its sensibility.
This has led me to look at his work in terms of its intersection of ballet,
especially Romantic ballet, and the avant-garde. Waring's works often
evinced yearnings toward romanticism, with its emphasis on intuition,
mystery, and voluptuous imagery; what he thought of most in making
a dance, and what "was the first thing that came about a dance," was
atmosphere.[14] According to Umberto Eco, "The concept of absolute
originality [was] born with Romanticism," and "the Romantic idea of
'creation from nothingness'" was challenged by such strategies of the
early twentieth century as "collage, mustachios on the Mona Lisa, [and]
art about art."[15] Waring, whose work was engaged with the beginnings
of postmodern dance, combined the vernacular and the "serious," disparate aspects that functioned simultaneously to call attention to themselves and to be considered with the utmost seriousness and sincerity.
His dances encompassed both a definitively romantic strain and the con-
tinuation of those early-twentieth-century strategies (which were fundamental to art of the 1960s and continue to be germane to contemporary
work) within an avant-garde frame.[16]

Literary critic Leslie Fiedler used the term "postmodernism" in the
1960s as a "challenge [to] the elitism of the high modernist tradition in
the name of pop."[17] I think here of Waring's *Terpsichore Explained*,
possibly a more overtly hilarious challenge than what Fiedler had in
mind. *Terpsichore* is a high-toned but absurd "lecture-demonstration"
that covers a vast range of dance historical eras through physical
and textual illustrations. The muddled dancers accompanying David
Vaughan's deadpan British professor's lecture are increasingly funny as
they refuse to respond to the hopeless entanglement into which their
pas de six has deteriorated or as they calmly illustrate the "hypotenuse

in neo-contemporary work in which the feet are placed in such a relation to each other that they have no relation to anything else." And Vaughan drily advises his audience at the start: "If you want to understand modern dance, you must have read Freud, and preferably have undergone analysis. Of course then you run the risk of not wanting to see any kind of dancing at all. But happily for us, not many people *do* modern dancing any more since it's getting so old-fashioned. But in between this and ballet lies a great yawning chasm, just chock-full of variants, mutants and hybrids." It is that "great yawning chasm" in which Waring's work lies.

Waring's relationship to the Judson was informed by his own work in dance and by his broader involvement across the arts. By the time the Judson Dance Theater was initiated, Waring had long been a participant in the experimental art movements of his time. His concerns with developments in dance and in other art forms were reflected in his choreographic collaborations with other artists, in his own activities as a writer, director, costume designer, painter, and collagist, and in his efforts toward education, outreach, and connection among artists and students.[18]

Waring's involvement with writers was of particular interest. Those with whom he worked as director or collaborator included Kenneth Koch, Maria Irene Fornes, Frank O'Hara, Robert Duncan, Paul Goodman, Diane di Prima, and Alan Marlowe; he also brought their writings, and that of many others, to his classes. Waring was a writer as well; he was a poet and essayist whose work appeared in literary publications (such as the 1963 *An Anthology,* edited by La Monte Young), and a playwright whose pieces were produced by the American Theater for Poets and the Judson Poets Theater, among others. He also reviewed other dancers' work and helped to inform nondancers, including critics, about dance. In 1958, Louis Horst, Martha Graham's musical director and a standard-bearer in the dance world, had asked Jill Johnston to write for *Dance Observer,* where she proceeded to write a favorable review of Waring's work. Later, choreographer and dancer Remy Charlip befriended Johnston at the New York Public Library dance collection and encouraged her to look at Cunningham and other avant-garde choreographers. Johnston says that it was Waring and Charlip who arranged for her to work at the *Village Voice,* where her dance writings would become an integral part of the dance movements of the 1960s.[19] David Gordon notes the importance of the retirement near that time of critic

John Martin. The *New York Times* then hired Allen Hughes despite the fact that he "had no knowledge of dance at all"; Hughes looked to his friend Freddie Herko for assistance, and as Herko was a protégé of Waring's, all of the parties involved met each other and Waring "began giving information that Allen Hughes would write about" to the fledgling critic.[20]

It was through theater that Waring first met Al Carmines, the minister and staunch supporter of, as well as participant in, the arts activities taking place in his church. Carmines dates the beginnings of their association with Waring's direction of Diane di Prima's *Murder Cake* at the Judson in 1963. About that venture, Carmines later wrote that Waring "was an exquisite director: room was found for the small gesture which he loved so much. The poetry of Miss di Prima's words found its perfect counterpart in Jimmy's direction and clarification. The characters posed on a sea of words, and they were serene or compassionate as the text called for." Carmines also pinpointed Waring's gift for the intertwining of dance and text in describing his direction of Arthur Williams's *Poor Little Match Girl* (1968), also at the Judson, saying that "Arthur's dry and passionate language came to life under Jimmy's fluid and exact direction."[21]

Waring was associated as well with the American Theater for Poets, also called the New York Poets Theater, founded in 1961 by di Prima (who had taken his composition class at the Living Theater) and Marlowe to produce plays by poets as well as dance and music; later it produced showings of music, Happenings, dance (including Waring's), and film.[22] Waring served on the organization's board of directors and contributed as a writer as well as a dancer and organizer. Also at this time, Waring worked, along with other dancers, on *The Floating Bear*, a literary newsletter edited by di Prima and Jones, which primarily published poetry and included performance reviews and announcements of events in the arts.[23] He participated in numerous other ventures that brought artists together: he organized and directed a play for the June 1963 Pocket Follies as a benefit for the Foundation for the Contemporary Performance Arts, which helped to support performances by the Judson Dance Theater and the Merce Cunningham Dance Company; he danced, with his company, in the New York City–wide Yam Festival of May 1963; and he organized two months of weekly "Events and Entertainments"—"dances, diversions, and what nots"—at the Pocket Theater in 1964.[24]

Waring collaborated, too, with many experimental composers, a number of whom worked with the Judson Dance Theater. He first worked with John Herbert McDowell, who frequently created music for him, in 1956, on *Adagietto: Flakes of Chance*. McDowell choreographed *Eight Pas de Deux, Pas de Trois, and Finale* (1963), subtitled "a small token for James Waring's Hallelujah Gardens," for a Judson concert: an extravaganza for seventeen performers, waltzes by forty composers, and a set of silver trophies on a wooden pillar by Remy Charlip. Waring also worked with Philip Corner, Malcolm Goldstein, Richard Maxfield, and Hy Gubernick. Waring's musical choices for his dances were extremely diverse, representing a broad range of classical, popular, and esoteric material as well as new work, including his own compositions. (True to form, though, Waring would at times advance his own remote and rather persnickety reputation: I recall him, in class, insisting—much of his actual choreographic history to the contrary—that it was unnecessary to use any music written after 1936!) On occasion he even participated in music-making for other choreographers; for example, in David Gordon's 1962 *Mannequin Dance*, in which Gordon performed a very slow sequence of rises and falls in a bathtub, Waring passed out balloons to audience members, directing them to first blow up the balloons and then slowly release their air.[25]

By the early 1950s, a decade before the Judson Dance Theater began, a small avant-garde dance community had already formed in New York City. Among its members were Merce Cunningham, John Cage, Katherine Litz, Merle Marsicano, Beverly Schmidt (Blossom), Paul Taylor, Aileen Passloff, Marian Sarach, and David Vaughan. In 1951, Waring, Vaughan, Taylor, Passloff, Sarach, and others (including dance writer Edwin Denby, New York City Ballet dancer Tanaquil Le Clercq, and actor Alex Rubin) formed the cooperative Dance Associates to present new work. The organization generated a great deal of work, but its annual concerts did not gain critical success; Vaughan points out that the critics "felt we were young upstarts thumbing our noses at the more established dance figures—which indeed we were."[26] Aileen Passloff adds that the group "would do performances at the Amato Opera House for which we'd get the audience by going out into the street and begging people to come in for nothing. And then there would be a handful of people in the audience, sometimes there were more people on the stage than there were in the audience."[27]

Much of that audience was composed of visual artists, writers, and musicians rather than dancers. Waring often invited artists to design sets or costumes for his dances; his collaborators included Julian Beck, George Brecht, Red Grooms, Al Hansen, Robert Indiana, Jasper Johns, Larry Poons, Robert Watts, Robert Whitman, and John Wulp. Many of these artists were involved in the creation of Happenings; Waring, too, was a proponent of Happenings, and he helped Allan Kaprow with one of his own first ones. The artists making Happenings shared with him, as well as with artists working later in the context of dance at the Judson, an interest in certain qualities, such as dadaist juxtapositions, the framing of ordinary activity as art, and nondevelopmental and non-hierarchical structures. These qualities, associated with Happenings, appeared also in the artists' collaborative efforts with Waring and in Waring's noncollaborative choreography, as suggested by the following examples:[28]

In Waring's *Peripateia* (1961), George Brecht created the decor in performance. He threw colored paint at a white scrim stretched across the rear of the stage, mixed with the dancers, swept confetti, and floated balloons. Richard Maxfield's music included a saxophone that sounded like "a faulty outboard motor."[29]

In 1958, Jill Johnston responded to Waring's *Dances before the Wall's* "groupings of random activities": dancers performing "sometimes in relation one dancer to another, sometimes in relation to the music, sometimes jumping with lights. . . . At times impression of an animated Klee painting, miniature idiosyncratic events juxtaposed and moving independently of each other at the same time in one space." She compared its "pure dance" effect to the "parts of a snake or a scorpion cut in pieces scattering in different directions, but all pieces of one life: uncanny." It included a wall designed by Julian Beck; Johnston described it as "a bright piece of magic, a hundred colorful eggcrates . . . filled with A&P saltboxes, busts of Chatterton, [and] copper fry pans" and added that the music, too—"classics, Cage, Presley . . ."—appeared "in juxtaposed order of their own volition."[30]

In 1960, Johnston reviewed Waring's *A Swarm of Butterflies Encountered on the Ocean,* a solo for Aileen Passloff; she observed that the "movements appear in piecemeal fashion; nothing is continuous, there are no phrases, something happens here, period—then there, period, and so on."[31]

Marianne Simon, in 1959, hinted at *Extravaganza*'s simultaneously "beautiful and hilarious" clutter: the performers "cavorted, burlesqued, chattered, sang, and climbed in and out of sublimely ridiculous costumes . . . to the chance accompaniment of tape, radio, musical instruments, and other unidentified missiles."[32]

Doris Hering noted that "a detached little girl with an umbrella; a tightly gowned amazon with squared arms and flapping hands; a timid male playing with his own footprints; [and] another male springing in repeated stiff jumps" coexisted in a single dance, *Intrada.*[33]

These descriptions reflect Waring's use of collage, an important property of all his work and one also reflected in his many paintings and visual art constructions, some of which were created at the collage parties he often held for friends and colleagues. Collage continues to be a widely employed strategy in contemporary art, associated with multiple layers of meaning and the clarification of processes. Its adaptation in the hands of the dadaists and, later, the surrealists captivated Waring. I recall that in his composition classes Waring often invoked a dadaist tear-down-the-walls spirit in his Marcel Duchamp–modeled proclamations about how anything one claims is art *is* art, and he orchestrated disruptive Happening-like events among unsuspecting audiences. He effused over the collages of dadaist-turned-surrealist Max Ernst and encouraged students to respond choreographically to the structural devices of paintings such as the work of surrealist René Magritte. And in line with dadaist notions, he urged students to look to the commonplace, the already-existing material they could reframe as art; many of the Judson experiments were concerned with Duchampian notions of "ready-mades" and the use of everyday material, with the meaning of making something new. I remember pointing blindfolded to notices on a bulletin board to find words that would form a dance's structural base, and dropping a strand of cooked spaghetti onto the floor to determine a dance's spatial path—an echo of dadaist experiments with string: Jean Arp dropped pieces of string onto paper and attached them to the paper in whatever form they assumed, and Duchamp's *Three Standard Stop-pages* began with the shapes created by threads dropped onto canvas.

By 1954, Waring had begun the dance company he maintained until 1969. He was a prolific dance-maker, and he presented his works consistently until his death in 1975. By the time the Judson Dance Theater came into being, he had been working, and respected, long enough to be regarded as a mentor. Although certainly a strong supporter of the Judson's efforts, he had mixed feelings about the work and about the space itself. Some of Waring's own commentary suggests both his wit and his attitude: in a group discussion, he claimed that "God was the organization's artistic director," that he was "distinguished in that [he] never went to any of the meetings."[34] Rainer says that Waring did not consider the church a venue for "real" concerts but rather as a place to work informally; she also notes that Waring "was critical of a lot that went on at Judson—thought it was dry and boring."[35] A number of Waring's Judson concerts were presented, though, by the Judson Dance Theater; his 25–26 August 1963 performance was the first such affiliation with the workshop. And that same year, he appeared in the Judson Dance Theater's Concert #12, opening it with his *Imperceptible Elongation No. 1.*

His dances, especially in the 1950s and pre-Judson 1960s, often perplexed and disappointed critics with their departures from traditional modern dance values and strategies: their lack of linearity, collage techniques, chaotic mise-en-scène, absence of consistent and recognizable emotion, and seemingly purposeless events. The last piece he considered a narrative dance was his 1954 *Freaks,* though many later dances "hint[ed] at story."[36] Doris Hering wrote that one concert "marked a vast improvement in Mr. Waring's ability to dominate the materials of his craft and create an organized theater impression. . . . [O]ne inevitably looks for a deeper creative purpose—for some semblance of a steady emotional or energy undercurrent. And there doesn't seem to be any."[37] In 1957 she noted that Waring's collage imagery could be moving if his aesthetic purpose were also apparent: "It is one thing to create an atmosphere. It is another to achieve an emotional goal with it."[38] Hering explained that the problem in one concert was "in the movement approach. . . . [There] were a profusion of beginnings that never developed into full statements or accrued to a climax." In the same review,

New England Dance Theater in *Purple Moment: An Interior Ballet in Two Parts, Dedicated to Joan Blondell* (1969). Photo by Theresa King.

she described "deadpan promenades," "arabesques piddling into finger-snaps," "sagging stances," and Waring himself as "rigid in the upper body, leaden in the face, [his dancing] not a happy experience."[39]

Even later, though, Waring's colleagues, including Judson dancers who were influenced by the choreographic freedom he introduced in his classes and dances, experienced difficulty with his dances. Even those who *liked* Waring's dances disagree over whether his work constituted a "mishmash," as evidenced in a 1976 broadcast discussion among David Gordon, Valda Setterfield, Yvonne Rainer, and Aileen Passloff, moderated by Marcia B. Siegel.[40]

Part of Waring's "mishmash" was his mixing of elements of high and popular art. From the beginning of his career, Waring felt a deep attachment to popular art and popular artists. In part this attachment was an outgrowth of his fascination and empathy with the offstage lives of those performers who were neither well known nor financially comfortable, who "for whatever reason—sexual or psychological or artistic"—were outsiders.[41] Many of his dances—including those made before 1955, when many of his works had a narrative base—concern a troupe of actors or dancers huddled together against the chills of cold and isolation, or observed, unmasked, in their private moments. Others celebrate their actual performing lives, drawing on vaudeville, the circus, commedia dell'arte, the music hall, and movie musicals.

A sampling of dances of the type that Yvonne Rainer referred to as Waring's "hybrid vaudeville"[42] includes *Pastorale* (1953), *Burlesca* (1953), *The Wanderers* (1951), *Phantom of the Opera* (1966), *An Eccentric Beauty Revisited* (1972), *Feathers* (1973), *Musical Moments* (1965), *A New Kind of Love* (1974), *Vaudeville for Lulu* (1971), *Extravaganza* (1957), and *Purple Moment* (1969).

Pastorale (1953): In this first dance in which he performed with Waring, David Vaughan played the part of a scarecrow. The story of two brothers and a group of traveling musicians, *Pastorale* was a dance about a "community of performers and their relationship to other people."[43]

Burlesca (1953): This was a performance-within-a-performance in which the troupe huddled together at the end. Vaughan, using the music hall performances of his past as part of his own performance, collaborated with Waring on the comedic, vaudevillian aspects of the dance. For example, he improvised a prologue in which he peeked through the curtain, counting the house and waving at friends. And in an extended "bit," Waring choreographed a crossover in which Vaughan pushed him across the stage: he would walk a few steps, be pushed, turn and glare resentfully at Vaughan, and repeat the process until he got across. Since the audience found this so amusing, Waring decided to do it again, roles switched, traveling in the other direction.[44]

Musical Moments (1965): This was a series of vignettes modeled on the Maurice Chevalier/Jeanette MacDonald movie *The Love Parade*. It included a procession of showgirls, composed of "various members of the avant-garde," including Barbara Dilley and Carolyn Brown, who joined the procession one by one, accompanied by song.[45]

Waring was still a youngster during the heyday of the Busby Berkeley films. John Herbert McDowell makes a case for these movies' extravagance, and what he calls their "monumentalities," that could be applied as well to the choreographic period of the late 1950s and early 1960s: "People are starved for the big fat gesture, the monstrous concept, the kind of nutty Dada grandeur that somehow appeared for a very few years in the midst of the depression."[46] He compares an event in one of Waring's dances to a cinematic corollary. Noting Berkeley's insistence on magic moments, such as a two-minute opening shot of Winifred Shaw's face growing "from a pin-point in a mass of black until it fills the screen," he considers the "beautiful daring of just going and going until it's done (like the moment in James Waring's *Arena* . . . where violent multiple activity, filling the stage, suddenly stops dead and a girl moves one finger, very slowly, exactly twenty-five times)."[47]

Waring had an affection for such extremes: the conventionally spectacular or the spectacularly small. In *Dances before the Wall* (1958), for example, David Gordon rubbed his thighs, slowly, twenty-one times. In the five-second-long *Imperceptible Elongation No. 1*, which Waring insisted was a Happening, "Everything happened together. There was this big white screen on the stage, and five or six jars of colored confetti. And suddenly, hands burst through the paper and grabbed the jars of confetti and emptied them. And at the same time big white puff balls were thrown from the balcony."[48] More "conventional" spectacles include his 1963 *At the Hallelujah Gardens*, which used any music "big, classical, and perversely overwhelming," a panoply of objects such as a white balloon tree, live geese, and potatoes, and intermittent dance sequences and events: a piece that "overran its bounds in all directions."[49]

Waring, of course, regularly "overran bounds" in his appropriation of historical material. In addition to their intersections with contemporary art experiments and their recollections of classical ballet, popular art, and early film, his dances also hark back to the dance of the 1910s and 1920s—Denishawn, Nijinsky and the Ballets Russes, plastique—and Andreas Pavley and Serge Oukrainsky, with whom his own teacher, Raoul Pausé, had studied. Based in plastique, Pavley and Oukrainsky's Chicago company encompassed ballet, opera, and vaudeville, grand spectacles and star-turn solos, fantasy and extravagance. Photographs that demonstrate a taste for Orientalia, art nouveau, and such technical and aesthetic extremes as men dancing on the points of their bare toes suggest imagery that would appear in Waring's dances forty years later.

Little Kootch Piece (1955): David Vaughan refers to this as "Jimmy's idea of a jazz piece." Dancer Marian Sarach's costume, designed by Jasper Johns, "had sort of a bare bosom, but it was painted, a leotard painted with nipples. It was vaguely kind of Etruscan, as I remember."[50]

Tambourine Dance (1965): Jack Anderson wrote that "Waring resembled a living *art nouveau* lampshade."[51]

At the Café Fleurette (1968): Gretchen MacLane wore a "fringed lampshade skirt" in the *Panamerica* tango, and Arlene Rothlein was dressed in "jewelled pajamas" in *Oriental Dance.*[52]

The men in the photographs of Pavley and Oukrainsky dances provide rich material in terms of gender imagery. In dances such as Oukrainsky's *Persian Dance,* a shoeless pointe piece he performed in a costume of gorgeous beading and bare skin, one is struck by the brief, gaudy attire of the male dancer; the appropriation and extension of the pointe work, which is conventionally the female province; the employment of a physical vocabulary stressing the serpentine over the straight; the preference for the occasional angled but still delicate pose over the weighted and earthy one. The men's faces, too, reflect gender/genre modes of performance of that day, either quietly intense beneath the beaded headdress or somewhat coy, the gaze less than straightforward: the conventionally feminine in compelling and erotic counterpoint to the dancer's maleness. Consider:

The Cobra Ballet (1970): Bryan Hayes—in gold-glittered blue net harem pants over orchid tights; orange lamé tunic; blue, red, and gold body makeup; and a crown—was a vision appearing to an opera devotee overdosing in a tenement hall. Slinking down a bannisterless spiral staircase, he was accompanied by a four-man corps de ballet fluttering and posing in long, gray shorts.[53]

Hayes suggests that Waring was especially interested in what he calls "the thing in the middle." One example of this is the vaudeville performers who did Indian dances; Waring studied photographs of such performers. Hayes recalls such dances as "very serious and dramatic, and then the rug was pulled out from under you by non sequitur. Some were the epitome of the worst kinds of opera ballets, pseudo-Orientalia, but it wasn't awful because it was done consciously, as parody."[54] Some of these cultural layerings in his dances, particularly as they employed elements of nontraditional gender imagery, brought the "camp" label to Waring's work.[55] The charge is not entirely unreasonable. Waring was concerned with stylization, with exaggeration, with androgyny, with extravagance, with looking beyond the bounds of "high culture" for artistic pleasure—the qualities Susan Sontag identified in her seminal 1964 essay "Notes on 'Camp.' "[56]

The categorization of camp implicitly dismisses the seriousness of the work in question.[57] While Sontag claims that some art considered camp may also be taken seriously, she makes clear that "many examples of Camp are things which, from a 'serious' point of view are either bad art or kitsch." She says, too, that camp's "way of seeing the world as an aesthetic phenomenon . . . is not in terms of beauty, but in terms of the degree of artifice, of stylization."[58] For Waring, an aesthetic viewpoint that bypassed beauty would have been a travesty. He was a very funny choreographer, and his sense of humor ran the gamut from the archly raised eyebrow to the no-holds-barred spectacle. In Sontag's words, he was, in camp tradition, "serious about the frivolous, frivolous about the serious."[59] But always, underneath the frivolity, the humor, and the extravagance was a profound belief in the beauty in human life.

Waring made less extravagant and colorful pieces also. In the late 1950s and early 1960s his work demonstrated its most evident connection to that of Merce Cunningham, whose dances had long been important to Waring.[60] Cunningham had a studio at the Living Theater; Waring watched him teach class there, familiarizing himself with Cunningham's movement vocabulary and the ways he put movement together. Later, in 1969, Jill Johnston suggested that Waring's use of space in particular was like Cunningham's but that Waring had arrived at that use of space without using chance methods.[61]

Dromenon (1961) might be considered Waring's signature work of this period. Photos and personal recollections suggest a "white" modern dance more like Cunningham's classicism than Waring's typically fanciful and poetic style; Doris Hering wrote that its appeal lay "in its spacious and softspoken use of the ballet vocabulary."[62] Still, Yvonne Rainer, who danced in the piece, recalls less traditional movements, basic to Waring's style, even within that framework: her entrance was a "combination of the classical line with quirky, rhythmic small gestures of the upper body."[63] Jill Johnston recalled the dance style as "peppered with personal gestures unique to Waring," and Marcia Marks noted the "liquid lyrical passages and sudden shock changes, competently executed movements and crude spasms of Mr. Waring's diaphragm."[64]

It was in Robert Dunn's composition classes that the Judson Dance Theater was born, but Waring had been teaching composition classes of a similar nature years before that at the Master Institute and the Living Theater, at the studio he shared with Paul Taylor, and at other venues. Dunn attended some of Waring's classes during his own Judson teaching hiatus; he recalled Waring reading to students from Herbert V. Guenther's book of Buddhist beliefs, *Philosophy and Psychology in the Abhidharma*, and he resumed teaching at Waring's urging.[65] Numerous students have expressed their belief in a sense of continuity between the work of the two composition teachers: David Gordon has written that by the time he began studying with Dunn in 1962, after taking Waring's technique and composition classes and dancing with him since 1956, "most of this stuff was not new" to him.[66] John Herbert McDowell noted the "historical import[ance]" of the lineage in the development of the Judson; Waring and Cunningham were among those he referred to in commenting that the Judson "was a focus for a number of things that had already been happening."[67] The concerns of these classes emerged, too, in the lectures Waring presented. He shared a studio with Rainer and Passloff beginning in 1961, and in 1962 the Judson dancers met there following his technique class; at that studio he also organized, with Diane di Prima, a lecture series whose speakers included Jill Johnston, George Brecht, and Judson dancers.

Waring regularly taught ballet technique classes, which were attended by students of all levels, including many Judson dancers; he demanded precision within the technique, attention to the minutiae of executing a step. Valda Setterfield recalls his quarter-inch pliés, and Sally Gross speaks of his painstaking analysis of a pirouette; others remember the intensity with which he exhorted his students to "close in fifth."[68] Waring was known always to be teaching both technique and composition classes—he could be counted on to hold classes on Christmas or to find time for a private lesson; it was through this route that he met many of the younger dancers who would often come to perform in his pieces, some of them moving back and forth between his company and the Judson, others making a more definitive choice in one direction.

It is impossible to say exactly how Waring influenced these students, of course. That he *did* influence them is certain; as early as 1962, after the first of the Judson Dance Theater's concerts, Diane di Prima referred to choreographers David Gordon, Yvonne Rainer, and Fred Herko as "working out of a tradition," and named the components of that tradition as their having studied with Cunningham, danced with Waring, and been "highly influenced" by both.[69] In 1969, Jill Johnston names Waring and fellow romantic avant-gardist Aileen Passloff, in addition to Cunningham, as "contribut[ing] to the climate that made the Judson Dance Theater possible."[70] Clearly, many of the dancers who studied and worked with Waring were inspired in their dancing and choreographing by his teachings, by the expansive nature of what he presented as art, or as the source material for making art; and many were excited about his dances, especially in the pre-Judson days. Others were urged along in their dancing careers by the opportunities he gave them to dance in his work and to make and present their own; those who danced in his work were also offered chances to work in dance different from their own concentration or in the work of their Judson colleagues. And for many of his students, the degree of attention, focus, and commitment that he gave, and that he demanded from his students and his dancers, to every detail of a movement, a phrase, a dance, an idea, was a model for making art.

Waring had a mixed-bag approach to choreography and to teaching. I have spoken with people who took his composition classes over the years in New York and with his students at Indian Hill, the summer arts camp in Stockbridge, Massachusetts, where he taught for ten years; I studied with him a decade after the Judson Dance Theater began. Certain elements apparently remained constant over time, while others changed. In 1987 David Gordon recalled that in Waring's early composition classes, he "gave you the ingredients of chance situations. He gave you a list of kinds of movement, and he said, 'make a piece in which you choose one of each kind of movement, but that's not chance.'"[71] Ten years later, in a memorial essay following the death of Robert Dunn, Gordon expanded this view, writing that Waring's "compositional assignments used chance procedure to arrive at arrangements of qualities of movements. Lyric, percussive, repetitive, etc."[72] Later classes included chance procedures as well as indeterminacy for creating movements and phrases and events. Waring adhered to his choreographic tenets with great thoroughness, demanding commitment to an unedited acceptance of whatever results emerged from dancers' choices and strategies, whether or not they "liked" them. Gordon and Setterfield recall that in the early 1960s classes Waring was very strict, even dogmatic, in his insistence that students not deviate from their material, that they not discard anything, that they retain even material they didn't like, saying, "if you *don't* get to like it, who said you have to like it anyway?"[73]

Waring's classes involved the presentation of an artistic and philosophical smorgasbord of meaningful models—in Gordon and Setterfield's description, "more a philosophy class than a physical class."[74] Waring offered, in addition to dadaist ideas and collage, the music and dance of John Cage and Merce Cunningham, Happenings, the writings of poets and playwrights and essayists. Gordon remembers being introduced to Morton Feldman, Fanny Brice, and Mahler; Mucha, Guston, and Rauschenberg; Cocteau, Buñuel, Berkeley, and Laurel and Hardy.[75] Waring called attention to art events going on at the time, urging students to see them. "At the very beginning of knowing him," Gordon recalls, "I had a sense that whatever this was he did and whatever this was he was telling me about connected to a *world*. . . . [Jimmy] made it clear that this was *another* art, not the *only* art, and that it was related to the other arts."[76] Lines of delineation between forms were unimportant to Waring. He recalled that when Yvonne Rainer "began to object and say, we're not making dances we're making objects. . . . [He] said what the hell does it matter so long as you're making something."[77] Waring analyzed movement and structure, breaking down the possibilities of phrases, their component parts (elements, textures, motifs, compounds, patterns) and combinations. His students made dances accompanied by silence or by the sounds created as part of their chance operations. And they altered their assumptions: I remember conceptualizing and carefully distinguishing between impossible and improbable dances.

In the classroom, Waring claimed that everyone was an artist, everyone could make dances. But (in my memory) he was a tough observer, clearly preferring the efforts of those who dove into compositional experiments with nerve, verve, and intellect; he simultaneously contradicted and preserved his own credo, too, reserving the right to differ with the artist's evaluation of his or her own work. And as a critic of professional work, he was not nonjudgmental. He was a severe arbiter of taste, and his own exquisite taste is referred to repeatedly by his colleagues and students. He often dismissed the work of major and less-well-known artists; he distinguished between "high-class boredom" and "low-class boredom," calling long and unvaried works "wallpaper movies" and disregarding dances he labeled "shit pie": a dance, like a pie, permeated by the smallest bit of shit.[78]

In his classes, Waring divided gestures into two categories: concrete and abstract. A concrete gesture is one that specifically stands for something else whose meaning will be understood by its intended audience: a palm-forward "stop sign," a thumbed nose. Waring called abstract a gesture that may indeed have meaning but whose meaning is not immediately or necessarily discernible by the audience. An example drawn from Waring's choreography is the torso contraction in combination with a hand over the mouth. Hering, in a review of *Burlesca* (1953), said the "dancers clapped their hands over their mouths as though they were about to vomit."[79] Vaughan recalls: "That was one of [Waring's] basic movements. . . . Whether it referred to throwing up or embarrassment, I don't know, but we did it a lot."[80]

Waring was very fond of florid and dramatic gestures that recalled earlier performance styles, but he did not call upon his dancers to develop these gestures from "the inward operation of the mind."[81] In his composition classes, Waring forbade what is conventionally understood in our culture to be acting. Instead, the dancer was to just do the movement fully and clearly; any "emoting" would be choreographed, the gestures, verbalizations, and facial expressions as much a part of the dance score—even one whose components were derived by chance operations—as any "dance movement." Several dancers who worked in his early pieces recall that Waring never advised them on issues of performance presence. Valda Setterfield said that Waring taught her that the performer's "conviction . . . translates itself to the audience as making the material real, no matter how curious the sequence seems to be."[82] David Vaughan says that Waring "trusted our intelligence and our intuition and our taste and our ability to project onstage. . . . It's that old thing—if you do the movement as clearly as you can, then the quality of it will come out. It's what Balanchine and Merce say."[83]

"Just doing the movement," though, is not so simple. There are vast differences of intention, experience, and actuality between what those words mean in relation to the work of Waring, Cunningham, or Balanchine or to what Yvonne Rainer meant when she coined the term "neutral doer," extending the Judson dancers' interest, as choreographic concept and performance style, in the dancer-as-object.[84] Waring, in fact, relied enormously on the individual characteristics of his dancers, and on the use of humor—but humor is tricky, and a delicate joke is easily lost. For example, Waring made considerable use of the straight face. Doris Hering, in the 1950s and 1960s, continually criticized his performance presence, calling him "detached" and "leaden," but other colleagues were attuned to his performance style; Vaughan recalls that "Jimmy was a supreme deadpan comic."[85]

Waring had a particular flair for choosing dancers who had something special to offer his choreography. He first "auditioned" David Gordon after meeting him at Washington Square Park and soon had him performing in works such as the 1958 *Dances before the Wall,* and he "discovered" Valda Setterfield immediately after she arrived from England, putting her into that same dance.[86] Yvonne Rainer first met Waring in 1961 through her interest in the work of his friend and colleague Aileen Passloff. That same year, he asked Rainer to perform two of her own solos for a program he was organizing for the Living Theater; Gordon, too, first performed his own choreography on a Living Theater program organized by Waring, in 1960.[87] Rainer, who says that Waring was "the first person to appreciate what [she] did," has spoken about how Waring made ballet steps she was able to execute and how he let her personality and performance style emerge in such dances as *At the Hallelujah Gardens,* where, as the Virginia Reel caller, she was given "free rein," and so "howled and made animal sounds" to his delight.[88] She recalls that "he had an uncanny ability to detect presence and whether a person could dance [in traditional dance terms] or not was secondary. . . . I think he almost invariably used quite intelligent people. And he also had this amazing gift for giving you things that were compatible with your temperament."[89]

Although Waring's casting reflected his great pleasure in locating or choosing performers whose special gifts he might reveal, it also reflected his dependence on which dancers were interested in working with him or able to work with him, or who was available to rehearse during a particular period. Gordon remembers that "sometimes the interest was because somebody was available and sometimes [it] was because no one else was. . . . He was very vulnerable about not being able to get anybody."[90]

Other factors Gordon and Setterfield recalled included the lack of information dancers possessed as to the general shape of a dance in which they were working, such as who the other dancers were and what these other dancers were doing, and the looseness of production elements, such as performance dates considered only when "enough of" a dance had been rehearsed.[91] The dancers who chose to work with Waring were generally drawn from the pool of experimentalists who were his friends, students, and colleagues. Their dance backgrounds, technical abilities, and talents were wide-ranging, and their choreographic concerns were focused on unconventional works such as Waring's. Those dancers whose accustomed milieu was ballet and who required, or could command, ballet company–level salaries tended to elude him.

It appears that Waring's influence on the lives of some of his early student-colleagues was extensive. For some, such as Gordon and Rainer, he was very important in the formative years of their career, but they then parted ways: Gordon wanted to make choices in his dances, and he rebelled against Waring's anti-editing stance.[92] Other dancers speak of Waring's extraordinary skill as a teacher of technique, his attention and commitment to detail in making and shaping movement. Sally Gross suggests that dancers felt obliged to take up sides, choosing as their mentor either Waring or Cunningham, opting either for "abstract choreography and bodies" or "expressive choreography and characters."[93] In the same vein, Lucinda Childs "stopped studying with Cunningham, because [she] was involved with Jimmy [Waring]."[94] Rainer recalls Waring's "sagacious posture—part mother hen and part sage."[95] Setterfield appears to remember Waring's range of knowledge and expertise with unblotched pleasure.[96] Some dancers suggest, though, that they eventually tired of the "camp" aspects of Waring's work, and also of the too-large presence he occupied in their lives. For all of his students, his erudition and generosity, the broad spectrum of the material he introduced to students and the openness with which he approached dance-making, encouraged students who were interested in expanding the parameters of dance and choreography.

Waring straddled certain principles of the Judson; his joint attachment to and evasion of them is clearest in relation to his division of teaching and choreographing. Waring's writings and the recollections of his colleagues lead me to believe that he generally distinguished between the principles he employed in teaching his classes and those upon which he relied in choreographing dances. Perhaps the most telling example, because of its central place in Judson work, is the use of chance procedures in dance-making. Waring's teaching was clearly influenced by, and later included, earlier efforts with chance. When he made dances, though, he worked using intuition, instinct, and impulse.

Chance's resonance lies in its suspension between positions, its balance achieved by the oppositional tensions of order and anarchy, choice and acceptance, autonomy and community, self-generated and externally composed acts, natural and cultural, subject and object. In dance-making, chance embodies or envelops the conflicts and ironies posed about possibilities of the body/the performer/the choreographer as a neutral figure, as object. These were the concerns—and the fabric— of the works made by the Judson dancers. But for Waring, I suspect, the usefulness of chance was in its potential as a backstage choreographic tool, one with which to expand and develop the choices of the artist, to find the widest possible range of elements outside the limitations of intuition, ego, and habit; nonetheless, it was his choreographic way to return to his own inner logic. In 1958 he considered the dances of Cunningham, "that eminent hoofer," made "by mechanical means. . . . You could call this process getting rid of yourself, and getting to the object. Or getting rid of karma. You never really get rid of yourself, anyhow. I mean, there you are! What nonsense!"[97] In 1965 he contemplated his own mix of attitudes: "I seldom know what I'm doing at the actual time of making. I work very much through intuition: I have been influenced by the chance techniques of John Cage and Merce Cunningham but never apply them directly or literally to my work. I have evolved no theories or rules about choreography. I don't believe that mine is the only way, especially since my way keeps changing. (I try to work through serenity and love and trust.) I think it is good to know as much as you can but not to depend on any of it."[98]

Later, in " 'Who's Counting?' Or, 'Over the Rainbow' " (1972), Waring suggested an assignment: "Make a dance coming from an attitude
you don't have, or hadn't thought of." A few lines later, he offers another
assignment, this one a devil's advocate variation on composer La Monte
Young's minimalist 1960 score, "Draw a straight line and follow it." Instead, advised Waring, "Draw a straight line and don't follow it."[99]
Throughout the essay, his insights, questions, and comments reflect
back on dance, both his own work and the work of the Judson. A few
examples:

How long should a dance be? Long enough to reach the ground. What
is minimal in minimal art? The audience? Does it take more effort to
get there to see it than the effort in making it? . . . What is so great
about effort, anyhow?[100]

Is a dance with no quantity, no length, really a dance? Is it conceptual
art? . . . Or just plain art?[101]

You have to measure, and divide, before you can count. Some people
can't count to one. Counting involves commitment, a commitment to
the moment, but a willingness not to cling to it. In relinquishing the
moment, one realizes it.[102]

In making dances, in teaching technique and composition, in writing
and conversation, James Waring asked many questions. Some were
shared by the dancers of the Judson Dance Theater in their choreographic explorations; others were integral to his singular sensibility.
Some questions he had asked for years before the advent of the Judson;
others were formulated in the years that followed, as he continued to
make dances and observe the art of his colleagues. Always, his resolu-
tions called forth an exchange of ideas, and a belief in the reciprocity
of the one who makes art and the one who actively returns the favor.
In his words: "Do we make dancing spectacular ourselves, in the way
that we watch? Does our pleasure depend upon our generosity? Is pleasure a meeting of generosities? Who's counting the moments?"[103]

Notes

1. Judith Dunn, "My Work and Judson's," *Ballet Review* 1, no. 6 (1967): 26.
2. This chapter is based on work I did for my master's thesis (Department of Performance Studies, New York University, 1989). I would like to thank Marcia B. Siegel for

her close readings and valuable suggestions, and the late Michael Kirby for his insights into 1960s performance. I would also like to thank David Vaughan for his invaluable assistance in researching the choreography of James Waring. Vaughan, who was Waring's friend and colleague, has spoken with me about Waring and his work on many more occasions than those "formal" interviews cited here, and he generously helped me procure photographs, documents, tapes, and other materials as well.

3. The dancers named here include active participants in the Judson Dance Theater workshops and concerts as well as those who joined the group's activities on an occasional basis or after the group had begun to disband.

4. Because of the focus of this chapter, most of Waring's dances to which I refer date from the 1950s and early 1960s; in some instances, however, I mention a dance made after the Judson years because it seems clearly representative of a long-term choreographic practice or style. My references to Waring's dances are largely based on published reviews and on historical accounts and personal memories of his colleagues. Moreover, I was fortunate to have studied and performed with Waring in the early 1970s, and I draw also on that brief, rich experience.

5. Linda Hutcheon, *A Theory of Parody* (New York: Methuen, 1985).

6. James Waring, *James Waring*, transcript, radio program of Jim D'Anna, WRVR-FM, New York, moderator Marcia B. Siegel, 10 January 1976, pp. 9–10.

7. Sally Banes, *Democracy's Body: Judson Dance Theater, 1962–1964* (Ann Arbor: University of Michigan Research Press, 1983), xviii.

8. James Waring, "My Work" [1965], *Ballet Review* 5, no. 4 (1975–76): 108–9.

9. Ibid., 108.

10. Jack Anderson, "The Paradoxes of James Waring," *Dance Magazine*, November 1968, 66.

11. David Vaughan, interview by the author, 2 December 1987.

12. Even Merce Cunningham, whose work has generally precluded balletic whimsy, in 1976 unveiled for television's *Dance in America* an excerpt of his 1953 *Septet*, a dance characterized by the kind of off-center charm and delicacy associated with Waring's ballets; the piece, which had not been in repertory since 1964, was performed again in concert in 1987.

13. Even so, in 1986 Lincoln Kirstein berated those choreographers who "appropriate ballet as a *style,* not a sequence of steps in an inherited academic vocabulary" ("The Curse of Isadora," *New York Times*, 23 November 1986, sec. 2, p. 28).

14. Aileen Passloff, qtd. in Waring, *Waring*, 14.

15. Umberto Eco, "Innovation and Repetition: Between Modern and Post-Modern Aesthetics," *Daedalus* 114 (Fall 1985): 178.

16. Renato Poggioli is among those who see romanticism and the avant-garde united by a continuous line "chronologically and historically," and he notes, too, that artists themselves have tended to be hostile to the connection between the avant-garde and romanticism, in the name of ridding themselves of past influences (*The Theory of the Avant-Garde,* trans. Gerald Fitzgerald [Cambridge: Harvard University Press, 1986], 46–47). And Octavio Paz, reflecting on the acceptance of prosaic elements into Romantic poetry, "the insertion of a foreign body—humor, irony, reflective pause—intended to interrupt the tripping of the syllables," might be speaking of the combination of elements that appeared in Waring's work (*The Bow and the Lyre,* trans. Ruth L. C. Simms [Austin: University of Texas Press, 1967], 71).

17. Qtd. in Ihab Hassan, "The Question of Postmodernism," in *Romanticism, Mod-*

ernism, Postmodernism, ed. Harry R. Garvin (Lewisburg, Pa.: Bucknell University Press, 1980), 118.

18. Numerous scholars and dancers have written about the Judson Dance Theater itself and about the visual, performing, and literary arts with which the Judson work interacted; a short list of these writers includes Sally Banes, Susan Foster, Jill Johnston, Deborah Jowitt, Allan Kaprow, Michael Kirby, Richard Kostelanetz, Yvonne Rainer, and Henry Sayre.

19. Banes, *Democracy's Body,* 32.

20. Waring, *Waring,* 8.

21. Al Carmines, "James Waring at Judson: A Chronology," prepared by the Judson Arts Program Archive Committee, April 1978, n.p.

22. During the October 1961–February 1962 season, for example, the group offered a program of plays including works by Waring as well as Michael McClure, LeRoi Jones (Amiri Baraka), di Prima, and others (Banes, *Democracy's Body,* 31–32).

23. Among these was the mention in November 1963 of "a proposed modern dance repertory company for the work of new choreographers," organized by Waring and sponsored by the American Theater for Poets (ibid., 170).

24. Ibid., 131, 132, 170, 194.

25. Ibid., 54.

26. Vaughan interview, December 1987.

27. Waring, *Waring,* 19.

28. Waring felt that the work of the Judson was distinguished from Happenings and that it did not come *from* them; he stated that the Judson "was primarily dance," that its work included "things that you could relate to Happenings but they sprang mostly from a dance point of view" (James Waring, John Herbert McDowell, Judith Dunn, Arlene Croce, and Don McDonagh, "Judson: A Discussion," *Ballet Review* 1, no. 6 [1967]: 50).

29. Vaughan interview, December 1987; Doris Hering, review, *Dance Magazine,* February 1961, 60.

30. Jill Johnston, review, *Village Voice,* 17 December 1958, 7.

31. Jill Johnston, review, *Village Voice,* 2 March 1960, 10.

32. Marianne Simon, review, *Village Voice,* 11 March 1959, 9.

33. Doris Hering, review, *Dance Magazine,* March 1955, 66–67.

34. Waring et al., "Judson," 31.

35. Banes, *Democracy's Body,* 153; Yvonne Rainer, telephone interview by the author, 16 March 1988.

36. Waring, "My Work," 110.

37. Doris Hering, review, *Dance Magazine,* March 1955, 67.

38. Doris Hering, review, *Dance Magazine,* June 1957, 87.

39. Doris Hering, review, *Dance Magazine,* February 1961, 60.

40. Waring, *Waring.*

41. Vaughan interview, December 1987.

42. Rainer interview.

43. Vaughan interview, December 1987.

44. Vaughan, telephone interview by the author, November 1987; Vaughan interview, December 1987.

45. Vaughan interview, December 1987.

46. John Herbert McDowell, "Movie Musicals: Being a Dissertation on Two

Books (Neither Brand New) and Mr. Berkeley," *Ballet Review* 2, no. 2 (1968): 106, 105.

47. Ibid., 106–7.

48. Waring et al., "Judson," 45.

49. Marcia Marks, review, *Dance Magazine*, March 1963, 59.

50. Vaughan interview, December 1987.

51. Jack Anderson, review of James Waring and Judson revivals, *Dance Magazine*, July 1966, 31.

52. Doris Hering, review, *Dance Magazine*, April 1968, 84.

53. Bryan Hayes, interview by the author, 8 December 1987.

54. Ibid.

55. Many of Waring's dances maintained traditional male and female roles; Yvonne Rainer characterized Waring's relationship to women as "Balanchinean—he was the gardener, they were the flowers" (Rainer interview). But the gender imagery in his work was varied and complex; for example, Marcia Marks noted in response to *Dromenon* (1961) that the faces of the dancers were "masklike," but that while the women were "beautiful but anonymous," the men were "insistently personal" (Marks, review, 59). I have discussed this use of gender imagery in "James Waring: Issues of Gender and Postmodernism," a paper presented at the November 1989 conference of the Congress on Research in Dance, Williamsburg, Virginia.

56. See Susan Sontag, "Notes on Camp" [1964], in *Against Interpretation* (New York: Farrar, Straus, Giroux, 1986), 275–92. Waring's solo *Feathers,* created in 1973 for dancer Raymond Johnson and dedicated to Barbette, the transvestite trapeze artist of the 1920s and 1930s, is a vivid evocation and commentary on the performance styles of this period, perhaps Waring's richest piece about sexual ambiguity, and one that has most often raised the suggestion of camp. Johnson, costumed in an extraordinary and lavish costume, his brief skirt like a tutu or toga and his beaded headdress a reminder of a "pseudo-Cleopatra silent film" (Ellen Stodolsky, review, *Dance Magazine*, November 1973, 27), creates a picture of ambiguity. His oblique glances and fluttering fingers, his "glamorous, vampy plastique poses" (Sally Banes, review of James Waring Festival, Judson Memorial Church, 21–30 April 1978, *Dance Magazine*, August 1978, 30), contrast, or conflict, with his muscular physique, his potential to move "big." Ronald Dabney, who learned the dance from Johnson, characterizes the dance as being about female impersonation, about "fooling and telling," and as an erotic interchange between the dancer and the spectator—the dancer teases the spectator, gives him the "privilege of seeing part of me" (Ronald Dabney, telephone interview by the author, 16 March 1989).

57. The concept of camp is still operative, but its connotations have changed since the 1960s. The continuing investigations into the performance of gender and sexuality characterizing contemporary dance, theater, and scholarship have recontextualized the term.

58. Sontag, "Notes on Camp," 278, 277.

59. Ibid., 288.

60. David Vaughan characterized these years as "an interim period between Jimmy's early works and the later works which became much more balletic, when he really wanted to work with ballet dancers [and] wanted the technical possibilities he could give them" (Vaughan interview, December 1987).

61. Jill Johnston, "The New American Modern Dance," in *The New American Arts*, ed. Richard Kostelanetz (New York: Collier-Macmillan, 1969), 181–82.

62. Doris Hering, review, *Dance Magazine*, May 1964, 64.

63. Waring, *Waring*, 30.

64. Johnston, "New American Modern Dance," 181–82; Marks, review, 59; also see Yvonne Rainer, *Work, 1961–1973* (New York and Halifax: New York University Press and The Press of the Nova Scotia College of Art and Design, 1974), 6, 315.

65. Banes, *Democracy's Body*, 208.

66. David Gordon, essay in "The Legacy of Robert Ellis Dunn (1928–1996)," *Movement Research Journal* 14 (Spring 1997): 19; Banes, *Democracy's Body*, 28.

67. Waring et al., "Judson," 31.

68. David Gordon and Valda Setterfield, interview by the author, 9 December 1987; Sally Gross, interview by the author, 19 September 1990.

69. Qtd. in Banes, *Democracy's Body*, 69.

70. Johnston, "New American Modern Dance," 182.

71. Gordon and Setterfield interview. Gordon remembers that in Merce Cunningham's composition classes, on the other hand, students "literally were tossing pennies until you were blue in the face. And then, after you got your whole score rigged up, you gave it to somebody else. And they did yours and you did theirs. So that was really chance. That isn't what went on in Jimmy's classes."

72. Gordon, essay in "Legacy," 19.

73. Gordon and Setterfield interview.

74. Ibid.

75. Gordon, essay in "Legacy," 19.

76. Gordon and Setterfield interview.

77. Waring et al., "Judson," 50.

78. Gordon and Setterfield interview; Waring, *Waring*, 31–32.

79. Doris Hering, review, *Dance Magazine*, January 1954, 46.

80. Vaughan interview, December 1987.

81. This phrase is borrowed from a 1919 study of plastique, or "fluid sculpture," which was sometimes echoed in Waring's dances. For some practitioners it was organized into a system of body shapes whose codified gestures, postures, and facial expressions represented particular emotional states. For example, "grief" might be represented by a kneeling position, elbow to knee, eyes shut, and "offering" by eyes to hands, arms raised, one foot slightly raised (Frank Leslie Clendenon, *The Art of Dancing: Its Theory and Practice* [St. Louis: Arcade Print Shop, 1919], 27).

82. Gordon and Setterfield interview.

83. Vaughan interview, December 1987.

84. Rainer, *Work*, 65.

85. Doris Hering, review, *Dance Magazine*, February 1961, 60; Vaughan interview, December 1987.

86. Waring, *Waring*, 1–3; Gordon and Setterfield interview.

87. Banes, *Democracy's Body*, 18, 28.

88. Rainer interview.

89. Waring, *Waring*, 5.

90. In an interview with David Gordon and Valda Setterfield, Gordon somewhat jokingly recalled how his duet with Setterfield in Waring's *Dances before the Wall* came into being "for the simple reason that I was leaving rehearsal at the time that she was arriving at rehearsal and I didn't get changed fast enough, while she changed faster." He and Setterfield elaborated on the responsibility of both "vagueness [as] an aesthetic that Jimmy was pursuing" (Setterfield) and "economics and expediency" (Gordon) in

Waring's dance-making. For instance, dancers' availability depended largely on who had outside jobs and on when those jobs left them free to rehearse. Dance material was accumulated over a long period of time, and Waring was always open to new input into his choreographic scheme. A month before the performance of *Dances*, he invited Setterfield, newly arrived from England, to join the dance; "He's just met this new dancer and he says, 'Oh great, come and be in the concert'" (Gordon).

91. Gordon and Setterfield interview.

92. Ibid.; Waring, *Waring.*

93. Gross interview.

94. Banes, *Democracy's Body*, 99.

95. Rainer interview.

96. Gordon and Setterfield interview.

97. James Waring, "Five Essays on Dancing," *Ballet Review* 2, no. 1 (1967): 71.

98. Waring, "My Work," 113.

99. James Waring, "'Who's Counting?' Or 'Over the Rainbow,'" *Ballet Review* 4, no. 2 (1972): 19.

100. Ibid., 18.

101. Ibid., 19.

102 Ibid.

103. Ibid., 19–20.

4

The Philosophy of Art History, Dance, and the 1960s

Noël Carroll

For more than a decade, in numerous books and articles, the art critic and philosopher Arthur Danto has advanced the controversial conjecture that art history has come to an end. In his 1997 book, *After the End of Art,* Danto goes so far as to offer a date for the end of art—namely, somewhere around 1964—and he has even dared to name the artist who he believes brought closure to the history of art. That artist is said to be Andy Warhol, whose exhibition of his *Brillo Box* at the Stable Gallery on East Forty-seventh Street in Manhattan is alleged by Danto to have brought art history to a climax.[1]

This is a bold if not foolhardy claim, courting paradox openly, since as anyone can see there are still tens of thousands of painters painting. But Danto, like everyone else, must know this. Indeed, Danto should know it better than many, since he is a practicing art critic, one who, among other things, has won the National Book Award for his discussions of the contemporary art scene. So Danto must mean something rather special when he talks of the end of art—when he alleges that Warhol liquidated the tradition in 1964. What might that be?

Before I try to answer that question, another question is likely to occur to you, the reader. It is: Why are we talking about Danto and his theory of the end of art, since that is a theory about painting and we are here to talk about dance? My justification for this apparent digression begins, of course, with the date that Danto has elected for the end of art—1964. For 1964 was not only the year Warhol rocked the art-world scene with *Brillo Box;* the 1963–64 season was also when the

Judson Dance Theater engineered a comparable revolution in the dance world. Nor are the two phenomena simply a matter of two ships passing in the night. The two revolutions trumpeted many of the same themes, such as the attempted blurring of the distinction between art and reality.

That is, if Warhol by means of his *Brillo Box* tried to problematize the boundary between artworks and everyday artifacts such as industrial packages, then, in like manner, Steve Paxton's *Satisfyin Lover* attempted to question any categorical difference that might be said to distinguish dance from ordinary, everyday movements like walking. Moreover, since Warhol's accomplishment, according to Danto, was to create artworks that were indiscernible from real things—Brillo boxes that were works of art which nevertheless looked just like mundane, ordinary Brillo boxes—then one wonders whether Paxton, Yvonne Rainer, and the other innovators of the Judson Dance Theater don't deserve the same sort of commendation for their attempt to level the difference between dancing and ordinary movement, between choreography and, for example, eating a sandwich.

Perhaps the Judson Dance Theater brought dance history to a climax in a manner that is strictly analogous to the way in which Danto alleges that Warhol brought closure to painting. That is, perhaps Danto's insights about Warhol might enable us to reconfigure the history of dance so as to enable us to see the significance of the Judson Dance Theater in a new light.

But before we think about the relevance of Danto's theory for dance, we need to come to terms with it on its home grounds, painting. Danto says that the history of painting came to an end somewhere around 1964. But what could "end" mean in this context? As we have seen, it makes no sense to say that painting stopped in 1964—that there were no more paintings made after 1964. People are still painting today; inasmuch as there are more people today than there were in 1964 and earlier, there are probably more people painting today, in the period Danto claims is after the end of art, than there were at work in the heyday of art. So when Danto speaks of the end of art, he cannot mean that people have stopped painting.

Instead, the sense of an ending that Danto has in mind is the end of a certain developmental process. Some of you may recall Woody Allen's humorous and altogether fanciful history of the sandwich. The Earl of Sandwich starts out with an assortment of ingredients: slices of bread, condiments, meats, and so forth. He wants to combine them in a convenient way for eating. His early experiments are failures. First he piles meats and condiments on a single piece of bread, but when he grabs it, he gets mustard all over himself. After years of brooding over this failure, he tries another experiment; he puts the single piece of bread between two pieces of meat, with the mustard spread between the salami and the bread. That's better, but his hand still gets greasy. Finally a lightbulb goes off in his head and the problem is decisively illuminated. He puts the salami and the condiments between two pieces of bread and waves the result triumphantly. The problem is solved. The sandwich is invented. The story of the sandwich is over. Or, to speak more precisely, the developmental history of the sandwich, the story of the progressive attempts to get the design of the sandwich just right, comes to a close. The problem has met with a solution; the evolution of the sandwich in terms of the purposes that set the process in motion is complete.

True, people still go on making sandwiches, even into our own day. And every once in a while modifications are made on the basic design of the sandwich: the triple-decker sandwich, the Dagwood sandwich, and so on. But in a certain sense, the story of the sandwich is over once the basic design of the sandwich is in place. The story of the sandwich, its developmental history, has come to a close; everything that comes after that, including all the sandwiches you and I might make, are, to change metaphors, icing on the cake. Our sandwiches, though undeniably sandwiches, are posthistorical sandwiches.

This is a silly example. A more serious one might be Newtonian physics. At a certain point in the nineteenth century, physicists dreamed of the possibility that complete knowledge of the physical universe was within their reach, if only some details of the Newtonian system could be worked out. Imagine everything had gone as planned. Then we might have spoken of the end of physics, even though engineers would have still gone on applying Newtonian formulas in the process of building bridges. The Newtonian project would have come to an end, even though children would continue to be taught physics and adults would continue to use it in the construction of various technologies. Perhaps adjustments or refinements of physics would be made here and there. But the story of physics, for all intents and purposes, would have been over.

When a practice has a project, one can imagine the project coming to an end. Narratives are our typical means for representing such projects. If the president is kidnapped near the beginning of the story, that sets in motion the problem of rescuing her. When that problem is solved (when the president is rescued), the story comes to an end. It has what literary theorists call closure. Presumably the president goes on doing things after she is rescued. But that is not part of the story. The story is over when the problem is solved and the project is discharged. There *is* life after narrative; it's just not part of the story.

So the sense of ending that Danto has in mind is the kind of ending—the kind of closure—that pertains to stories, to the past configured as a historical narrative, indeed configured as a developmental, historical narrative. Just as Hegel did not mean that the sun would never rise again after the end of history, Danto does not mean canvases will not be painted after the end of art. He, like Hegel, only means that a certain story has reached its terminus: that Warhol, somewhere around 1964, had solved a certain problem, or, more accurately, brought a certain project as far along as it was possible to bring it. That is, when Danto says that we have reached the end of art, what he means, stated less paradoxically, is that a certain developmental project has evolved to a point at which no more progress is possible. It turns out that Danto does not think that Warhol, like the Earl of Sandwich, completely solved the problem that confronted him. Rather, Danto argues that Warhol brought his problem as close to a solution as any painter could.

Of course, this is an obscure way of speaking, unless I divulge what Danto takes to be the problem that challenged Warhol, along with indicating its place in the evolving tradition of Western painting. In order to do that, I must offer a brief sketch of Danto's account of the history of painting. Here it is important to remember that Danto thinks of history in terms of narratives, and of narratives as underwritten by human purposes and projects that aspire toward solutions.

The earliest stages of art history for Danto, as for many others, essentially involve the history of pictorial representation. This history starts in Greece and then is taken up again in the Renaissance. It is underwritten by a project: verisimilitude, or the approximation of the perceptual appearance of real three-dimensional things by means of flat surfaces. The aim of this sort of art (which we might call mimetic after the theories of mimesis of Plato and Aristotle) is vividly, if hyperbolically, captured in those Greek anecdotes about birds mistaking pictures of grapes for real fruit and artists mistaking trompe l'oeil drapery for actual curtains. Call this aspiration: the conquest of perceptual reality.

This project is the engine that drives art history for centuries. It is the existence of this project that enables art historians from Vasari to Gombrich to compose a narrative history of art. There is a problem: the representation of the appearance of three-dimensional things on flat surfaces. Succeeding generations of artists can be plotted along an evolutionary trajectory inasmuch as each development, such as the refinement of perspective, brings the project closer and closer to realizing its aims. The construction of pictorial space via perspective is followed with even more heightened realism with respect to shadow and texture. And so on. Art movements such as realism and even impressionism can be explained as stages in the evolving story of approximating the look of perceptual reality. Moreover, this process is abetted by theory; philosophers of art repeat in treatise after treatise that art is essentially representational.

This is the first stage of the history of art, its beginning, in the Aristotelian sense; it contrasts with a middle and an end. It is clearly a developmental history, the history of a project that informed the practice of painting for generations. Perhaps it was not the project of every painter, but it is of such overriding concern both practically and theoretically that it renders a rather comprehensive chunk of art history intelligible. As a story, it is more comprehensive than any other competing story we know.

But stories require complications; they are not just beginnings. There are also middles. And the story of art as the history of representation reaches a crisis point. This occurs roughly in the nineteenth century and can be marked by the invention of photography. Photography, it might be said, realizes the project of mimetic art only too easily. Photography, as it is refined, is capable of capturing the visual appearances of things automatically. And when photography is developed into cinema, it seems to surpass the wildest dreams of mimetic art, for cinema not only represents the visual appearances of things mechanically in a way that comes to rival painting; it goes painting one better by capturing a dimension of visual appearances categorically denied to painting—namely, movement. Thus cinema is even more realistic in this respect than painting could ever be.

Photography and cinema, in effect, bring the project of art—construed in terms of perceptual verisimilitude—to a conclusion. But this, then, raises a new problem: what will be the vocation of art after the conquest of perceptual reality? Would the history of art construed as a developmental story end with masses of painters queuing up for job retraining programs?

Of course, this is not what happened. Instead, at the level of both theory and practice, artists and philosophers identified new projects for painting. Noteworthy among these are formalism of the sort championed by Clive Bell with help from Kant, and expressionism of the variety defended by many philosophers of the first part of the twentieth century, including R. G. Collingwood and Susanne K. Langer.

According to the formalist program, art was never really about representation; it is about the creation of significant form, which raises in spectators a species of aesthetic experience that earlier theorists would have called beauty.[2] For formalists, painting is about the play of structure and color—the play of formal elements. Historically, one can read this as an act of recuperation in the face of the fact that photography and cinema put representational painting out of business. Moreover, it presents a way of radically recuperating art history. Art history, on this view, was never really about the conquest of perceptual appearances according to the formalists. All genuine art of the past was really about formal invention. At the same time, the demotion of representation and the concomitant elevation of form by the polemics of theorists and critics such as Clive Bell and Roger Fry made experiments in abstract painting more intelligible.

Formalism, however, was not the only available reaction to the end of the representational project. Expressionism is another. For the expressionist, art is not about capturing the appearances of the perceptual, external world but rather about clarifying the inner world of feelings. Through strategies such as distortion, German Expressionists sought an iconography of the soul, while abstraction, in the case of artists such as Kandinsky, also provided a serviceable medium for expression.

But even if formalism and expressionism provided vocations for art after the closure of the developmental history of representational painting, these vocations were different in kind from the one afforded by mimetic art. Why? Because mimetic art gave painters a project—a clear-cut target to hit, namely, perceptual verisimilitude. One could gauge progress toward that end in a fairly straightforward manner; one could gauge closer and closer approximations of perceptual appearances. And inasmuch as there was a clearly defined end to the project, an assessable solution to the problem, it enabled painters to live in a story that promised a climax.

But that is not the case under either the formalist or the expressionist dispensation. Artists could discover formal structure after formal structure, or clarify an indefinitely large number of emotions. But there was no specifiable end that could be conjectured to either enterprise. There was no formal structure whose discovery would herald a completion of the formalist agenda, nor was there any emotion whose expression would mark the end of the trail. Formalism and expressionism provided artists with ways to go on after the goal of representation was effectively closed off. They did not, however, generate new *developmental* narratives; they lacked a project with clearly defined closure. Thus they did not provide the grounds for a continuing narrative of art—one with a beginning, middle, and end.

This pause in the forward-moving propulsion of the story of art, however, was only a momentary stopping point. For during the period of reaction to the closing of the mimetic project, another option, an alternative to both formalism and expressionism, appeared, which once again afforded a project for painters. It was a project with a clearly defined target, a project, therefore, that opened the possibility that painting could once again tell of itself a developmental story. That project is what has come to be called modernism.

According to modernist theory, as enacted by painters and recounted by critics, the role of art was to define its own essential nature. Painting became a form of critique, an interrogation of its own conditions of possibility. Given the fate of the mimetic project, the nature of painting was no longer thought to reside in representing perceptual appearances accurately; it was to be sought elsewhere. Like the mimetic project, the modernist project had a clear-cut target. For presumably painting had an essential nature. Successive approximations of that nature would move the modernist project toward completion. Artists had a definable goal once again, which, among other things, meant that painting could once more be characterized by a developing narrative.

One version of that story, as told by Clement Greenberg and repeated by many others, is that modern art is an adventure in clarifying the nature of its basic elements: the two-dimensionality of the picture plane, composed essentially of line and color. Cubism, on this account, works in a shallow pictorial space, one to be contracted virtual centimeter by virtual centimeter until it appears coextensive with the canvas in the work of Morris Louis, while the work of Jackson Pollock is said to be about exhibiting the ontological fact that line and color are the fundamental constituents of painting. The painting itself was thought to be a real thing, rather than a representation of something else. That real thing belonged to a certain category, painting, a category with its own integrity, its own nature, constituted of features such as flatness.

For Danto, it is into this modernist narrative, this story of art's project of self-definition, that Warhol and kindred spirits make their decisive interventions. Pop artists such as Lichtenstein and Johns challenge the modernist oppositions such as flat painterly things versus representations by making paintings of comic-book panels and flags that are at once, in certain senses, both flat *and* representations—since they are representations of flat things. Perhaps it was their devilish deconstruction of his basic categories that so ill-disposed Greenberg to Pop Art.

A basic presupposition of modernism à la Greenberg was that paintings are real things rather than representations. Nevertheless, they were a distinct sort of real thing, painted things with their own essential perceptual characteristics, such as flatness. Put bluntly, paintings were still thought to be different from other sorts of real things in perceptually discernible ways. The importance of Warhol for Danto is that Warhol undermined this presupposition by creating objects such as *Brillo Box*, which were artworks at the same time they were perceptually indiscernible from other sorts of real things, notably ordinary Brillo boxes by Proctor and Gamble. That is, Warhol in effect proposed that something could be a work of art irrespective of the way it looked; a work of art could look like anything.

This challenged Greenberg's version of modernism, since that was based on the presupposition that the critique of painting could proceed by using the means of painting, the visual elements of painting, to show *for anyone to see* what differentiates painting in its essential nature from everything else. But the argument implicit in Warhol's *Brillo Box* is that whatever makes something art is something the eye cannot descry, since though Warhol's *Brillo Box* looks just like an ordinary Brillo box, his *Brillo Box* is art and Proctor and Gamble's is not. Warhol demonstrated, in other words, that artworks could look like anything, that they did not have necessary self-defining, perceptible features. Warhol proposed that artworks could just look like ordinary, everyday things.

Warhol's achievement, then, according to Danto, is a contribution to the definition of art, but one that brings the modernist project to a halt rather than to a conclusion. For by proposing that art can look like anything else, Warhol places an insurmountable barrier in the way of the modernist project. The idea behind modernism was that painting could interrogate its own nature by deploying its own means, its perceptible properties, reflexively. The modernist painter, in other words, could discover and make others *see* the nature of painting in virtue of the way the relevant paintings *looked*. In contrast, Warhol's experiments implied that what made something art was not a matter of the way things looked, an insight perhaps already presaged by Duchamp's readymades. This, of course, represents a contribution to the discussion of the nature of art initiated by modernism. But it also indicates a limit to how far painters operating as painters, that is, as people whose medium is how things look, can contribute to such a discussion. For if how things look is ultimately irrelevant to art status, then visual artists using the media at their disposal do not possess suitable means to show what makes something art rather than something else—just because whatever that differentia might be, it is something that is indiscernible perceptually.

Warhol proposed that the difference between artworks and real things is not something you can eyeball. But if that differentia is not something you can show or see, then it is not something to which painters as visual artists can give us perceptual access: it is not something they can *show* us. Thus, according to Danto, Warhol and other artists of the sixties brought the modernist narrative to a halt by making works that implied that the nature of art was not a topic that could be pursued to the bitter end in the medium of painting. It required another medium. And predictably enough, Danto, a philosopher, says that that medium is philosophy. So, for Danto, with Warhol's work, art history as a progressive narrative reaches a stopping point, a point beyond which it can go no further. This is no tragedy, however, for the work of Warhol and others is also liberating. Inasmuch as it implies that art can look like anything, it ushers in an era of radical pluralism when art can take on any form, from performance art to installations of every configuration. Thus, art in posthistorical times (Danto's name for our own epoch) has given up the prospect of having a story, a progressive myth to tell about itself, but in return it possesses a newfound freedom and diversity.

There are, of course, a number of problems of detail with Danto's theory of the end of art. And yet, the large movements Danto traces in the coordinated development of Western art practice and theory do concur with much of the tradition's self-understanding. That is, Danto has retold the story of painting in terms that the art world already, if only vaguely, acknowledges, though he has, perhaps, told it with more explanatory elegance than is customary, linking the different moments in the dialectic into a seamless narrative network. And for our purposes, this raises two questions: first, to what extent, if any, can the model Danto has constructed for the history of painting serve as a model of the history of dance; and second, if it is so serviceable, can Danto's observations about Warhol help organize our understanding of the significance of comparable choreographic artists such as Yvonne Rainer, Steve Paxton, David Gordon, Lucinda Childs, Douglas Dunn, and others?

The answer to the first question is that Danto's history of fine art tracks the evolution of dance practice and theory to a remarkable degree. That is, the history of dance—as the development of choreographic practice and theoretical speculation—can readily be told as a story whose major moments correspond very closely to the major movements in Danto's history of painting.

If Western theatrical dancing proper can be said to begin roughly in the eighteenth century with the theoretical writings and practice of Jean-Georges Noverre, it must also be agreed that Noverre operated within a context dominated by representation theories of art.[3] For example, in 1747, Charles Batteux published a treatise entitled *The Beaux-Arts Reduced to a Single Principle.*[4] For Batteux, everything that is to count as a work of art meets the same criterion, which is imitation, an idea common, as we have seen, to Western philosophers as early as Plato and Aristotle.

Noverre was a man with a mission. As a choreographer, he was committed to getting dance taken seriously. To do this, he aspired to have the dance recognized as an art form. And since the presiding theory of art was that art is essentially imitation or representation, this committed Noverre to arguing that dance is representation.

Of course, like other philosophers, such as Adam Smith, Noverre

knew that not all dance was representational. As Smith put it, much of
the dance of his and Noverre's time, from peasant jigs to court masques,
was not representational but rather a succession of airs and figures, a
matter of cadenced steps functionally aimed at displaying grace and agil-
ity.[5] But Noverre was not concerned with describing dance as it was.
He was concerned with saying what dance should become—what dance
should become in order to be considered art, the most obvious means
at Noverre's disposal for having dance taken seriously.

Thus, Noverre advocated that dance forsake its ornamentalism and
airs and become an art of imitation. Noverre writes, "A well-composed
ballet is a living picture of the passions, manners, customs [and] cere-
monies . . . of . . . nations."[6] And he argued that ballets must be devised
with action in order to achieve this purpose. Of course, the *drama* Aristotle correlates with mimesis derives its name from the Greek word for
"doing." So in calling for dance to become the imitation of action (or
of doings), Noverre is effectively calling for dance to become a kind of
theater rather than a collection of charming steps. The development of
the *ballet d'action,* the form associated with Noverre's writing and practice and which dominates the period of the Romantic ballet as well, is
essentially linked to the mimetic or representational theory of art.

Noverre's constant analogies between drama and painting, the two
arts Plato used to exemplify mimesis in his *Republic,* are especially telling in this regard. Throughout his letters, Noverre is at pains to claim
that dance has powers comparable to painting and theater and that the
appropriate line for the evolution of dance to follow is to exploit these
powers. Otherwise, dance will not assume its proper place in the system
of the fine arts. Thus the upshot of Noverre's practices and polemics is
to segue the initial development of dance in the modern period (the only
period of Western dance about which we can speak with confidence) to
the first stage of the grand story of art that we have heard from Danto.

If the first act of dance history corresponds to the beginning of
Danto's story of art, what of later episodes? As the authority of the view
that representation is the essence of art eroded in the late nineteenth
and early twentieth centuries, we find that serious thinking about dance,
like serious thinking about painting, turns in the direction of alternatives
such as formalism and expressionism.

The formalist moment is perhaps best articulated by the critic-theo-
rist André Levinson, who worked in Russia and later France. Perhaps

struck by the aesthetic superiority of the divertissements of the Russian Imperial Ballet over its story elements, Levinson locates the value of dance in its capacity to create compelling patterns of movement that command our attention for their own sake. Levinson is also what we might call an essentialist about dance; he believes that dance should exploit those of its capabilities that differentiate it from every other art form. He disparages the notion that dance should be drama on the grounds that choreography should be its own art and not a subaltern to theater.

Assembling a theoretical heritage that he believes includes Théophile Gautier, Stéphane Mallarmé, and Paul Valéry, Levinson argues:

I can not think of anyone who has devoted himself to those characteristics which belong exclusively to dancing, or who has endeavored to formulate specifically the laws of this art on its own ground. . . . No one has ever tried to portray the intrinsic beauty of the dance step, its innate quality, its esthetic reason for being. . . . It is the desire of the dancer to create beauty which causes him to make use of his knowledge of mechanics and that finally dominates this knowledge. He subjects his muscles to a rigid discipline; through arduous practice he bends and adapts his body to the exigencies of an abstract and perfect form.[7]

Just as we find in the history of painting, in dance, formalism provides one option for responding to the collapse of the representational theory of art. But as in the history of painting, expressionism in dance is another. Modern dance—the dance of Graham, Humphrey, Wigman, Limón, and others—coalesces around the conviction that the proper function of dance is the expression of feelings. These convictions find voice not only in the writings of certain choreographers but in the theoretical speculation of critics and theorists like John Martin and Susanne K. Langer.[8]

Both Martin and Langer are committed to expression theories of art. Both see the substance of dance in expressive movement, which Martin calls "meta-kinesis" and which Langer locates in what she calls the realm of virtual powers. For Langer, that the scope of dance proper is delimited to the domain of virtual powers distinguishes it from drama, which for her is an affair of destiny. In contrast, Martin's view, that the arrangement of dance forms is dictated by "the logic of inner feeling," signals a necessary departure from the regulative standard of theatrical imitation (insofar as the logic of feeling is different from the logic of action, i.e., from the logic of narrative). Thus expressionism, like formalism, eschews Noverre's ideal of dance as essentially a theater art. Moreover, expressionism, especially as it figures in modern dance, will become one of the major provocations leading to the development of what is now referred to as postmodern dance.

Furthermore, as Danto's history of art predicts, by the middle of the twentieth century a form of dance modernism begins to appear alongside formalism and expressionism as a response to the decline of representation. In some of the abstract ballets of Balanchine[9] and the dances of Merce Cunningham, choreography that appears committed to disclosing the basic constituents of dancing begins to command increasing attention. However, as a critique of the nature of dance, this work retains the appearance of dance. No matter how pared down, Balanchine's vocabulary is still balletic, while Cunningham's leaps and partnering, though subverting the tradition, clearly look like dancing. Like the heroes of Greenbergian modernism, Balanchine's and Cunningham's critiques of dance remain, so to say, from the inside. They pursue the question of the nature of dance through an idiom of forms that are usually still perceptibly dancerly, forms that contrast discernibly from what might be called "everyday movement" or even "real movement."

Of course, it is at this point in the story that what we refer to as postmodern dance begins to assume a significance parallel to that which Danto attributes to the work of Warhol and his 1964 exhibition of *Brillo Box*. For Danto, Warhol's achievement resides in bringing the art world to the realization that works of art could look like anything, including mundane, ordinary objects. Likewise, at roughly the same time, in and around Judson Church, choreographers were creating dances with similar theoretical commitments. Just as Warhol problematized the distinction between artworks and ordinary objects, these choreographers challenged the distinction between dance movements and ordinary movement.[10]

Judith Dunn's *Acapulco,* for example, comprised hair brushing, playing cards, and ironing a dress. In Robert Dunn's composition class, Steve Paxton presented an untitled piece in which he ate a sandwich. In *Satisfyin Lover,* Paxton sends a platoon of people across the space walking in the unaffected way that one might stroll down the street, sustaining our interest by means of a structure that invites the comparison of different styles of walking. And Paxton returns to the subject of ordinary walking again in *Flat*, where he undresses, dresses, and ambulates in circles punctuated by moments of arrest. Likewise, Simone Forti's *See-Saw* presents an ordinary child's game as an opportunity for spectators to notice the microphysics of everyday movement. And Douglas Dunn composed a chair piece that involved nothing more than ordinary, though very deliberate, standing up and sitting down.

A strategy of postmodern dance with particular significance for leveling the boundary between dance movement and ordinary movement was the task. In *Room Service,* Yvonne Rainer has her performers carry a mattress through the space. Here everyday work movements are presented in a dance-world context in order to recall to mind the intelligence exhibited by the body in discharging mundane tasks. Theoretically, however, the work also suggests that movements that do not look like dance can be dance when framed in a way that underscores neglected properties of movement.

In Deborah Hay's *no. 3,* three helpers toppled and dragged three stacks of bricks while Hay ran evenly in circles. Similarly, the invented tasks in Simone Forti's *Slant Board* and *Rollers* present the audience with movements that do not look like dance but which become dance when exhibited in an aesthetic context in which our attention is less concerned with what is being done or accomplished and more concerned with how it is done: its mechanics, energies, and qualities. Task performances insinuate, in other words, that if a major subject of dance is the exhibition and perception of movement for its own sake, then the movements that we shall count as dance need not look at all like those bequeathed to us by tradition as dancerly. A dance movement can look like anything, even ordinary movement and work.

An important strategy of Pop artists for leveling the perceptual distinction between art and other things was, of course, to create artworks that were indistinguishable from the artifacts of popular culture. By presenting comic-book panels or movie stills as artworks, people like Lichtenstein, Claes Oldenburg, and Warhol attacked the distinction between high art—or art proper—and popular art. This line of attack is also evident in the work of postmodern choreographers. In Elaine Summers's *Suite,* the last section is organized around the then-popular dance, the Twist. Not only did the dancers twist, but the audience was invited to join in. This not only suggested that popular dancing like the

Twist was dance properly so-called but also, insofar as earlier sections of the dance were named "Galliard" and "Saraband," *Suite* insinuated that the distinction between high art dance and ordinary social dancing has frequently been quite porous.

If, using Danto's account of Warhol, we identify a major aim of early postmodern dance as articulating the perspective that dance movement can look like anything, then we are in a position to explain why Yvonne Rainer's *Trio A* has always been regarded as so theoretically important. Although this dance suggests the kind of energy levels expended in ordinary movement, it does not look like everyday movement. But at the same time, it does not look like anything our culture could readily recognize as dance. It is designed in such a way as to thwart the traditional categories we use for recognizing movement as dance movement, thereby insinuating that something can lack all the *perceptible* features we associate with dance movement and yet still be dance.

Trio A eschews arresting gestural shapes, using neither frozen moments nor movements like pirouettes or jetés that evoke a sense of an abstract, choreographic geometry or gestalt. No special parts of the body are privileged. Head, hands, and legs all move, not only defying the idea of a balletic line but also making it difficult to summarize the style in terms of a part of the body, as one might with the style of Limón in terms of emphasis on the upper torso. There are no repetitions or variations, as the dance forgoes even the vaguest rhythmic structure, and there is no demarcation between phrases. Perhaps needless to say, there is no story, character, attitude, or action. The dance even lacks a legible floor plan; it is not organized by means of an abstract geometry. In a sense, *Trio A* is a study in negations, an eschewal of the relevance of many of the central cultural criteria that we typically mobilize in order *perceptually* to recognize movement as dance. All these negatives, however, do add up to a positive thesis: namely, that any movement can be a dance movement, no matter what it looks like. In this way, Rainer and others managed to bring the evolving conversation of dance history roughly to that point to which Danto claims Warhol brought the conversation of art history in 1964.

One question that always arises in discussions of postmodern dance is, why isn't Merce Cunningham regarded as a postmodern choreographer? Certainly, he is respected as a forerunner. But why isn't he accorded a central place in the visionary company of postmoderns? Perhaps we can answer that question by recalling Danto's history of art. For Danto, modernists, notably those of the Greenbergian persuasion, were committed to pursuing the critique of painting via emphasis on the perceptible properties of painting: things like flatness, line, and color. They presupposed that art had certain discernible features, features you could eyeball. Warhol raised the ante in the game of critique, proposing artworks indistinguishable from real things.

In this light, one might say of Cunningham that his important work is analogous to the Greenbergian stage of modernism. Though many still might find his work incomprehensible (in the same way that spectators may still be confused by abstractionists like Stella), they nevertheless are able to recognize perceptually that Cunningham's movements generally fit into traditional categories of dance movement. In contrast to Paxton's *Satisfyin Lover*, Cunningham's leaps, however small, don't look like ordinary walking. Cunningham seminally advanced the critique of dance, but he stopped short of attempting to erase the boundary between dance movement and ordinary movement. That boundary (what Danto calls with respect to Warhol the indiscernibility question) remained to be crossed by Paxton, Rainer, and others. It was not until that border was pierced that these choreographers became postmodern and even, in a certain way of speaking, postmodern*ist*.

I hope that I have been able to show the relevance of Danto's philosophical history of art to dance history. I would not wish to endorse all of Danto's theses.[11] For example, Danto claims that Warhol has ended the progressive narrative of art for all time, and I am not convinced that anyone, including Danto, can know that.[12] Danto also points to another way in which Warhol is important to the history of art: he contends that Warhol liberated art, initiating a period of great pluralism, insofar as after Warhol, anything can be art. In this sense, Warhol is the founding intelligence of our posthistorical art world.

Surely a similar place of honor is due those choreographers who were Warhol's contemporaries: Rainer, Paxton, Gordon, Forti, Dunn, and many others. They, too, demonstrated that anything could become dance no matter how it looked—from Contact Improvisation to we know not what. In retrospect, they have extended the range of possibility for contemporary dance momentously. They have opened a new world of dance: not an end to dance, but perhaps a new beginning.

Notes

1. This article originated as a talk at the festival Talking Dancing in Stockholm, Sweden, in August 1997.

2. Arthur Danto, *After the End of Art: Contemporary Art and the Pale of History* (Princeton: Princeton University Press, 1997).

3. See Noël Carroll, "Beauty and the Genealogy of Art Theory," *Philosophical Forum* 22, no. 4 (1991): 307–34.

4. See Jean-Georges Noverre, *Letters on Dancing and Ballets,* trans. C. W. Beaumont (New York: Dance Horizons, 1966).

5. Charles Batteux, *Les Beaux-Arts réduits à un même principe,* ed. Jean-Remy Mantion (Paris: Aux Amateurs de Livres, 1989).

6. Adam Smith, *Essays on Philosophical Subjects* (Oxford: Oxford University Press, 1980).

7. Noverre, *Letters on Dancing and Ballets,* 16.

8. André Levinson, "The Spirit of the Classic Dance," in *Dance as a Theatre Art,* ed. Selma Jeanne Cohen (New York: Dodd, Mead, 1974), 113.

9. John Martin, *The Modern Dance* (New York: Dance Horizons, 1972); Susanne K. Langer, *Feeling and Form* (New York: Scribner's, 1953).

10. See, for example, David Michael Levin, "Balanchine's Formalism," *Dance Perspectives* 55 (Autumn 1973).

11. For an overview and description of dances by members of the Judson Dance Theater, see Sally Banes, *Democracy's Body: Judson Dance Theater, 1962–1964* (1980, 1983; reprint, Durham, N.C.: Duke University Press, 1993).

12. For my criticisms of Danto's *After the End of Art,* see Noël Carroll, "Danto's New Definition of Art and the Problem of Art Theories," *British Journal of Aesthetics* 37, no. 4 (1997): 386–92.

13. For criticism of Danto's thesis that art history is over, see Noël Carroll, "The End of Art?" in *History and Theory,* theme issue no. 37 (1998): 17–29.

5

Dance Quote Unquote

Jill Johnston

Dear Sally,

I'm studying a list of performances I did in the 1960s, looking for a common thread, or at least some sweeping reason for having done them. There were thirteen performances altogether, although two had only one audience member. That was Andy Warhol, who was shooting them as home movies. One took place the day of JFK's funeral in November 1963 at Billy Klüver's house in New Jersey. I doubt that it was premeditated, and I have no memory of what we were both doing there. But while the funeral was in progress on TV in the living room, Andy was shooting me in Billy's muddy backyard running around in circles with a rifle slung over my shoulder, wearing a beret, a red jacket, cut-offs, and tall black boots. Afterward, we drove into the city to a party where Larry Rivers, taken with my outfit, asked me to pose for him at the Chelsea—he lived there then perhaps—for a painting as a Moon Woman. When he was finished I appeared life-size in one panel of a diptych; the other panel would be occupied by a painting of an astronaut in full gear. Was posing for Larry also a performance? I suppose so, by the lights of the sixties. But my list includes only dancelike or dance-contextualized activities. Or things that were Happenings, the form that a number of "dance" performances assumed then. Dance quote unquote was a leading conundrum of the day. If it was done at the Judson Church by the Judson Dance Theater, no matter what it was, it was called dance.

Running in circles, even or especially in the mud, was definitely an appropriate dance activity by Judson articles of faith. I never "danced" at Judson, though I presented an entire evening there, in 1962, before the first Judson Dance Theater performance in July that year. I know someone asked me to do it. Probably Al Carmines, the Judson minister. I would never have offered or asked to do it myself. Had I heeded that fact, I wouldn't have done anything when asked either. So there you have it. The whole evening was a nightmare, beginning with the martinis I consumed beforehand to dull the violent edges of my fear. The effect of course was to prolong the night's agony, my multifaceted field of action, involving quite a few people, slowing down considerably while I performed under the influence. John Cage, the man we all believed had the last word on art then, was unaccountably present, and he came up at the end to tell me he wished *he* could be so "free."

I don't believe for a moment he meant that. On second thought, maybe he did. His own work, which he promoted shamelessly, was extremely contained, despite its indeterminacy, often leaving his performers to make choices under various conditions—advancing an unfortunate sense at large that art could be just a lot of commotion, could take place virtually in a playpen of permissiveness. That in fact anybody could do it, not only so-called artists. And that it is going on all the time, whether we see it or think so or not. Sometime later that year John corralled me at a party where I was wearing the same red dress in which I had done my infamous evening at Judson, and he asked me to perform with him and David Tudor at the Y on Ninety-second Street in his 1958 piece *Music Walk*. Again, I honored a request. And again, I asked myself no significant or leading questions. But I must have felt buoyed up to realize that the primary responsibility was not going to be mine and that I would be appearing in very good company. How could anything go wrong? Moreover, I was billed as a "dancer," lending me a certain legitimacy. *Music Walk* was originally for one or more pianists. Then in 1960, dancers were added, and the piece was retitled *Music Walk with Dancers*. John took it on tour with Tudor, and with Merce Cunningham and Carolyn Brown, the most legitimate dancers around. Now for our upcoming version of it at the Y, it would have yet another title: *Music Walk with Dancer*.

At home in my fifth-floor walk-up in Washington Heights, I puzzled over John's "score." I was supposed to select any number of activities, then obtain readings for them by placing a transparent rectangle having five parallel lines on it over nine different sheets with points. The order of their performance and allotted times were the things to arrive at.

Armed finally with my red dress, a stack of three-by-five index cards with the proper notations, and a carload of household equipment including a baby bottle, a toy dog on wheels, and a vacuum cleaner, I arrived at the theater for a brief rehearsal before the performance. Right there something went wrong. My stack of cards came afoul of a pool of water, blurring the inked notations on them. After a moment of consternation I coolly abandoned them, and during the performance I proceeded from station to station where my things were set up, in whatever order occurred to me, and without much regard for time spent, except to stay within the ten-minute frame of the piece. John and David were all the while fiddling with their radio dials and monkeying around with the insides of a grand piano, following instructions on their own graphically immaculate—intact, of course—cards. Everyone seemed happy with the event until afterward, when we were partying at a restaurant and I told John, with a certain misplaced glee, about my accident with the cards. Learning that I had forsaken his score, he scolded me for not giving up my ego. He meant I suppose for not giving it up *to him*—an ulterior design I would grow to suspect him of.

My list tells me I became a para-Judson performer or dancer, a wall-flower in waiting for an opportunity, usually upon being asked, to create some disorder at large. There was one arena, however, where I needed no invitation, and that was the world of parties, many of them in artists' lofts, where I excelled at making rare spectacles of myself. My signature tableau vivant was hanging upside down on horizontal loft pipes close to the ceilings. A torn dress or a lost shoe was the expected result. Otherwise I was a very enthusiastic party dancer, making the most of the step or move du jour and of the new style of pretending to be dancing with a partner while really doing one's own thing. As for performances proper, I may be lying to myself, but I never felt left out of the Judson Dance Theater. I saw it as a serious professional forum, its leading participants having come up through some ranks or other, like the class Bob Dunn taught before it began. My own serious profession was writing, and at that moment I was specializing in writing about Judson. I saw their church space as sacrosanct. At the same time, in the boundary-dissolving spirit of the time, I became quite entangled personally with some of the choreographers, especially those I helped promote as an emerging elite group—not only in writing but in producing concerts of their work. As producer, I had opportunities to perform with them outside the inviolable space of the church.

Jill Johnston. Photo by Vicki Lawrence.

One such chance was a series I produced at the Washington Square Art Gallery in August 1964. A carte blanche feeling about the situation evidently overcame me. People were away for the dog days; key members of the Judson scene were on tour dancing with Cunningham in Europe. I asked Yvonne Rainer, a captive on my program, to do an improvisation with me, and I suppose she could hardly say no. An evening that would live in infamy was under way. Yvonne chose a lush operatic Berlioz to accompany us, perhaps with intent to drown us out. By the time we started I was already drowning—in alcohol, a half of a fifth of vodka as I recall. Thus while I know I stayed on my feet in fulfilling my obligation to perform, I thankfully had and have total amnesia as to what transpired. A single photographic record shows me in dark shades hovering menacingly from the top of a gallery staircase, legs astride its ironwork, in black tights and my well-traveled tall black boots. I was, it seems, about to jump onto and kill Yvonne on the floor below, at that moment having an intimate relationship with a gallery pillar, her arms wrapped lovingly around its circumference. Afterward I learned that she was displeased, not with the event per se (necessarily), but with my need to perform blotto.

I took the criticism to heart and never performed blotto again. At the Buffalo Festival of the Arts in the spring of 1965 (here I had been asked to present Judson choreographers, and decided to include myself) I did another duet, this time with artist Robert Morris, and became very particular about its form. He would build a structure onstage out of two-by-fours; it would have a horizontal crossbar strong enough to hold me when I got ready to hang from it, and unhinged enough to cause the whole structure and myself to crash to the floor. While Bob fabricated this damage-worthy assemblage stage left, I busied myself to his right stuffing a box with crumpled newspapers, in preparation for making a daring leap into it from the height of a chair. I must then have walked casually over to Bob's shaky skeletal frame to self-destruct on or with it, a finale that was surely fraught with significance, perhaps a dire warning about the future. I think I was very ill that time with a Shanghai flu or something. Photographic evidence shows that I had advanced from the tall black boots to white pants. However, I was not through yet with the boots. They had been so serviceable. In June 1963 at the Pocket Theater on Third Avenue, I had done a really successful performance in them.

It was called *In an English Country Garden.* I had asked Malcolm Goldstein to play that famous tune over and over again on his violin onstage. My garden was further set with a round tin tub of water, artificial flowers floating in it. While Malcolm sawed away, I appeared in the boots and heavy black rain gear, a slicker hat and slicker coat, stepping into the tub of water and flowers. Bob Morris in the meantime was walking down the aisle of the theater toward the stage dressed in a sheet with a sign on the back that read HILL. When he climbed onstage and approached the tub, he stood on a chair there (like a hill—get it?), produced a watering can from under his sheet, and sprayed its contents over my head. When his can was emptied I threw off my slickers, appearing in a skimpy black dress, and showered the audience with the soaked plastic flowers, tossed with much gusto and great merriment into its midst. The audience was happy (they were cheering and laughing); the next performers, David Gordon and Valda Setterfield, were not. The stage, I would hear later, had been left flooded with water that they had had to mop up. Morris, by the way, has recently claimed that he was not costumed in a sheet at all but a kind of "hoop dress" of a beige color, with possibly suspenders or harness or bra on top. He remembers being like part of a bell. He felt "upholstered more than gowned." I just cannot imagine how he could have been a "hill" in a hooped skirt. But with no photographic evidence, it's his word against mine. Anyway, the piece was great. And it didn't stop there. It went on into the night, an endless party at an Egyptian belly-dancing place where I got uncorked and became seized with the inspiration to dance like Isadora on a restaurant tabletop, as I had read about her doing someplace in Europe or Russia. The black boots, of course, went there too.

And on to Los Angeles in the spring of 1965 at the L.A. County Museum, where curator Jim Elliott had invited Bob Rauschenberg to bring his Judson friends out to perform. We were kept for three weeks in an apartment on the pier over a merry-go-round. Besides Bob, Deborah and Alex Hay, and Steve Paxton, Barbara Dilley and Trisha Brown were there. We drove go-carts and played multiple solitaire, which Deborah won handily, whiling the time away until we had to perform. I never found out why I was included. But summoned within the clique, I gave my contribution my very best thought and put on a most organized effort, free of spilled substances or other unwanted disturbance. As a sort of guerilla performer, I seemed containable when asked "inside." In October 1964, Allan Kaprow asked me to join a host of other performers in a presentation of Karlheinz Stockhausen's *Originale*—a big, teeming Happening to take place at the Carnegie Recital Hall. Here a formless situation—a bewildering pileup of unconnected activities—became a prescription for unlimited lawlessness. Kaprow made the mistake of casting me as a "free agent," and I got into all kinds of trouble there—denounced, for instance, by a painter and his wife for interfering in their act. On my own, one way or another, I was reliably unpredictable and reckless.

During 1967 and 1968, I presented three panels at New York University's Loeb Student Center. The first was relatively conventional; the next was a deranged critique or commentary on panels. Lists of Q's and A's were passed out to panel members beforehand. Any Q could be answered by any A, to be interpreted at will. Steve Paxton, who was there, remembers Barbara Dilley in a large turban walking a pig around; I remember Willoughby Sharp taking all his clothes off, and someone else parading or dancing across the long panel table. The plan called for replacing ourselves as panel members at random from the audience. A steady march toward disintegration was afoot from the start. I was shocked myself by the chaos I had let loose. A man at the back unleashed a scare, yelling "FIRE, FIRE, FIRE . . ." And a young woman, evidently new in town, began to have a public breakdown. I thought she was demonstrating, but Steve, who took her in hand to calm her, tells me no, she was just pleading for humanity. My third NYU panel was my last performance of the sixties. It was 1968, by which time I had passed through various transitional fires.

All of which had led to an abandonment of criticism, and to a column representing my life. I was no longer split between serious writing and theatrical hijinks. Serializing my life, the things I now covered were completely self-generated. *I* was the performance; the writing was an extension of it, a running account and commentary. And freed of criticism, the writing got very twisted, guaranteeing a continuance of attention. My last panel at NYU, titled "The Disintegration of a Critic," heralding this new life, or memorializing the old, called for my absence. Critic David Bourdon, armed with some of my phone bills and bank accounts, moderated it. Cellist Charlotte Moorman participated, accompanied by her cello; Andy Warhol was there, probably with recording equipment. And I don't remember the rest—well, except for John de Menil, the oil tycoon. I never tried to find out what they all said about me, if anything.

During the 1970s I performed once more, but then as a common lecturer at large. A microphone, I discovered, was a great crutch—lending confidence and shelter. A mike and a lectern were the only objects involved in the performances. I didn't have to bring them, and they stood still, like a house or a tree. I had had lots of trouble dealing with objects. I could just dance, no quotes around it. But the object-ridden sixties dictated dangerous collisions for someone like myself, living essentially in her head. The general form of my lectures was a reading of my last column followed by audience interaction. I construed these gigs differently from my presenters—universities most often. While addressing the radical subjects upon which I was invited to speak, I subversively viewed my writing as the raison d'appearance. Indeed, what else brought me there?

Love, Jill

Thanks to Robert Morris and Steve Paxton for helping with their memories.

6

Dancing in New York

The 1960s

Gus Solomons jr

When I came to New York in 1961 to dance in Donald McKayle's Broadway-bound show *Kicks & Co!*, written by Oscar Brown, Jr., starring Burgess Meredith, Nichelle Nichols (later, Uhura on *Star Trek*), and Al Freeman, Jr., I was fresh out of MIT (Massachusetts Institute of Technology) with a Bachelor of Architecture degree and a burning itch to perform and make dances. At that age, twenty-one, when one has more energy than wisdom, the immediacy of dance was overwhelmingly more appealing than the relative infinity of time between conception and completion of a building.

Compared to Cambridge, where I had feared I'd spend my entire life as a big fish in a little pond, New York was a plethora of exciting choices; it lived up to its nickname, Fun City. One could survive on virtually no money. Pork 'n' beans was a dime a can, cottage cheese was twenty-five cents a pound, and a friend introduced me to "dark tuna" pie, a concoction of canned peas, Velveeta, onions, and (gulp!) cat food, baked in a crust. Transit fare was fifteen cents, and the monthly rent on my first apartment, a sublet, sixth-floor walk-up railroad flat on the Upper East Side with tub in the kitchen and toilet down the hall, was $28.36.

After four previews in Chicago, the show closed for want of a better book. Instead of rewriting, the producer fired the director and hired a writer (his wife) to redirect it! (As is so often the case in showbiz, if it's broke, break it worse!) So, there I was in New York and not about to leave, now that I had tasted the fruit. I got a scholarship to study at the

Graham School and also struggled through ballet classes from Bill Grif-
fith (at the Joffrey School) and Richard Thomas.

I went to Broadway auditions and always made it to the final cut.
The choreographers would take me aside and tell me my dancing was
terrific, but "we don't have a [black] partner for you," or "the producer
won't go for mixing couples." I was flattered that they liked my dancing
and just accepted as a the fact of life that a "colored" dancer only did
"colored" shows. The Kennedy/Johnson administrations in Washington
illegalized discrimination, and race relations seemed to get better for a
while. Most people tried to get along; I felt bigotry only when apartment
hunting.

I found myself rehearsing endless hours with various choreographers, but my projected income would be around fifty dollars a month,
which covered only the rent. Yes, a floor-through sublet on West Sev-
enty-second Street rented for a hundred dollars a month in 1962! But
in those days I ate a lot, so in 1963 to supplement my income I got a
"real" job with a Fifth Avenue interior design firm, Barbara Dorn Associates, the closest I came to practicing architecture. Though the position
was full-time, Ms. Dorn allowed me to start work at 7 A.M. so that I
could leave the office by 3 P.M. to take my classes at the Graham studio.

After six months I was laid off during a stock market slump, but in
the same mail with my pink slip was an offer to teach at the Dance
Circle in Boston. I could fly to Boston on the Northeast Shuttle for
eleven dollars each way and teach two classes for fifty bucks, on which
I could live comfortably. From then on I earned my living performing
and teaching dance.

From the start of my modern dance training with Jan Veen at the
Boston Conservatory, making dances was synonymous with dancing; I
enjoyed choreographing. Several defectors from the Helen Tamiris/
Daniel Nagrin Company found a loft on East Ninth Street, where for
ten dollars' rent a month each, nine of us could share a workspace.
Members of Studio 9 included Gail Ewert, Becky Arnold, Cliff Keuter,
Phoebe Neville, Margaret Beals, Elina Mooney, and her husband, photographer Guy Cross. I spent many wee hours capering around the studio, creating. We danced in each other's dances and showed them at
the Ninety-second Street YMCA and the Clark Center, mostly. This was
before the Judson Church, most famous of the downtown venues of the
time, began presenting dance.

Gus Solomons jr. Author's private collection.

I was part of the original group from which the Judson group sprang. It began as an informal seminar on composition, led by Robert Ellis Dunn at the old Cunningham studio on West Fourteenth Street and Sixth Avenue. We wanted to find new forms, ways of making dances that were different from those of our mentors: Doris Humphrey, who wrote the rule book; Martha Graham and disciples, who delved into the emotions; José Limón, the artistic scion of Humphrey; and even Merce Cunningham. We tried to break all the rules to get at the essence of dance.

Although I, too, was interested in deconstructing forms and structures, I was too in love with technical dancing to abandon it in favor of pedestrian, minimal movement. Hence, I went my own way and wasn't part of the "official" Judson group of legend. Because I am African American, critics and historians generally assume that I was not of the avant-garde, an almost exclusively Euro-American clique. This was in spite of the fact that I grew up in a white, middle-class neighborhood and was educated at Cambridge High and Latin School and MIT.

Early in 1962, I was rehearsing for a concert with Deborah Jowitt and John Wilson when I heard that Pearl Lang might want me to dance for her. I had attended a performance of her *Shira* in Boston the previous summer and thought it one of the most beautiful dances I'd seen, but technically much too difficult for me. Friends convinced me to try out, and I danced the work several times over the next few years, moving from the corps to the role of Messenger, who spent most of the dance jumping and leaping. Bruce Marks had originated the role. Following in his footsteps was strenuous to say the least, and I spent many a rehearsal nearly in tears, trying to stay in the air long enough to make full circles with my torso before coming down. Pearl was a taskmaster. Once I tried to pull my MIT education on her, advising her that the laws of physics made such-and-such a step impossible. She declared, "You're not a physicist now, you're a dancer!" I did it.

In the spring of 1962 I was one of a group of hot New York male dancers who did the first reconstruction of Ted Shawn's *Kinetic Molpai* at the Jacob's Pillow Summer Festival, directed by Norman Walker with Barton Mumaw, one of the original dancers. Among others in the piece were Louis Falco, Sam Huang, Bruce Becker, Wesley Fata, and Robert Powell. Most of us tried to emulate Powell's sexy pelvic-motivated rendition of Graham's style, which was seductively feline and egocentric, but for Shawn's work we had to learn to surrender our egos and dance as a team. It was a very enlightening and stimulating experience.

I danced with Joyce Trisler, Flower Hujer, Hava Kohav, and others and from 1961 to 1964 with the Donald McKayle Company. I created the role of the King in *District Storyville*, among other of McKayle's ballets, and got to do a performance of Donny's role in *Rainbow Round*

My Shoulder with Carmen de Lavallade. (I was aching to be in *Games*, but Donny felt I was too tall to be believable as a kid.) During one season Paula Kelly and I were Adam and Eve in both a McKayle ballet and one by Lang. Kelly was one of the strongest humans I'd ever met.

By then, for some insane reason, I'd decided to trim down my already lean frame and believed that energy was not related to dietary intake. I tried to eat nothing but a couple of pastries a week. So, I was cranky and weak. Kelly had more than enough power for both of us. I think that was my first minor bout with depression; I was moody, sluggish, and hard to work with, and McKayle fired me.

There was a lot of drug use in the 1960s, even among us normally disciplined dancers. People generally had not yet become health conscious. Steak was considered the "perfect food," and nearly everybody smoked pot, took pills (uppers and downers), and drank. I enjoyed scotch, gin, and vermouth, but because I hated losing control I didn't experiment with chemical mind-bending. In connection with my campaign to maintain maximum energy with minimum body weight, I took doctor-prescribed dexamils (amphetamines) for a few years, but nothing hallucinatory. I was also not sexually adventurous. The combination of depression, dieting, and New England guilt obliterated my libido, so the sexual revolution was wasted on me. Drugs were the "plague" of the era, and many people lost acquaintances, friends, and lovers to fatal "bad trips."

In 1964 I had danced with advanced scholarship students from the Martha Graham School in a lecture-demonstration at Lincoln Center. The following year Graham invited me to join her company. I loved all that emoting and dramatic make-believe, so I jumped at the chance. But studying with Cunningham, learning to dance from stillness, was giving me technical control rather than sheer muscle power, on which I'd been dancing until then.

Graham dancers would get themselves into a state of high anxiety to dance well. I, on the other hand, spent rehearsal time between run-throughs lying in a corner, deep-breathing, finding inner calm, becoming still. That season I danced *Phaedra*, *Secular Games* (replacing Dick Gain, he of the awesome technique!), and the Ghost of Samuel in *The Witch of Endor*, a role I created. And I carried a spear in the epic four-act *Clytemnestra*.

I loved the physical and emotional indulgence of the Graham

repertoire, even though the Cunningham approach was more sustaining. I never aspired to dance with Cunningham, however, because his group was entirely without dancers of any color but white. In fact, that same season Merce did invite me to dance with his troupe. Utter surprise! Sheer delight! The company had returned from a six-month world tour, and all but Carolyn Brown and Viola Farber resigned. He asked me to dinner at a small Italian restaurant on Sixteenth Street and popped the question. (Back then Merce loved to eat and ate everything—including steak, the perfect food, on performance days.) I floated home, ecstatic.

Logistics got complicated that spring: I was rehearsing with Cunningham and Graham at the same time, and M.G. didn't know I was dancing with M.C. The day after the Graham season closed at the Fifty-fourth Street Theater, I flew to Chicago to meet the Cunningham Company for my debut performances at a theater-in-the-round on the south side. I don't remember the repertoire, but I do remember that the stage was tiny and the postperformance reception was great.

For the next three years, I toured the United States and Europe with the Cunningham Company. Some of the tours and most of the receptions were luxurious. Once we went to Europe for four weeks for just two dates, one in Spain, the other, I think, in Paris. In the days between gigs one of John Cage's wealthiest pals, Jean de Menil, housed us at his château outside Paris, which was so huge all the dancers had their own bedrooms! The domestic staff fed us lavish meals, and we went horseback riding in the Forest of Ardennes. Sandra Neels and I were so gung-ho (read obsessive) that we schlepped into Paris and rented a studio to give ourselves class. I feared if I missed a day of practice, I'd forget how to dance.

Once in Spain, we went to a disco after the concert with some new fans. I left my dance bag in their car, but when we were ready to leave for the hotel there was no sign of our ride. The company had to leave town the next morning, I without my bag, thinking I'd been had. But it turned out the driver had found it in his backseat; he returned it to the hotel next day, and it caught up with me in Marseilles. I still have that red canvas, expandable bag.

I spent the coldest February of my life in Buffalo, New York, where we had a residency. That was where Merce created *Rain Forest* and started *Walkaround Time*. The decor for the former dance by Andy Warhol was big silver Mylar balloons, which were supposed to fill the

Gus Solomons jr. Photo by Guy Cross.

stage space and collide with us as we danced. It was an exciting prospect, but the helium wouldn't keep them aloft properly. Some kept drifting out into the audience, and finally we had to go out of our way to bump into the half dozen or so that remained onstage. There were also camera-men crawling around the wings, filming a documentary on Cunningham and Cage.

My most vivid recollection of that opening night, however, was the stabbing pain in the ball of my left foot every time it touched the floor. My fifth lumbar disc had begun deteriorating, and that was the first symptom. I had to get through the concert, trying never to put weight on the left foot. Numbness in the leg started shortly after that, and by March I was unable to jump or balance. I had to leave the company with a doubtful prognosis for a continued dance career.

I had been choreographing on the side during my time with Cun-ningham, but after a summer's recuperation I decided to continue danc-ing and form my own company. My dances experimented with game rules to create accidental juxtapositions and unpredictable images. For instance, I was fond of giving dancers, musicians, and light operators interdependent tasks for determining their activities: when a dancer does X, the sound does Y, and the lights do Z, and so forth. Everyone had to stay alert to the instantaneous situation. I used as accompaniment words, ambient sound like the noises the dancers made while dancing, or commissioned music.

I even had the audience provide accompaniment by following taped instructions to do, on purpose, the distracting things audiences do unconsciously: clearing throats, rustling programs, whispering. In another piece there were no dancers at all. The audience was instructed to execute the sympathetic physical responses we normally make when we watch movement—stiffen your back, hold your breath, tap your feet— even though no dancing was happening onstage. The only "performers" were two tape recorders: one with instructions, the other with musical background.

One of the most exciting projects I made was the dual-screen video-dance *CITY/MOTION/SPACE/GAME* (those four words in any order), produced in 1968 by Rick Hauser at WGBH-TV in Boston. It was taped on location (Prudential Center, Public Gardens, and a south Boston scrap yard) as well as at the TV studio. The half-hour piece, which appeared simultaneously on the VHF and UHF public broadcasting channels, was an investigation of the unique properties of the video medium that are unlike live performance: reduced scale, flattening of spatial dimensions, and accelerated visual pace.

Now, thirty years later, I'm still making my living dancing and having a great time experimenting, performing, choreographing, and breaking rules. It's fun to watch trends repeat and to review dance concerts so that today's young dancers don't think they've invented the wheel when they discover that you can talk and dance at the same time, or mix media, or get naked onstage. I've been there; we did that already, and it was at least as good, if not better—albeit at a somewhat slower tempo.

7

Monk and King

The Sixties Kids

Deborah Jowitt

In 1965, Jill Johnston, the dance critic of the *Village Voice,* retrospectively announced the demise of Judson Dance Theater in 1964.[1] She had hinted at the possibility even earlier. Johnston, an engagingly partisan commentator on the radical activities that had begun in 1962 at Judson Church, nevertheless acknowledged that it was only the collaborative, consensual, fairly nondiscriminating zeal of Judson's early years that were over.[2] Performances at various sites, both in New York and elsewhere, had begun to isolate Judson's "stars," such as Yvonne Rainer, Trisha Brown, Steve Paxton, Deborah Hay, and Robert Rauschenberg, from others who had shown work at the church. Curatorship was but one of the concepts that separated the early 1960s from the later years. The artists went back to their studios, and, increasingly, choreographers stopped sharing concerts and appearing in one another's pieces. They went to work honing individual styles, probing deeper into the Pandora's boxes opened during the permissive first years of Robert Dunn's seminal composition classes and the Judson workshops and concerts.

Johnston's *Voice* article on the end of Judson was reprinted in *Ballet Review*'s Judson issue of 1967, along with a postscript on developments since she had written the original piece.[3] In it she put a wary imprimatur on a possible second generation of Judsonites—Kenneth King, Meredith Monk, and Phoebe Neville—who were beginning to be highly visible at avant-garde venues, including Judson Church. Constance Poster contributed an article on Monk's and King's brave new works to the same issue of *Ballet Review.*

Johnston, in fact, had come down rather hard on two works of King's that she had seen at the Bridge Theatre on Eighth Street in July 1965: *cup/saucer/two dancers/radio* (1964) and a premiere, *Self-Portrait: Dedicated to the Memory of John Fitzgerald Kennedy.* He was, she thought, "applying vanguard tactics to a moribund expressionism."[4] However, for reasons not entirely clear, she changed her mind and provided discerning and sympathetic analyses of the dances shown by Monk, Neville, and King on a shared concert at Judson Church in April 1966: Monk's *Portable* and a revised version of *The Beach* (1965); Neville's *Move,* a trio featuring the three of them, and *Terrible,* made in collaboration with Joe Jones; King's *Camouflage* and *Blow-Out,* with Laura Dean as his partner. All three choreographers participated, along with seven others, in William Meyer's *Lecture on Thunder.*

It may have been in part the collaborative spirit that made Johnston link these very young choreographers with the Judson tradition, although their work had received no imprimatur from the founding Judsonites. King and Monk appeared with others at the Washington Square Galleries in September 1964 and at Clark Center a month later. Neville performed in King's works at the 1965 Bridge Theatre concerts. In September 1965, Monk and King both appeared in Jackson Mac Low's *The Pronouns* in the Second Avant-Garde Festival organized by radical cellist Charlotte Moorman at Judson Hall on Fifty-seventh Street, and Neville and Monk performed Monk's *Radar.* A month later, *Radar* and King's *Spectacular* (with Monk in the cast) were shown on a program at the recently established Dance Theater Workshop (then a fluctuating group of choreographers who shared programs in Jeff Duncan's loft at 215 West Twentieth Street). At the end of 1966, a few months after the 1966 King-Monk-Neville concert at Judson, Monk and Neville shared a Judson concert in which King danced. (He remembers Neville's *Dance with Mandolins* for the three of them as "Phoebe's 500-sissones closing work.")[5]

I won't be dealing with Neville's work in this essay. Her bent for dramatic dance—as opposed to dance theater—set her apart from Monk and King, despite mutual admiration and shared ideas.[6] Today, Monk and King too have dissimilar interests and careers. Monk, acknowledged worldwide for her virtuosic singing voice, her distinctive musical compositions, and her extraordinary music-theater fables, doesn't even like to label the movement element in her performances "dance." King, like Monk, has been the subject of a chapter in Sally Banes's *Terpsichore in Sneakers*[7] and a segment in Michael Blackwood's film *Making Dances,* although he no longer maintains a company or a full-time performing schedule, concentrating more on writing. Half of his recent oeuvre consisted of nonprogrammatic dances in a leggy, attenuated, erect-spined style that showed Merce Cunningham's influence and in which the performers often improvised with prechoreographed themes. Other of his works featured elaborated linguistic acrobatics: words were dissected, recombined, rhymed, and punned on; the solos he still, on occasion, performs frequently contain hilarious tirades by eccentric characters who lecture on politics, semantics, philosophy, and art.

Yet, different as the two choreographers may have appeared later, their development as artists owed a great deal to the influences of Judson and to their work together in the 1960s. Their interest in nonlinear theater, personae, the technique of collaging, the use of film, and nontraditional approaches to space and time took them in different directions, but for the four-year period between 1964 and 1968, audiences considered them to have much in common.

They hung out together and bounced a lot of ideas off each other then. Says King, "What interested both of us—quite ferociously—and what made our friendship imaginative and freewheeling and persevering was the way the different arts can come together . . . sometimes fragmentation is just a set of techniques to break the boundaries between things."

According to Monk, they thought, with the hubris of the young, that they were hot stuff—the next wave. Monk and King (and Neville) were involved with dance theater at a time when most choreographers considered to be on the cutting edge were concerned with bedrock of movement and form, with unheard-of combinations of mundane, playful, and/or outrageous elements, with the presentation of the dancer as unmoved (and often unpolished) executant. As King explains, "Judson really enabled all these grammatologies or methods of mixing performance formats to happen—the breaking of the barriers . . . but [those choreographers] had eliminated a certain kind of expressivity or expression that still interested me—something about acting and performance and projection that was character-based."

Although Johnston's somewhat misleading phrase "moribund expressionism" pejoratively linked King to the dominant modern dance figures—specifically to Charles Weidman in his declining years—Monk and King were far from being direct or literal in their handling of expression. When artist Robert Rauschenberg smeared a pillow and patchwork quilt with paint and arranged it on the wall (the "combine painting" *Bed*, 1955), he was not, despite the loaded nature of bed imagery and the metaphoric power of a "stained" bed, making an explicit subjective statement. (A German Expressionist painter earlier in the century might well have used the same theme to express and elicit powerful emotion.) Similarly, neither Monk nor King approached character in ways that came across as emotive. Nor was "motivation" an issue. Reviews by mainstream publications (*Dance Magazine, New York Times*) often referred to their blank or frozen expressions, their apparently impassive presentation of the body, and accompanying images that could be shocking, cruel, or bizarre (like Jeff Norwalk's films of a snake devouring a mouse and of the eviscerated corpse of a rat beneath a flower, which figured in King's *m-o-o-n-b-r-a-i-n with SuperLecture* [1967]).

Detaching performers from appearing to own any emotions that might be involved and pruning their responses of behavior that looked instinctive had become something of a Judson convention. (One can also note an impassive performance of implicitly dramatic events in *Geranium* and *Carnation* by Lucinda Childs, who began choreographing at about the same time, but whose work was included on programs directly or indirectly sponsored by Judson Dance Theater.) Speaking in 1984 of *Duet with Cat's Scream and Locomotive* (1966), which Monk made for herself and King, Monk mentioned that she had tried to deal with extremes of motion and emotion that were "not with us."[8] The tape loop of a speeding train and its horn was interrupted in the middle by the screech of a cat, the drastic sounds contrasting with the calm, deliberate behavior of Monk and King as they moved through and with an array of yellow objects (Monk thinks of the duet as a "desert piece"): curved yellow blocks worn by King as shoes, two different-sized, straight-edged structures with photos of legs on their legs ("a little like a sphinx," she remembers), two pairs of stilts (a tall one and a short one), and wooden crescent mouths all painted with smiles except for one that was crying (these were rocked by means of invisible strings stretched offstage). When Monk held up a mouth in front of her face, it amplified emotion, just as, she explains, in the theaters of ancient Greece a megaphone concealed within a mask could both intensify and distance the actor's voice. Despite this distancing, however, it seemed to me then that the works of Monk and King fostered the regrafting of implicit emotions back onto the performers by the audience—a concept that sometime later began to interest Rainer and another Judson founding member, David Gordon.

In King's *cup/saucer/two dancers/radio*, there was a moment in which King and Neville—she in a bra, girdle, curlers, and pointe shoes, he in underwear and a tie—held cups and saucers just below their mouths and, as they stared grimly straight ahead, their hands began to tremble with increasing violence, causing the cups to chatter against the saucers. When they'd gotten the cups rattling frantically, they tilted them as if to drink, but without the usual accommodation of mouth to hand. Colored dye slowly spilled down the white of their chests and bellies. The effect was shocking—not only in its messiness but in the disassociation of this couple from their bodies and their appetites.

Issues of role-playing were implicit in the works even before King began to assume personae and develop characters, before Monk began to use biography as material. However, neither constructed linear time structures. For them, as for many visual artists of the day, collage and assemblage replaced hierarchical arrangements in space; and, like the artists who produced Happenings, they fragmented time in an analogous manner, accruing meaning through the juxtaposing or layering of elements. The technique is one that Monk brilliantly employs today, likening herself to a mosaicist: the overall design may only gradually become apparent, even though every small piece is fastidiously chosen and set. And, despite the fluidity of King's dances and the build-to-a-climax nature of some of his word pieces, he continued to work by layering, juxtaposing, and repeating small modules.

When Kenneth King began showing works in New York in 1964, he was still enrolled at Antioch, a small, radical liberal arts college in Yellow Springs, Ohio. Interested in becoming an actor, he had begun playing character roles in summer stock and children's theater before he entered college, and he was advised to take some dance classes if he wanted the role of the Scarecrow in *The Wizard of Oz* (tall, long-limbed, and drastically lean, he was a natural for the part). Although King made and presented his choreography at Antioch, there was no dance department there, so he combined reading philosophy with yearly breaks in

New York of about three months (Antioch's work-study plan encouraged this). He picked Syvilla Fort's name out of a phone book, took ballet, modern, and African classes with her, and found them inspiring. (It was to come up with music to match Fort's African American vitality that John Cage has created his first prepared piano pieces back in the 1930s.) King also studied for three years (with time out for Antioch) with choreographer-dancer Paul Sanasardo. He says that Sanasardo, who had trained with Martha Graham and Antony Tudor and danced extensively with Anna Sokolow's company, taught him a lot about projection, motivation, and emotion.

It was in Sanasardo's classes that he met Phoebe Neville, who told him he should go down to Judson Church and see what was happening. When he showed *cup/saucer/two dancers/radio* in September 1964 on the same series at the Washington Square Galleries that featured Monk's *Break*, he had not only been sharing space at a studio on Ninth Street with Monk, Neville, Gus Solomons jr, Fred Herko, and Deborah Lee; he had been hanging out with the avant-garde film crowd. This time he had managed a nine-month break from tolerant Antioch, and he appeared in Gregory Markopoulos's *The Iliac Passion* (along with Andy Warhol and Jack Smith), among other films. In 1965 he imported Neville to Antioch and presented a concert that included *cup/saucer/two dancers/radio* and *Spectacular*, in the meantime completing a senior thesis. While his classmates were graduating, he was already back in New York, preparing to show *Self-Portrait: Dedicated to the Memory of John Fitzgerald Kennedy*.

King's early pieces were kinetic agglomerations of Pop Art imagery with little or no dancing. In *Spectacular*, various of the four performers lay on the floor and languidly built themselves phalluses out of shaving cream. At one point they repeatedly entered, congregated around a chair, and formed a pietà. All were elaborately made up, and all wore white. (Monk appeared as a pregnant housewife, and at some point a doll fell from under her short nightgown.) I innocently asked King after one performance why he felt it necessary to repeat the pietà pose so many times, and he replied, "I want to make sure you never have to see it again." Slowness, repetition, and the pictorial clarity of the images did, indeed, make the spectator feel as if the dance were being burned onto his or her retina.

Remembering these works and reading about them, I'm struck by

how painterly they were. The Happenings and gallery events that pro-
liferated in the 1960s and the choreography of visual artists such as
Rauschenberg, Alex Hay, Robert Morris, and others associated with
Judson Dance Theater helped to develop choreographers' eyes for arrangements in space, for correspondence in terms of color and shape,
for unlikely combinations of materials. In King's "Toward a Trans-
Literal and Trans-Technical Dance-Theater," an essay he contributed
to Gregory Battcock's *The New Art,* he honors the role of certain artists associated with Judson in what he terms the "blow-out" of dance:
"For example, 'painter' Robert Rauschenberg and 'sculptor' Robert
Morris trans-connect time-space *as* Theater Events in which paint, objects, light, sculptured forms and human beings all become objects or
performers."[9] The objectness of performers and the performative tension of the objects that shared the stage as equal partners were under-
lined by King's title *cup/saucer/two dancers/radio.*

In a 1991 interview, King mentioned that with *Blow-Out* and *Camouflage* (1966) he was coming to the end of his interest in *Vogue, Harper's Bazaar,* and "all that pop imagery that was circulating in the culture." But these two dances were his most expert to date in finding
kinetic ways to express that imagery. In *Blow-Out,* he seized on the
persona of the tough motorcyclist (as did filmmaker Kenneth Anger in
his notorious 1963 *Scorpio Rising*). But although King's motorcyclist
may have worn black leather and shades, he also wore orange gloves
with elastic strings connecting every finger with the corners of Judson
Church, creating the illusion of gestures that reverberated in expanding
perspective. He and Laura Dean (who also wore shades) inhabited a
fragmented cubist space furnished with a chair and a tilting table (it
had legs of different lengths, with fake fruit and a wineglass glued on).
King began sitting on the chair; he filled his mouth with marbles, then
stood up and let them all roll out in extreme slow motion. Demosthenes
as Hell's Angel. Character became vivid at the instant of presentation,
without the baggage of motivation and background, "liberated," as King
puts it, "from happening, without having to be anchored in narrative."
Dialogue, characterization, and functional movement were variables to
be ordered by the dancers in performance. The sounds that accompanied the slow repositionings of performers and objects were a text by
Descartes (on examining the evidence of the senses), music of Vivaldi,
a siren, and the "Hallelujah Chorus."

King based another collage, the surreal solo *Camouflage,* on a haunting excerpt from Alain Robbe-Grillet's novel *In the Labyrinth* that had to do with a shell-shocked soldier lost in a snowstorm. His structure was as fragmented as Robbe-Grillet's. Wearing a bicycle bell on his hip, green gloves, green toe shoes, a helmet, and camouflage-green tights and leotard with a square cut out like a television screen to show his blood-smeared stomach, King performed a number of seemingly disjunct activities. He mimed throwing a hand grenade; he jumped on pointe; he stood on a small green rug while an overhead bag rained sugar down onto him; he spoke into a telephone, paced on the rug, shivered and wiped the "snow" off, fell dead. The Vietnam War was on his mind.

In 1967, King's interest in semantics and linguistics generated the first of many radical writings that began to accompany his dances: spoken by him on tape, spoken by him live in performance, read by others, and/or projected onto a screen. The text for *Print-Out,* which was published in Richard Kostelanetz's anthology *Future's Fiction,*[10] was both projected and spoken by King on a tape made in an echo chamber. King wore a lab coat and had a black hood over his head. There was no dancing in this at all, and not a lot of action, but he did make use of a rubber snake and a rubber salamander, having read, he says, about a Mexican tribe that used these animals to prophesy. ("It was also sort of like science fiction.")

The lecture in *m-o-o-n-b-r-a-i-n* with *SuperLecture,* later published in Kostelanetz's *Young American Writers,* dealt, perhaps, with the death and rebirth of art. "Dancing was about moving until moving got in the way. The abstract expressionists expressed everything. Now there is nothing left to express, not even alienation. That's why the most perfect imaginable dance would take place in some sealed-off, empty white-walled room with nothing in it."[11]

In keeping with ideas about the decay of art as we know it, King entered as a derelict—wigged, masked, and wearing a shabby overcoat. Under the old-man mask, King had rigged rubber tubing: "He takes off his hat, and I just blow up. The audience can't see any rubber tubes. This balloon [on top of the old-man's head], which is stuffed with powder, inflates until it's huge, and then it breaks and white powder goes all over (obviously a hallucinogenic image). And then I take off the mask, and you see that it's me, and that I'm young. Then I take off the overcoat, and I have this foam rubber suit on." A coiled rubber snake was embedded in the stomach of the suit, an apple over the heart. The other two embedded props, King thinks, may have been a stuffed gloved hand and a fish. These were all connected by a fishing line. King lay down on the floor and cast out the line; it pulled the props right out of him, leaving their imprints. After that, the suit came off, leaving King in light gray underwear; he held out stuffed gardening gloves on sticks, giganticizing the reach of his now slim form. Norwalk's controversial films of snake and rat approached the subject of omnivorous tradition and decay from another viewpoint. Many people found the piece disgusting; others, like the film critic Gregory Battcock, compared King to Beckett and Artaud.[12]

King now considers *m-o-o-n-b-r-a-i-n with SuperLecture* "a culmination of my collaging dance-theater activities. In 1968, I really began dancing with *Extravalalaganza* at Judson." The dance style he demonstrated in the late 1960s and early 1970s stands as a primer in relation to the semaphoric, Cunningham-influenced style of his later choreography. I remember it as an almost unstopping stream of light traveling steps—a chaining together of runs, skips, hops, small leaps, and springy tiptoe walks that made him look about to leave the earth. His arms kept curving around his long body as if he were carving the symbols of an unknown language onto the air. He seemed to be able to keep this up for astonishingly long periods of time. The connection between his words and movements had a mystical edge. He was honoring dancing as a catalyst for knowledge, a kind of motor that generates words and stimulates thought: "It was a way to rev up the body to know certain things." Watching him dance, one could easily believe this to be true and accept what he did as the "mapping of an open field." And when, in the early 1970s, his texts began to deal—in witty, fanciful, and frighteningly credible ways—with government conspiracies, King could convince you that, in the guise of Joseph K. Devadese of the Inner Seercret Service, he was using dancing as a telepathic device to field messages from outer space. He had admired the openness generated by Happenings, by the idea of making discoveries about material in performance, and much of the dancing was improvised around a structure. (King continued to use improvisation in his later, very "dancey" group works. The

Kenneth King in his 1990 *Dancing Wor(l)ds* as Patrick Duncan, a persona he developed in the early 1970s. Photo by Johan Elbers.

performers made decisions about when to perform what prerehearsed modules of material or how to space their dancing within the various grids King devised.)

The texts were not improvised. They were dizzyingly dense. The words themselves seemed to be dancing, buzzing about the spectators' ears, trying to insinuate themselves into the brain. Consider this excerpt from a dissertation on the double negative read aloud during *Metagexis* (1972): "No conditions cannot *not* be m e t. This is maybe why and also not *not* an explanation either as such *why* aesthetics and theology do not see eye to eye. One is busy a p p e a r i n g—while,—or so that the 'other' can be *being being* busy disappearing."[13] Or, from the same text, "The hoard hides the herd but the hurt hurls hearing. The herd hides the hurt but the Heart hurls healing."[14]

During these years, King was experimenting with altered states. (He jokes that when people asked him if he went to graduate school, he'd reply, "No, I took LSD.") His interest in Jungian archetypes (perhaps abetted by drugs) began to spawn personae. There was Pablo, the guy in the lab coat and the black hood who appeared in several pieces during

1968. King describes him as being "like a dream figure, or a phantom fragment. An oracular figure that resides in the consciousness, that announces or directs like a guardian or guide." I think it was Pablo whom I saw pushing a heavily bandaged figure in a wheelchair in 1970 in *Secret Cellar,* dedicated to the critic Edwin Denby (ironically, King had asked that it not be reviewed, being temporarily down on critics). On 4 January 1968, according to Jill Johnston, Pablo appeared, sitting motionless for a very long time, in a performance at Judson Church, for which it had been announced that Sergei Alexandrovitch would be performing *A Show*.[15] Sergei was "a Russian dancer discovered by Zora Zash of Global Arts Shows International" (another King persona). Sergei had already appeared at the Youth Pavilion at Expo 67 with Alfred North (a performer who also worked with Monk) for a free 10 P.M. show on a Saturday, and *Print-Out* was shown several times. (One wonders what the world's fair crowd made of this.) Sergei did dance later in the evening Johnston described, wearing tails and sneakers: "Stiff torso, looser extremities. Skitter-running. Improvised inertia. Appealingly whimsical. Le Petit Prince."[16] Looking remarkably like Kenneth King. Once, at the New School, Sergei had been scheduled to perform, and Pablo had shown up with a letter from Zora explaining that he wouldn't be there.

King speaks of these personae as "plastic semblances" of the performer, or "exemplifications of an archetype." There was the Heavy Man, a character in a padded white suit who danced with light-footed ease in *Extravalalaganza* in 1968 at Judson and who resurfaced, played by Robert Wilson, in King's *The Phenomenology of Movement* in 1969. (That same year, King played him in Wilson's *The Life and Times of Sigmund Freud*.)[17] Later there was Joseph K. Devadese, the medium, born of the reading King had been doing (Gurdjieff; Susanne K. Langer—one of his heroes, to whom he dedicated the major work *Battery* in 1975), and the ensuing experimentation with the dervish ideas of ropedancing and whirling. There was Patrick, the reincarnation of the drowned son of Isadora Duncan—an avatar of Sergei and an expression of King's lyrical side. There was Mater Harry, the androgynous blond spy, who spoke in hoarse whispers from behind a fan. The most fully developed of the characters was Pontease Tyak. The old man in *Print-Out* was a forerunner. Tyak is the curator of the Trans-Himalayan Society—an old man with woolly gray hair and beard, an overcoat, hat, and dark glasses. He had a thick Slavic accent with a touch of Yiddish, and on his appearance in *Metagexis* he told, with many wheezing, self-congratulatory chuckles, a story based on a William James anecdote in "What Pragmatism Means." In Pontease's hilarious version, three philosophers argue wildly about the nature of reality as they follow a squirrel running around a tree. Tyak some years later impersonated Nietzsche (another King hero) reading from *Thus Spake Zarathustra*. Like many of King's recent characters, and like the text-pieces in which he and others speak of themselves, Pontease is a scream.

In the 1960s, the collaging and the personae and the cracked-open words could easily be taken as part of the neo-dada scene, but it seems to me that King's work has always had a deeper unity of which these devices are symptoms. He whirls words, images, and phrases of movement as if in a cyclotron, reducing them to small units. The original identity is not always fully knowable, and a new identity often crackles tantalizingly at the peripheries of one's brain. In King's brain, one imagines the usual synapses bypassed, and meaning flaring along the nerves and muscles like wildfire.

Meredith Monk tends to date her career from the solo *Break* in 1964; however, having grown up around New York City and in Westchester County, she was aware several years before then of the radical changes going on in the arts. At progressive Sarah Lawrence College, she studied not only with legendary composition teacher Bessie Schönberg but also with Beverly Schmidt (Blossom)—a former Alwin Nikolais dancer who was busy freeing herself from the master's aesthetic—and with Judith Dunn, one of the founding members of Judson Dance Theater. And the trip from Sarah Lawrence, in Bronxville, to New York's studios and theaters was a short one. Monk was still in college in 1963 when her *Diploid* was shown on one of Clark Center's Young Choreographers concerts; this duet, which she describes as architectural, kept the two dancers—herself and dancer-choreographer Elizabeth Keen—in constant contact.

It was evident from the beginning that Monk's talent was a remarkable one. Another piece made in college, *Timestop,* featured five women in stop-start motion, like an assemblage of atoms. "My ultimate dance piece," she calls it now. And *Break,* made after her graduation and premiered on 28 September 1964 at Washington Square Galleries, was an indisputably original work. Seeing it in a later revival, I was struck by the fastidious and painterly way in which Monk had dissected and recombined sounds and images. The intermittent taped noises of a motor starting, brakes squealing, glass shattering, and so on not only create a disturbing atmosphere but allude to the black-and-white visual presentation. Imagine that shards of a shattered mirror had each captured part of something and were reflecting it oddly tilted in space and severed from context. The performer's repeated walks into a horizontal lunge are arrested each time at a different moment. Not only are the sparse, blunt, occasionally witty actions apparently independent of cause and effect, but the dancer's isolated limbs appear and disappear from behind parts of the performance space architecture or theatrical "flats." Once, her head sticks out from behind a white panel, horizontal to the floor, twisted toward the audience. The coolly architectural carving up of space and figure hangs in curious tension with the aura of forced fragmentation (i.e., visions of shattered structures and possible dismemberment) induced by the tape and the distortions of the figure. It's something like a live movie (a term Monk actually used to describe her 1970 outdoor piece, *Needlebrain Lloyd and the Systems Kid*). But Monk, I think, also intended the piece to convey a break with tradition. At one point the dancer briefly leaves the performing area and stands among the spectators, contemplating where she or he has just been (*Break* has also been performed by a man in later revivals).[18]

This breaking of the frame is oddly shocking, even today, especially if the space is the traditionally inviolate proscenium stage. The act is part of Monk's ongoing concern with perception and perceptual stances. In the duet *Radar* (1965), Monk and Neville wore featureless masks and beeped gently to locate each other in space. When the piece began, Neville was sitting in the audience, and Monk lugged her to a place onstage. Years later, in the 1971 *Vessel*, it was arranged that if the phone should ring during the first part of the performance (the part that occurred in Monk's loft), Ping Chong, one of the performers, would answer it. At one performance, he told the person at the other end of the line that he couldn't talk now because there was a performance going on. Since all the actions happened very close to the audience, and some were mundane, the phone call was a startling reminder of the separation—and the closeness—between art and life.

Studying in New York studios, taking Robert Dunn's composition workshop in the summer of 1964 (his third and final one in the context of Judson), and sharing rehearsal space introduced Monk to other young experimenters. Up until 1967, she not only appeared in works by King and Neville but participated in a number of other performances, ranging from traditional (Fred Berk's Hebraica Dancers) to vanguard. When Fluxus artist Dick Higgins staged the events titled *Celestials* and *The Tart* at Sunnyside Gardens, a boxing ring in Queens, Monk was in the cast. When artist-choreographer Carolee Schneemann presented her "kinetic theater" piece *Water Light Water Needle* at St. Mark's Church, Monk was one of those who clambered on ropes that crisscrossed the room high above a floor littered with newspaper. Accomplished as a singer and musician, she participated in *Pomegranada* (1966), a Judson musical by H. M. Koutoukas and Al Carmines, choreographed by Aileen Passloff. She remembers being part of a Satie evening at Dick Higgins's house in the spring of 1966; some of Satie's music hall pieces were performed, and the concert culminated with the twenty-four-hour relay performance of the composer's *Vexations* (it began at midnight, and Monk was one of the pianists). In the New York Avant-Garde Festival of 1965, Higgins, his wife, Alison Knowles, the Japanese artist Ay-O, and Monk realized the dada scenario of Satie's *Relâche*. It was for the same festival that she created her *Radar*, along with *Blackboard*, a response to one of the poems in Jackson Mac Low's *Poems for Dancers*. In this, Monk, smartly dressed and wearing high heels, simply wrote words on a wheeled blackboard, which she crisply rotated; the loaded content of some of the words and the "hot" medium of print contrasted with the ambiguity, the "coolness," of the presentation. It could be seen in relation to Marshall McLuhan's book *Understanding Media*, which had come out the year before, with its influential analyses of how various media shape and control human understanding and behavior.

From the beginning, members of Judson Dance Theater indicated that they could do without proscenium stages, and the alternate spaces they used fostered new spatial vistas. By the time Monk and King appeared on the scene, this was a given. Monk, however, was from the beginning particularly adventurous about unusual uses of space and uses of unusual spaces. This may be in part because she has always had to cope with a vision problem that causes her to perceive the world in two dimensions, her principal method of determining depth being that of comparing sizes. Her way of seeing seems to have contributed to her interest in deep space and in layering events on one another. It was inevitable that film, with its flat surface and manipulations of close-up

Meredith Monk in *Sixteen Millimeter Earrings* (1966). Photo by Charlotte Victoria.

and long shot, would attract her; her *Sixteen Millimeter Earrings* (1966) incorporated three film sequences by Kenneth Van Sickle.[19]

Already in this piece, Monk showed herself to be a master of visual and aural rhyming, with spare and elegantly designed effects that echoed each other hauntingly: the red paper streamers that blew upward, the long red wig that she donned, the film of flames consuming a long-haired doll, and Monk—naked like the doll—standing up from inside a trunk so that the filmed flames played over her body. The stiffness of two red sticks that she whipped contrasted with the flexibility of the red streamers and the different sounds they made. She presented, for us to connect if we wished, analogies among the anatomical eye, the artist's eye, and the camera's eye. She allowed us to contrast a smooth and noncommittal movement sequence, performed in profile and in place, with her taped description of the virtuosic dancing she should perhaps be doing at this point. She placed a large paper globe over her head, and when images of her face were projected onto it, she lifted her real hand to wipe her filmed eye.[20]

As art critic John Perrault pointed out in the *Village Voice* early in 1967, *Sixteen Millimeter Earrings* drew attention to surfaces: the skin as covering for the body (a taped voice speaks of this), the retina as a screen for receiving and transmitting what enters the eye, the dancer's body as a screen for filmed images, and the performer's studiedly neutral persona onto which the audience projects imaginings induced by text and actions.[21]

Sixteen Millimeter Earrings was the first important work whose score Monk took full credit for (she also sang, both live and on tape), even though music did not play the role it now plays in her career. As King turned to text—and at about the same time—Monk turned to music and spoken words as a way of amplifying and underscoring her visual imagery.

The ambiance of Monk's pieces then as now was one of fantastic visions, or of the mundane dislocated and charged with elusive drama. They had something, even then, of modern myths in the making. Yet although, in keeping with 1960s vanguard performance traditions, they were presented without artifice on the part of the performer(s), they made some of the senior Judsonites uncomfortable; I remember one of them saying that Monk's work seemed autobiographical, too "personal" (a charge Monk disagrees with).

Although Monk still shies away from linear narrative, elements of storytelling and role-playing have been important in most of her pieces since 1971 and *Vessel*. In the 1960s, her work, like King's, was scarcely narrative at all. The vivid elements resonated against one another but remained mysteriously fluid in intent.

Monk continued to excavate the roles of performer and observer, especially in regard to space and perception. The 1967 *Blueprint*, as performed in the small Judson Gallery next door to the church, began with Monk and Alfred North sitting side by side on chairs facing the audience. With their straight posture, expressionless faces, and long hair, they might have posed for Grant Wood: Hippie Gothic. At the end of the short, extremely spare piece (a living, moving art show rather than a dance), the two arose, and while increasingly loud knocking came from the tape recorder that Monk carried, they walked with extreme slowness away from the audience on a long diagonal, toward a white door that slowly creaked open and cast a beam of light on them. When they had (finally) passed through the door and disappeared, a "hostess" gestured to the audience to walk across the performing area to a window at the rear and look through it. There in the now-illuminated garden sat life-size dolls of Monk and North, side by side on chairs but with their backs to us, as if we were now the backdrop for another performance.

Portable (1966) had enlisted the participation of spectators in moving a small furnished room on wheels, a stage within the stage. Other works more deliberately reversed the usual stationary audience/mobile performers situation, juxtaposing a traveling audience and performers located at various points in a given area like living art displays. Several years earlier, visual artists had broken out of the aesthetic of static gallery/museum displays by bringing perambulating audiences into the time-space structures of dance and theater. Now Monk was wittily reversing the process. In *Co-op*, performed continuously for one and a half hours in 1968 at New York University's Loeb Student Center, spectators could watch a film by Monk, *Ball-Bearing*, downstairs, stroll past four cubicles made of stacked beach umbrella boxes that contained performers in relaxed poses, or (guided by the program) proceed to staged events like *Hippie Love Dance*, in which Monk and William Dunas—in what amounted to a sly dig at censorship and prurience—alternated explicitly sexual dancing, while fully clothed, with stripping to G-strings and moving very little. During an ambitious dance season in 1969, Charles Reinhart took the controversial step of presenting several offbeat choreographers (Yvonne Rainer, Twyla Tharp, Don Redlich, Deborah Hay, and Monk) at a Broadway theater, the Billy Rose. Monk installed "lobby exhibits"—several large cardboard cartons with peepholes. Inside them, people read by flashlight, slept, ate.

Of these static displays, Monk says, "I wanted to break open the proscenium situation . . . to break down things you take for granted about performance. I was very interested at that time in how something was seen, that you didn't always have to be looking at this rectangle from far away. I was curious about the psychology of the audience's relation to the performer—what it does if you do something right in front of somebody's eyes."

Toward the end of the 1960s, many sculptors, such as David Smith and Carl Andre, were combining monumental scale with forms and materials that in appearance all but denied the shaping role of the artist's hand. Certain choreographers—the work of Trisha Brown and Twyla Tharp was especially notable—became increasingly adventurous in their use of large public spaces. The practice appealingly blurred the distinction between art and the reality on which it was superimposed and jolted the spectator's eye loose from a habit of central focus nurtured by centuries of viewing composition on the proscenium stage. In some of the large-scale outdoor or museum pieces, there was too much for the audience to take in at one time. Merce Cunningham's radical experiments with dislocating the spatial hierarchies of a proscenium stage and forcing spectators to choose what to look at were nothing next to sitting at dusk in Central Park, straining to see the crowds of dancers in everyday clothes performing Twyla Tharp's *Medley* (1969), some of them tiny figures way across the Sheep Meadow, vanishing into the background of passersby, dogs, babies, and darkness.

At a time when King became involved with more and more complex redesigning of space simply by dancing, Monk created three massive pageants—*Juice* (1969), *Needlebrain Lloyd and the Systems Kid* (1970), and *Vessel* (1971)—that offered stunningly theatrical insights into landscape, architecture, and the vagaries of perception. In all these pieces, the audience traveled from place to place, either immediately, between sections, or by coming to a different site on another day to see the next installment. More than with Monk's previous pieces, to be a spectator for any of these was to feel oneself on a pilgrimage or a treasure hunt.

Juice began at the Guggenheim Museum on 7 November, picked up at the small Minor Latham Playhouse at Barnard College on 29 November for several performances, and reconvened on 7 December at The House, Monk's loft. As Monk says, "It was really about architecture. The content was the building." At the Guggenheim, the audience sat in the main-floor lobby and watched an exotic pageant wind its way up Frank Lloyd Wright's corkscrewing ramp. Monk was one of four travelers (Dick Higgins was another) wearing red clothes and boots, their hands and faces stained, clinging to each other as they marched—half caterpillar, half phantom hikers. Singing choruses appeared at various points on the ramp, disappeared by backing up, reappeared in new places. Several women in the costume of Marie Antoinette's day revolved in place, tiered one above another. During the second section of part one, the audience was free to move up the ramps and branch out into galleries, where they found Monk's dancers—all in red boots—executing movement sequences, more or less in place. A signal sent all the performers racing down the ramp; the audience, crowding to the railings, could see them briefly far below, dancing and playing Jew's harps as they exited.

Three weeks later, certain key episodes and images from the Guggenheim reappeared, pared down in terms of scale and personnel, reordered, and augmented by new material. A clue to the change in scale was offered by the contrasting preambles: at the Guggenheim, a woman had galloped up and down Fifth Avenue on horseback while the crowd was waiting to enter the museum. At Minor Latham, a child sat by the steps to the theater, astride a rocking horse. The proscenium setting engendered a play of sorts in which the four red people performed solo acts. The final installment, in the loft, was an exhibit of photos, costumes, and props from the previous two parts. The only human presence was provided by the four red people, on black-and-white video and in extreme closeup, as, one by one, they described their involvement with the work. The increasingly intimate perspective was offset by the ruses of theatricality and ultimately by the medium that rendered the performers exceedingly close but incorporeal.

Needlebrain Lloyd traveled the summertime campus of Connecticut College in New London, then the home of the American Dance Festival. This "live movie" offered a dreamlike assemblage of events structured by landscape. It began in the afternoon in the Arboretum and moved to the immense grassy quad. After a dinner break, spectators returned around 9 P.M. to the lawn and then were led back to the Arboretum. A spooky couple, who had seemed to appear from the pond near the beginning of the piece, ended it by getting into a boat and rowing away into the darkness.

Those who saw *Needlebrain Lloyd* say they'll never forget the magic of it. The four red people were in it, and a woman in Marie Antoinette attire, and scores of others. Pioneers (all the women pregnant) pitched camp on the lawn and lit fires. In the distance, a croquet game was in progress. Stiltwalkers and dragons appeared; nymphs danced in trees; Monk sang eerily by the torchlit pond; the windows of a building suddenly lit to display people in bizarre poses. In the afternoon, horses galloped across the quad, performers following; in the evening portion, motorcycles blared and blazed over the same lawn. The pilgrimage not only negotiated the distance between two points on the same campus and from day to night but also seemed to hopscotch centuries and dredge up elements and phantoms from who knew what mythologies.

It was also during 1970 that Monk gave her *Raw Recital* at the Whitney Museum, and in June 1971 her first record, *Key,* was released. Always a gifted singer, she had been making discoveries about how to extend the range of her voice, how to alter it to create a style and vocabulary as flexible and idiosyncratic as her movement style. As her body often seemed to be slipping in between the expected shapes—always a little off guard, suspended, awkward—her voice slid between tones of the Western scale. King's wordplay fractured spoken English; her singing dissected traditional melodic practice. Given the modal melodies she favored, she could sound like a plainchant angel, but the next minute her voice could scratch and growl and whine uncannily. She could sing overtones. Music critics compared her repetitive, wordless vocalise to Asian music, to African, to Indian. Her singing conjured up characters—young, old, male, female. And *Key* was a kind of aural travelogue; you followed her voice through what sounded like a haunted house and many transformations.

Later in 1971, Monk presented the culminating work of this period and one that pointed the way to her music theater pieces of the 1980s and 1990s. *Vessel,* like *Juice,* took place in three locations: Monk's loft on Great Jones Street; the Performing Garage, a non-proscenium theater a little further downtown; and a nearby parking lot. Most people saw the first two parts together (Monk hired a bus to transport the audience) and returned to see the third at a later date. All three parts were given together on Halloween. In a sense, *Vessel* reversed the perceptual changes one went through in viewing *Juice.* Some events seen and heard in the immensely long, narrow space of the loft (one hundred by twenty-five feet) proved to be microcosms of what happened later in the theater or lot. Monk was still concerned with the effects of distance and architecture on perception, as shown in a lengthy interview published in *Drama Review* where she talks about the moatlike gulf between audience and performers in the first part: "I'm putting a bracket around my living situation by making it so that you are actually looking into a real room, but from a great distance away."[22]

But in *Vessel,* subtitled "an opera epic," Monk built her strongest narrative continuity to date, not by conventional storytelling but by the selection of materials and the way she structured them to echo one another. Also, *Vessel* introduced the element of impersonation into her work. It was clear throughout that her subject was Joan of Arc; that even though she might wear contemporary dungarees and a bowler hat, as she did in part three, she was standing in for Joan; and that when she danced into the distance of the darkened parking lot toward the sparks of a welder's torch, we were seeing Joan's fiery immolation. Soldiers fencing with rakes, pioneers lighting their campfires in the lot, and, in the theater, tittering brocaded courtiers, a dopey king and his domineering queen, two people reciting Bishop Cauchon's speech from Shaw's *St. Joan,* and members of her company (The House) serenely tearing lettuce on a "handmade mountain" of white muslin—all these images resonated against the fable of the visionary maiden-warrior and the portrait of the contemporary artist-seer in the deteriorating landscape of downtown Manhattan where she lived and worked. (It is interesting to think that the church across the street from the parking lot, where Joan's three saints were suddenly, magically illuminated, was some years later found to be sinking into the ground and torn down.)

There was something childlike, as Monk acknowledged, about the appearance of *Vessel.* Its decor and costumes had the charm of the handmade, the found, the make-do. "Wryness" was a word Monk used in connection with the mise-en-scène.[23] The air of "anything can happen now" heightened the sense of fable, of fairy tale. Yet there was immense sophistication in the way Monk layered her materials, letting one event echo another, making the spectators' minds travel over an aural and visual landscape, picking out motifs.

In the two years prior to *Vessel,* Monk had begun to tour by recycling material, combing House members and local university students, and generating new pieces in response to new sites (*Tour 2: Barbershop, Tour 7: Factory, Tour 8: Castle,* etc.). After *Vessel* she began to create works like *Education of the Girlchild* (1972–73) that involved smaller casts and could be performed in a variety of available theaters. Even her large-scale masterpiece *Quarry* (1976) required only a non-proscenium theater space of a certain size and shape.

But *Vessel,* which won an Obie Award for outstanding achievement in the theater, was more than the culmination of the second period of Monk's career. It expanded her interest in visual structuring to a franker exploration of the structures and rhythms of emotional states. Her mosaic techniques more consistently set up narrative tensions. *Vessel* also crystallized Monk's interest in the past as another layer of the present. As Monk superimposed the story of Joan on present reality, so she continued in later works to juxtapose past and present, to use archaeology as both theme and device. And *Vessel* articulated the motif of the questing heroine or artist that was to inform other pieces—most notably *Quarry, Specimen Days,* the film *Book of Days,* and the opera *Atlas.*

Both Monk's and King's techniques and interests remained remarkably consistent. The range and the skill deepened and matured. The element of fiction in Monk's work has become clearer and more daring; music has engendered more overarching structures. Yet her handling of character and action is as untraditional as it ever was. And though King's later dances seemed at first consideration to have little to do with the painterly theater events he once made and his comic pieces with text, the technique of reassembling fragments in new combinations continued to subtly mold his work and to influence the writing he now focuses on. More importantly, the notion of dancing and theater as mystical events that relate us to the myths and prophecies of our culture— and perhaps to universal powers—is one that has guided the careers of both these visionary artists.

Notes

1. Jill Johnston, "Judson '64: I," *Village Voice,* 21 January 1965, 12, 19; Johnston, "Judson '64: II," *Village Voice,* 28 January 1965, 11, 28.

2. The last officially numbered Judson concert occurred in 1964 (Concert #16, 29 April), yet some of the best-known charter members of Judson—Yvonne Rainer, Steve Paxton, Trisha Brown, Judith Dunn, and David Gordon—presented work at the church

through 1966 and, along with Carolyn Brown, Lucinda Childs, Tony Holder, Robert Rauschenberg, Alex Hay, Robert Whitman, and Claes Oldenberg, contributed to the 1965 shared programs at the 1st New York Theatre Rally, co-produced by Alan Solomon and Steve Paxton.

3. Jill Johnston, "Judson 1964: End of an Era," *Ballet Review* 1, no. 6 (1967): 7–14.

4. Jill Johnston, "Horizontal Baggage," *Village Voice,* 29 July 1965, 8, 12.

5. Unless otherwise noted, all remarks by King and Monk are drawn from interviews with the author that took place in 1991.

6. Neville has never achieved the prominence of Monk or the less-widespread recognition of King. She developed over the 1960s the kind of works she is still cherished for—her own performing has something of the dark, delicate intensity one associates with Mary Wigman—her ritualistic solos and small-scale group works combine highly distilled gestures and restrained performing with such foreboding and often macabre images that they affect one like inexplicable nightmares.

7. Sally Banes, *Terpsichore in Sneakers: Post-Modern Dance,* 2nd ed. (Middletown, Conn.: Wesleyan University Press, 1987).

8. Meredith Monk, interview by the author, April 1981.

9. Kenneth King, "Toward a Trans-Literal and Trans-Technical Dance-Theatre," in *The New Art,* ed. Gregory Battcock (New York: Dutton, 1973), 121.

10. Kenneth King, "CELE((CERE))BRATIONS: PROBElems & SOULutions fir the dyEYEing KING," in *Future's Fictions,* ed. Richard Kostelanetz. Special issue of *Panache* (1971): 48–60.

11. Kenneth King, "SuperLecture," in *The Young American Writers,* ed. Richard Kostelanetz (New York: Funk and Wagnalls, 1967), 223.

12. Gregory Battcock, "Notations on a New Dance Program," *Film Culture* 43 (Winter 1966): 4.

13. "Metagexis (Joseph's Song)," 1972, unpublished manuscript. Excerpts have appeared in *Eddy* 8 (Spring–Summer 1976): 27–32.

14. Ibid.

15. Jill Johnston, "Where's Kenneth?" *Village Voice,* 18 January 1968, 24. Reprinted in Jill Johnston, *Marmalade Me,* rev. ed. (Middletown, Conn.: Wesleyan University Press, 1998), 139–41.

16. Ibid., 141.

17. In charting the early careers of Wilson, King, and Monk, the question of inter-influence has caused some confusion and hostility. On 30 June 1980—by which time Wilson had already achieved international fame as a creator and director of nonlinear theatrical spectacles—the *New Yorker* published an article by Arlene Croce entitled "Slowly the History of Them Comes Out" (reprinted in her *Going to the Dance* [New York: Knopf, 1982], 285–93). In the article, Croce presented Wilson as an influence on Monk, King, and several other choreographers. (The infuriated responses to this and other theories of artistic lineage proposed in Croce's articles are referred to in *Going to the Dance* in an addendum to the review.)

Certainly Monk and King were choreographing in distinctive ways before Wilson began to present work in New York. His first notable production, *The King of Spain,* appeared in 1969 (it was later incorporated into *The Life and Times of Sigmund Freud,* 1970). The three artists initially were friendly. Wilson appeared in works by Monk, replacing Alfred North for tour dates of her 1967 *Blueprint* and performing in *Co-op* (1968). In 1968, Monk, Wilson, and Robin Stoughton improvised in an L-shaped alley off Great Jones Street for part two of *ByrdwoMAN*—with Monk taking over the role of Byrdwoman from Wilson, who had played it during part one in his loft. (In those years, Wilson occasionally went by the name of Byrd Hoffman, an early teacher he revered.) King appeared not only in *The Life and Times of Sigmund Freud* (as did Audrey Monk, Meredith's mother) but also in two small-scale events of Wilson's in 1967 or 1968, one of which took place at the Bleecker Street Cinema, the other at Jerome Robbins's American Theatre Laboratory. Later the friendship soured, with Monk and King feeling that Wilson had appropriated ideas from them.

18. Lutz Forster performed *Break* with the José Limón Company in 1986 and in the Megadance concert (part of Serious Fun! at Lincoln Center) in 1992, and Rob Besserer took Monk's role in the 1991–92 tours of Mikhail Baryshnikov's White Oak Dance Project.

19. Monk's best-known works for film and/or video are *Ellis Island* (1979) and *Book of Days* (1988).

20. A film was made of *Sixteen Millimeter Earrings* in 1980, produced, directed, and photographed by Robert Withers.

21. John Perrault, "Out of Time, In the Center," *Village Voice*, 15 December 1966, 12–13, 36 (reference to *Sixteen Millimeter Earrings* appears on 36).

22. " 'Vessel': An Opera Epic," *Drama Review* 16, no. 1 (1972; T-53): 87–103. Reprinted in Selma Jeanne Cohen, *Dance as a Theatre Art*, rev. ed. (Princeton, N.J.: Princeton Book Company, 1992), 210.

23. Ibid., 212.

8

One Route from Ballet to Postmodern

Wendy Perron

On 6 July 1962, the day of the first performance of Robert Dunn's workshop at Judson Memorial Church, I performed with my ballet teacher on Cape Cod. Miss Fokine (Michel's niece, Irine) took a group of students to Nausett Lights Beach, where we had class for two hours every morning and late afternoon on an outdoor platform and swam at the beach down the block in between. At the end of this idyllic summer, we gave a recital for local residents. I was fourteen.

After every performance, summer or winter, Miss Fokine would pick on one poor kid who had done something transgressive, like letting dirty toe shoe ribbons drag on the floor. On this occasion, after our performance of the "Grand Pas" from *Paquita,* she entered our dressing room and came right at me, pointing and yelling, "Look at your hair! You look like an African Fujiyama!" We had been on the Cape for six weeks, and whenever my mother wasn't around to cut my hair it grew like a bush. From that moment on, I grew it long so I could tie it back in a bun like the other girls. When not in class, I ironed it or applied a god-awful-smelling chemical to straighten it. I never found out what a "Fujiyama" was, but I don't think it's African.

That fall the Bolshoi was coming to the Metropolitan Opera House, and they were looking for American teenagers to be extras in the crowd scenes of Leonid Yakobson's new *Spartacus.* Miss Fokine's mother, Alexandra Fedorova, still had connections to the Bolshoi, and she arranged for a bunch of us to audition. I was among the lucky group chosen to perform. We were onstage when Vladimir Vasiliev leaped like a panther

137

and turned like a gyroscope. When Maya Plisetskaya dragged the cart like a beggar woman, we all had to point at her and laugh. Backstage, Galina Ulanova walked a few steps behind the meltingly lovely Ekaterina Maximova. My fantasy was to become the next Anastasia Stevens, the American girl who danced with the Bolshoi and also translated for us. Plus, she had beautiful reddish frizzy hair (frizzy—like mine!).

In the summer of 1963, I went to the Delacorte Theater in Central Park to see the new Joffrey Ballet. Because the performance was free, crowds of people would come, so you had to get your ticket in the morning and camp out in the park all afternoon. I remember seeing Gerald Arpino's *Sea Shadow*, with Lisa Bradley, hair long and free, undulating on top of a man. She was both pristine and sensual, and utterly gorgeous. The possibility of this kind of dancerly sexuality appealed to my budding sense of myself. That night I decided to study at the Joffrey school (officially the American Ballet Center) starting in the fall, even though it meant commuting from New Jersey.

I loved the Joffrey school, especially Françoise Martinet, who wore white tennis shoes even for pointe work. The classes seemed less strict than at the School of American Ballet, where I had studied during the summers of 1960 and 1963, and the atmosphere was not quite so hallowed.[1] Lisa Bradley, Noël Mason, Ivy Clear, Trinette Singleton, Charthel Arthur, and Marjorie Mussman were all taking the advanced class, which I watched whenever I could. I usually took the intermediate class with Miss Martinet, Lillian Moore, or occasionally Mr. Joffrey. I tried hard to be a worthy ballet student, and when Mr. Joffrey asked me to stand front and center as an example to the others, I was thrilled almost to the point of delirium.

A few modern dancers took class too. I didn't want to be a modern dancer—that's what my mother had been. I had studied "interpretive dance" with my mother and other teachers since I was five. I had taken the June course at the Martha Graham School of Contemporary Dance that summer of 1963, and I continued to go every Friday, but it remained a sideline for me.[2]

One day as I was walking to Washington Square Park between classes, I saw one of the modern dancers from the Joffrey class—Sandra Neels—on the steps of a church on Washington Square South. She called out to me, saying, "You should come to some performances here. They're really interesting." I just said, "Uh huh." I didn't go to see modern dance unless my mother dragged me. (Sandra danced with Merce Cunningham from 1963 to 1973.)

I've gone back to that moment many times, wondering if anything would have mobilized me to check out the performances at Judson. My two magnetic poles at that time were *Swan Lake* and *West Side Story*. I would listen to the radio, roving up and down the dial in hopes of hearing one or the other. I had seen *West Side Story* on Broadway and memorized all the songs. The same year, I danced in my ballet teacher's *Swan Lake* and adored it. I could have rippled my arms to Tchaikovsky's music for days.

As my high school graduation approached, I developed three possible plans. The first was to attend New York University and continue studying at the Joffrey school, with the hope of getting into the company. The second was to go to Juilliard, where I could study both modern dance and ballet. The third was to go to Bennington, which was my mother's first choice, and for that reason it was my last.

I forced myself to assess my prospects in ballet realistically. Although I was a lyrical, musical classical dancer, my turn-out and pointe work were less than sparkling. In the Graham technique you had to dig deeper into yourself, and that intensity had a gritty psychological appeal. So, after being accepted at Juilliard, I watched some classes there. I realized that if I chose that route, the next four years would be entirely familiar to me, as I had taken modern and ballet classes virtually all my life. On the other hand, the day I visited the Bennington campus in Vermont happened to be a beautiful fall afternoon, and somehow that day illuminated my desire to enter into the world of art and literature and learning. I opted for the unknown rather than the known.

It took me my whole freshman year to change over from being a ballet dancer to being a modern dancer. I had to be broken like a horse is broken before you can ride it. Bill Bales lit into me for my habits—the swanlike neck, the rippling arms, the prissy footsteps, the jutting chin, the delicate fingers. I had to purge myself of these mannerisms and find the ground underneath me.

During my college years—1965 to 1969—I often came to New York City and saw early Dance Theater Workshop performances. Jack Moore, one of the three founders, was teaching dance at Bennington. On one of these trips I saw Rudy Perez do *Countdown*. He sat on a chair and took a drag of a cigarette in surreal slowed-down time while the *Songs of the Auvergne* played on tape. When he stood up, you could see stripes of blue paint on his face. Was it war paint? The tears of a clown? The markings of a quarterback? The dance was ineffably sad, yet rooted and powerful.

And I went back to the Delacorte in 1966 and saw Carmen de Lavallade in a solo by Geoffrey Holder. She was the most beautiful woman dancing I could imagine. The vision of her spiraling in a white dress lingered in my mind for days. It was the first "modern dance" I fell in love with, but it wasn't weighty and angular like "modern dance" or insistent in any way. It was like dreaming of an island far away.

I was feeling more comfortable as a modern dancer and wanted to choreograph, simply because it was so hard to do well. (I was quickly developing a critic's eye and could see the pitfalls clearly.) I remember a time in Jack Moore's composition class, probably in my junior or senior year, when the assignment was to make a beginning and an ending. We would each then choose someone else's beginning and someone else's ending and make our own middle to sandwich in between. I was in the studio alone, trying to begin my beginning. I started with a big reach up with my head and arm—an ecstatic reach to the heavens. I was playing with it, trying out different ways of doing it. I started breaking it up into parts. Through endless trials, I found a way of reaching the head up, then bringing the arm up sharply, and then as the head came down, leaving the arm up. Within two seconds, the arm movement intercut the head movement. I worked on it until I could do it without thinking. It was an unusual coordination, but a certain energy came from breaking it up. It was no longer a breathy or ecstatic thing, but broken, like shards. When I showed it in class, everyone responded immediately, and more than half of them chose it for their beginning. I felt something had happened. I had undermined a unit of assumed movement and made something new. Looking back, I see that I was deconstructing a standard reach—my first encounter with postmodernism. I feel that much of my choreography can be traced to that moment.

College changed me, but the 1960s did too. I remember sunny days when we would take our dormitory furniture out on the lawn. Someone's stereo would be blasting Aretha Franklin's voice from a dorm window, and everything was fine in the world. To me that was the sixties: wearing a filmy Indian shirt and beads and hearing Aretha wail over the Commons lawn. Some of us were dancing and some were reading. Ooooh it felt good. Singing "R-e-s-p-e-c-t" along with Aretha was a glorious way to grow up.

One night during our college dance tour in the winter of 1968, I stayed at a friend's pad in Boston. She sat me down and said, "You have to hear the new Beatles album." It was *Sgt. Pepper's Lonely Hearts Club Band,* and I was overwhelmed. The ingenuity, the drive, the lilting but somehow rebellious melodies, the camaraderie, the lightheartedness, the trippiness (yes, we got stoned first), the sense that *anything* can follow *anything,* were astounding. (Did the Beatles know about John Cage?)

So my new poles were Aretha Franklin and the Beatles. The go-for-broke, sing-from-your-guts celebration of womanhood on the one hand and this zany collaboration, the revelation that you could be brainy and also have fun, on the other.

College taught me that while it's worthwhile to be a good girl, it's also worthwhile to break the rules. The Bennington campus had 350 acres of rolling hills and picturesque landscape. Viola Farber, a former Cunningham dancer who taught at Bennington briefly, asked us to choreograph for an out-of-doors spot on campus. I was feeling pretty dismal, nursing a broken heart that I pretended was "sophomore slump." I wasn't in the mood to celebrate the joy of life on the grassy knolls or under a lushly spreading oak, so I found a small area between a garage and a chicken coop that was littered with hangers, old tires, and beer cans. Mostly I got entangled in some wires and looked at the ground. Decades later, Viola, recalling that assignment, enthusiastically blurted out, "And you picked the ugliest place on campus!"

In the fall of 1968, Judith Dunn came up to Vermont to teach, with musician Bill Dixon in tow. Also a former dancer with Cunningham, Judy had assisted her husband, Robert Dunn, in giving the composition workshops that led to Judson Dance Theater. She had since separated from him. I loved her yoga class and learned the sun worship from her. To demonstrate the lion posture, she would get preternaturally calm and then, with a ridiculously fierce thrust of her head, stick her tongue out and down and pop her eyes wide open. She would hold that posture for two full minutes. I was impressed with her commitment.

But I hated Judy's technique class. Her idea of the new relation of music to dance was that Bill would play any loungey jazz thing on the piano while we did the combination. She emphatically did not want the piano to set the tempo and did not want us to do the steps "to" the music. But she scolded us when, inevitably, we each did it with different timing. This seemed illogical and irresponsible, and I quit the class.

But Judy's presence opened things up. She challenged the tradition of a single end-of-semester concert in Commons Theater so that we could do performances in other spaces and times. But one such performance, masterminded by Cathy Weis, one year behind me (now a video/dance/performance artist), and an MFA design student named Mary Fussell, was already in the works. Cathy and Mary turned Jennings Mansion, where music classes were held, into a complex, dreamlike environment. On the ground floor was a genteel ballroom where Ulysses Dove[3] and I danced with guests and graciously escorted them to the level below. The basement practice rooms had been transformed to represent organs of the body: one room was the heart, another the lungs, another the liver. Audience members entered rooms with billowing fabrics and throbbing sounds. They were given costumes to don, so the separation between performers and audience was blurred, and people went from room to room in a pleasantly confused state. Tuli Kupferberg of the Fugs came to campus to heighten the confusion.

I knew that Judy was conducting a serious improvisation session on Friday mornings, but I never went. Out of that class came her strong improvisation performance group of the next few years. I knew that something very interior, very intuitive was going on that I wasn't privy to or didn't have access to in myself. Just the fact that it was a three-hour session was daunting.

Also, I had had an experience that crystallized my fear of improvisation. One Thursday afternoon during the weekly dance division workshop, Jack Moore decided, for a change of pace, that we should improvise. He named a few people to go up onstage and "improvise." (This was Commons Theater, where Martha Graham and the other modern dance "pioneers" had premiered major works.) Someone put a box full of hats onstage. As Jack was calling out names of people to go up and experiment in front of everyone, his eyes alighted on me and he added my name. I froze like a stone. Even if my future had depended on it, I couldn't have budged from my seat. I shook my head vehemently. "Oh, come on, Wendy, it'll be fun," said Jack. "No," I said. This went back and forth a few more times as I totally humiliated myself.

Jack finally dropped his case, and I got to sit back and watch the adventurous ones onstage. They played with the hats. They covered their eyes with the hats, stomped on them, tossed them around. At best, what they did was either cute or clever. I was glad I hadn't acquiesced. But amid the sea of silliness, one phenomenon surfaced: Lisa Nelson, a student one year behind me. Her concentration was a thing to behold. Her quickness and connectedness between her dance self and the hat self were astonishing. She did things with the hats that I was sure no one else on earth had ever done. I couldn't take my eyes off her. She seemed to be getting signals from outer space, or I guess inner space. (Many years later, she teamed up with Steve Paxton, and they created *PA RT* [1978], a collaborative duet which they still sometimes perform.) To this day, she is my favorite improviser.

During my freshman non-resident term (now called field work term) I studied at Paul Sanasardo's studio at Sixteenth Street and Sixth Avenue. His class was known as the most difficult modern technique class in the city. I was up for it. In that class were Sara Rudner, Cliff Keuter, Elina Mooney, Kenneth King, Diane Germaine, Manuel Alum, Sally Bowden, Bill Dunas, Mark Franko, Judith Blackstone, and Laura Dean. I loved watching these dancers as I had loved watching the dancers at the School of American Ballet, at Joffrey, and at the Graham School.

But studying with Paul Sanasardo was a mixed experience. As galvanizing as his rigorous barre and combinations were, his narcissism was out of control. After giving orders in his richly booming voice, he'd watch himself in the mirror, his eyes glued to his own image. He treated his dancers brutally. Manuel Alum and Diane Germaine, his two star dancers, were routinely scorned and humiliated in class. It was disturbing. I did not aspire to work with a man like that.

One person who seemed not to belong in an advanced technique class was Bill Dunas. He would do triplets across the floor with his head wagging back and forth, which I interpreted as an excuse-me-for-living attitude. I was then blown away by his performances at the Cubiculo in which he appeared between blackouts in intensely characterized roles. Every move he made, every look on his face, was drastic. No complex movement, no virtuosic technique emanated from his performing self—just an existential hunger and rawness. Later, in 1972, I learned *Gap*, the basic three-minute dance that he put into each piece in a different way. I remember outstretched arms with fists, feet planted apart. The head dips and the arms loop around each other, then you come up strong, as defiant as before. I fell in love with him—and this love, for a change, was requited.

During the summers of 1967 and 1968, I attended the American Dance Festival at Connecticut College. I took Sarah Stackhouse's ecstatic classes in Limón technique, Graham classes with David Wood, Doris Rudko's course in Louis Horst's choreographic method, and Lucas Hoving's eclectic technique class. For those of us already having back trouble, Betty Jones offered extracurricular sessions in the "constructive rest position," based on the work of Lulu Sweigard. The second summer I danced in a reconstruction of Doris Humphrey's *New Dance* (1935), directed by Jennifer Muller and supervised by José Limón. But more important was that Martha Wittman, of the Bennington faculty, had asked me to assist her in teaching, and I got to observe her serious but unorthodox approach to composition. She experimented with group process and improvisation as routes to choreography.

So when I graduated from Bennington and came to New York in 1969, I was no longer satisfied by modern dance as I had known it—the austere beauty of Limón's *Moor's Pavane,* the chiseled angst of Martha Graham in *Lamentation.* I was drawn to performances of the Grand Union—these family reunions where you wondered who was going to misbehave, and we'd watch them get on each other's nerves—brilliantly. They were our Beatles. We all had our favorites. "Were you there the time Trisha stayed under a blanket for about an *hour*?" "Did you see how David insulted Nancy? Do you think he really meant it this time?" "Did Douglas wear that preacher outfit 'cause he felt alienated?" "The women's dance was really silly this time." "I don't know what David and Barbara were doing with those pillows, but I loved watching them."

I remember the Grand Union performance at New York University's Loeb Student Center when they played the popular song "Lola" by The Kinks about a hundred times. One of the performers would just walk over to the phonograph and turn it on. This was against all the rules of what we had been taught in college about using music, not to mention the choice of a popular song. But this alluring yet insolent song about ambiguous sexuality captured the moment perfectly. Everyone was trying out everything. Choosing that song exemplified the conflation of high art and popular art that was heralded by Susan Sontag. This was like bringing your furniture out on the grass and listening to Aretha. The defiance, the sensuality, the do-your-own-thingness of it!

My first year after graduating, while I was on scholarship at the Martha Graham School, I danced with Rudy Perez. I learned a lot about applying collage techniques to dance, but after a year I realized that he too had a kind of narcissism that seemed to leave no room for anyone else's reality.

I was taking class with Maggie Black, a popular ballet teacher whom modern dancers trusted because of her emphasis on alignment. At the end of one class, Sara Rudner and Rose Marie Wright, scouting new talent for Twyla Tharp, approached me and invited me to come to Twyla's studio. In a one-candidate audition, I was told "You'll do," but I felt uncomfortable in the movement. I had not yet seen *The One Hundreds* (1970), the piece that blew my mind with its inventiveness and sent me scurrying to the audition for the "farm club," the temporary group of seventeen young dancers and nondancers she assembled to learn repertory. Working with her was a juicy challenge for me as a dancer and an observer. Out of Twyla's body came a stream of ingenious, intricate, infinitely varied, and open-ended movement. A clear love of the body in motion—as opposed to positions, and as opposed to motion in the service of narrative—was the motivating force. "You must feel personally about every move," she told us while showing the steps, thus confirming what I had always felt and known about dance.

In 1971, at the Whitney Museum, I saw Trisha Brown's *Walking on the Wall,* in which her performers, aided by specially made harnesses, walked on the wall. The illusion was so strong that you could swear you were looking out a window and down to the sidewalk. It was very trippy, as though everyone in the room was having the same hallucination. She also performed *Skymap* (1969), for which she asked those of us in the audience to lie on our backs, look up, and listen. We heard Trisha's voice inviting us to use our imagination to cross a fantasy terrain. It was an amazing feeling to know that everyone was making similar thought pictures while packed like sardines on the floor. (Is this a descendant of Anna Halprin's community pieces?) I wanted to remember every word and write it down.

In 1973 I saw Yvonne Rainer's *Inner Appearances,* her prelude to *This is the story of a woman who. . . .* It was on a program, organized by James Waring, called "Dancing Ladies." Her sole action was vacuuming—a decision that was both logical (considering so many women spent so much time at it) and daring (in that vacuuming was not traditionally considered the stuff of art). I was completely engrossed in her written text, projected sentence by sentence onto the back wall. One of the lines, which I wrote down on a scrap of program, was, "Social interaction seems to be mostly about seduction." I felt that Yvonne was like Susan Sontag, her high-pitched intelligence joining together with high-pitched emotions. There was a force to this piece (which was before the term "performance art" was commonly used) but also a restraint that was moving. And I was knocked out by the protest she embedded in her biography in the program notes. Although James Waring had been her mentor, she railed against the title "Dancing Ladies": "Five years ago I might have appreciated the humor and quaintness of 'Dancing Ladies,' but in a time when more and more women are struggling for a sense of individual identity in ways that are new and unsettling, such a title is—at best—anachronistic in its ignoring of that struggle and—far worse—condescending." I loved that she just couldn't leave it alone. Yvonne was one of the few people who had the guts to live the slogan of the times—"the personal is the political."

Through Bill Dunas I met Kenneth King, and I danced in his pieces *Praxiomatics* and *The Telaxic Synapsulator* (both 1974). The cast of *Praxiomatics* included David Woodberry and three people who had performed with Robert Wilson: Charles Dennis, Robyn Brentano, and Liz Pasquale. I loved dancing with Kenneth. Somehow, he created an environment that dissipated my fear of improvisation. By now I had done some improvisation with Art Bauman (a cofounder of Dance Theater Workshop) and a little when Daniel Nagrin started his Workgroup (which I ultimately was not accepted into). But I really felt free with Kenneth. He is a very technical dancer and appreciates technique in other dancers. I was fascinated by his character work and his willingness to go out on a limb. Kenneth is the philosopher/artist, wizardly in his thinking. His *High Noon,* based on Nietzsche's writings, was dark and mysterious, studded equally with moments of Nietzsche's truth and Nietzsche's craziness.

Talking about truth and craziness: around this time I was reading Jill Johnston's collection of *Village Voice* reviews entitled *Marmalade Me.* It sizzled with her highly personal take on dance and art. Her writing bypassed the usual logic and organization of paragraphs and cut to the heart of her searing and poetic vision. Hers was a real sixties voice. I understood enough about my limitations as a choreographer not to try

Wendy Perron in *The One of No Way* by Francis Alenikoff. Photo by Eric Reiner.

to emulate what I learned about the sixties from her account. But it got me curious about Judson and interested in writing. I took three cycles of a course in dance writing sponsored by Dance Theater Workshop that was co-taught by Deborah Jowitt and Marcia B. Siegel. (I may have this backward: it could be that the course is what led me to read Johnston.)

When I started dancing with Trisha Brown in 1975, I felt I had come home. In addition to seeing her walk on walls, I had seen some of her dances in a gallery. The year before, I had written a survey of new dance for *New York Magazine* (which never made it into print), and in it I declared Trisha my favorite choreographer. I described her dancers as having "collapsible bodies." I was trying to identify not only the special quality of looseness but also the possibility that they could drop to the floor at any moment. It was like collapsing your assumptions, like emptying your mind. Whatever you were thinking, it could just end. Trisha's quicksilver mind matched her collapsible body. No need to hold on to the uplifted body, the virtuosic, the heroic. Just a need to keep dancing. It was radical almost like Jerry Rubin and Abbie Hoffman were radical.

In Trisha's studio in Soho we were making a piece called *Pyramid*, whose score was a diabolical progression of accumulating and de-accumulating. The first day, Trisha explained the structure and asked us to make our own series of movements. When we asked what kind of movement, she said something like, "It should be simple and complex, steady and erratic, strong and delicate, logical and irrational, grand and humble." This series of paradoxes whetted my movement-making appetite. I had a great time working on this piece. About Trisha, I wrote in my journal, "Her movements are more natural than natural. . . . You can see her thoughts in the dancing and she questions everything." And Trisha didn't mind my bushy hair. By that time Angela Davis had emerged as a cultural icon, so I started thinking that my natural hair state was a Judaic version of the Afro.

During this period, I was also writing reviews for the *Soho Weekly News*, right around the corner from Trisha's studio. Since I wasn't crazy about reviewing my friends, I mostly kept away from dance. Instead I covered the new, anything-goes performances—stemming from experimentation in theater, dance, and visual art—that were later dubbed "performance art." Robb Baker edited a section called the "Concepts in Performance" page, and it was the only place where this type of thing could be covered. When Robb left, I became the editor of that page. And after I left, Sally Banes, who had started writing for it, took it over.

Tragically, in the late 1970s Judith Dunn developed a brain tumor and could no longer teach. While she was on medical leave, the Bennington College dance division looked for a replacement—and found me. Soon after I arrived in 1978, we were discussing ideas for the next repertory class at a dance division meeting. Martha Wittman, who was still on the faculty then (and, in her sixties, started dancing with the Liz Lerman Dance Exchange in the mid-1990s), suggested teaching Judy's *Dew Horse* (1963/1966). I wanted to expand the idea to doing a semester's worth of works from Judson Dance Theater. Another faculty member, designer/videographer/performer Tony Carruthers, loved the idea. Between Tony and me, the project grew to include residencies with Trisha, Yvonne, Steve Paxton, and Lisa Nelson; a lecture by Sally Banes (who was writing her dissertation on Judson at the time);[4] reconstructions of Steve's *Flat* (1964), Yvonne's *We Shall Run* (1963), and Trisha's

Wendy Perron in rehearsal for *Rocks* by Jack Moore (1970). Photo by Eric Reiner.

Homemade (1965); a series of videotaped interviews; and an exhibit of photographs that toured internationally. Later we reconstructed many more pieces at St. Mark's Church. All of this was the Bennington College Judson Project, and it took up much of my time from 1979 to 1982. (I continue to give a slide lecture on Judson Dance Theater, incorporating the White Oak Dance Project's reconstructions.)

Much of the work I saw in the 1970s led me to look for its roots in Judson: the mind trip of Rudy Perez, the intensity of Kenneth King, the paradoxical nature of Trisha Brown, the mythmaking improvisation of the Grand Union, the hard-won intellectual feminism of Yvonne Rainer, the brazen writing of Jill Johnston, and the emergence of performance art. Judson was a time to clear the slate and start over. The allure for me was returning to a heady beginning that I hadn't witnessed, when sparks of possibility flew across the skyscape of the American mind.

Notes

1. But I thoroughly enjoyed my training at the School of American Ballet. In my diary of 1963, I paired the name of each of my teachers with her or his most repeated utterance: Antonina Tumkovsky ("Cheek to me"), Maria Tallchief ("Stomach in, chest out"), André Eglevsky ("Arms simple"), Lew Christensen ("Learn to listen"), and Muriel Stuart ("Now rest, darling").

2. Nevertheless, I was very involved in the Graham classes. The Friday class was the advanced teenage class, and many kids from the High School of Performing Arts took it, including Christian Holder. One Friday, 22 November 1963, while in my high school history class, I learned that President Kennedy had been shot and killed. After general chaos and crying in the girls' room, I took the bus in to New York City anyway. Only about six kids showed up, but David Wood taught class as usual. He said, "We're dancers, and dancing is what we do no matter what tragedy has occurred. We will work through it."

3. Dove later danced with Merce Cunningham and Alvin Ailey and became an internationally acclaimed choreographer who mounted works on many companies until his death in 1996.

4. This dissertation was later published as *Democracy's Body: Judson Dance Theater, 1962–1964* (Ann Arbor: University of Michigan Research Press, 1983).

9

Radical Discoveries
Pioneering Postmodern Dance in Britain

Stephanie Jordan

It is received wisdom that the major development in British dance in the 1960s was the foundation of a professional contemporary dance tradition.[1] This tradition was of an expressionist bias and took as its model the style of Martha Graham, whose company had visited Britain in 1954 and 1963. The turning point was the transformation of Ballet Rambert from a classical into a contemporary dance company in 1966 and the founding by philanthropist Robin Howard of the London School of Contemporary Dance (LSCD) and the company London Contemporary Dance Theatre (LCDT) in 1966 and 1967, respectively. It is much less well known that a countermovement of alternative dance activity sprang up almost immediately after the establishment of a Graham-based tradition, a small countermovement—after all, this was the beginning of any professional community outside ballet—but nevertheless a forceful one. Indeed, this alternative activity seems already to have been under way by the end of the 1960s.

Paradoxically, perhaps, this counter-activity was promoted by Howard's own Contemporary Ballet Trust (in 1970 renamed, more appropriately, Contemporary Dance Trust), which was the umbrella for LSCD, LCDT, and their home from 1969 onward, The Place. Under these auspices, the new activity continued to flourish until the mid-1970s.[2] The choreographers responsible were either students at the LSCD or artists who had developed a close association with The Place, using it, for instance, as a rehearsal base and performance venue.

Howard welcomed this countermovement. It is important to realize

151

that, as well as having a passion for Graham's work, Howard took a great interest in experimental dance. He had brought Twyla Tharp over to London in 1967, in the days before she was a "proscenium" choreographer. In the late 1980s, reflecting upon the development of the LSCD, he recalled his belief in cultivating opposition, that one of the purposes of such an institution was to stir up countermovements, as long as a "dialogue" between differing schools of thought could be kept going.[3] As a sign of his more radical interests, Howard organized for the opening of The Place a series of performance events for different spaces in the building, entitled *Explorations*. He also invited Patricia Hutchinson to be the LSCD's first principal in 1967. This was an important decision: students remember her as someone who responded openly and with flexibility to their needs and creative ambitions.[4] If some students felt out of sympathy with the Graham-based work, they found plenty of opportunities for making and showing a different kind of work that was more aligned with the new activity in the other arts. The term "postmodernism" was not yet in currency, but some of this work certainly demonstrates what we might now recognize as postmodern tendencies.[5]

This "postmodern" British work has not been well documented. There are reviews, and a few short retrospective writings to the effect that there was some kind of alternative movement;[6] however, there is a dearth of rigorous discussion of the conceptual basis of the work or of the intentions of the artists involved.

Several factors have unwittingly helped to hide this activity from view. LCDT dominated Contemporary Dance Trust activities by the mid-1970s. By then, The Place and the LSCD had changed image and become less of a creative force (Howard himself recognized this),[7] much more focused on training performers in Graham-based style. Alternative work only acquired a label and a magazine, *New Dance*, in 1977, as if indeed this were the real beginning of the movement (the term "New Dance" was coined in preference to the American term "postmodern," thus establishing an independent British identity). The late 1970s saw a proliferation of independent groups outside the two main contemporary dance companies. In the mid-1980s the notion of backdating the use of the term "New Dance" was proposed.[8]

Very important too is the fact that several students left The Place and the LSCD to work under the banner of performance art, theater, or film, finding official notions of what constituted dance too confining and the support of a dance community small. The line of continuity therefore from the late 1960s and early 1970s was thin. Richard Alston is one of the few to have remained prominent in dance after this period. Later (from 1986 to 1993) the artistic director of Rambert Dance Company and then of the Richard Alston Dance Company, he founded Strider, the first independent dance group to emerge from the LSCD, which existed from 1972 to 1975. The irony is that Alston's work has long since embraced more traditional fundamental forms and concepts, and he now considers himself a modernist, not a postmodernist.

It could be, too, that some of the dance work of the early period was overlooked, not seen as part of dance. After all, in Britain modern dance itself was new, not to mention postmodern dance. It seems that, conscious of the boundaries between media, many dance critics and representatives from the dance funding bodies needed to see technical steps in order to classify a work as dance or to see it as falling within their domain.[9]

Now we might review the past in relation to a developed theoretical understanding and broader notions of what could be considered part of our dance history. The context of innovation across all the arts is revealing.

American avant-garde art exerted a strong influence in Britain during this period. There were the visits in 1964 and 1966 of John Cage and Merce Cunningham (then an inspiration to artists from almost every discipline other than dance),[10] the exhibitions of Robert Rauschenberg and Jasper Johns in 1964 and of the minimalists in 1969, and appearances of radical theater groups like Living Theater in 1964 and La Mama and Open Theater in 1967. However, British and European radical movements had their own powerful voices. There was the counterculture in theater and the related mixed-media Happenings and performance art (this "fringe" movement blossomed in Britain from about 1965, while the European Fluxus group had existed since 1962); avant-garde film, painting, sculpture, and poetry; and the very lively British art school scene at the time, decidedly antielitist and as open to producing pop music as to fostering fine art.

It is important too that The Place was an arts center presenting theater, performance art, films, and art exhibitions as well as dance, and that in the early days, many people who attached themselves to the LSCD as full- or part-time students came from the other arts, some as mature students. Alston, for instance, had already been to art school. Such students arrived versed in the new kind of activity. Dance therefore had direct links with this broader artistic context, especially with the visual arts. There is a parallel here with the first generation of American postmodern choreographers, who likewise developed visual arts connections, for instance, with Pop Art, minimalist sculpture, and avant-garde film.

Dance in the late 1960s and early 1970s also represented a physical immediacy, a potency, a liberation from the word that was sought by artists from many disciplines. Related to this, there was at that time a flamboyant move away from painting and sculpture into performance, for instance, by Barry Flanagan, Gilbert and George, Richard Long, and Bruce McLean, all of whom attended St. Martin's School of Art during the 1960s. Flanagan even attended dance classes at The Place and formed a link with Strider during its first year of activity.

In addition to promoting the Graham work, the LSCD introduced to its students a number of teachers and choreographers who were in tune with recent artistic developments. There were, for instance, the young composer Michael Finnissy, who encouraged the more independent kind of relationship between music and dance that Cage and Cunningham had pioneered, and the drama tutor John Roche, who introduced a breadth of techniques from the new fringe theater movement. There were also visiting American teachers who had come from Cunningham's way of thinking: Cunningham himself, Viola Farber, and Margaret Jenkins, all of whom taught briefly at Berners Place (the LSCD's first base), and later, Rosalind Newman, who taught at The Place. Twyla Tharp held open rehearsals at The Place during her season at the Round House in 1974. In 1972, Meredith Monk incorporated thirty students into a performance of her *Juice*.

Examining the radical British dance work created during this period, we find examples of practice in Sally Banes's two main postmodern categories. First, there is work that emphasizes the nature of the medium itself, the analytic, "modernist" kind of postmodern dance and, closely related to this, work that uses Cunningham's principles. Second, there is work that has meaning beyond the medium of movement itself.

In the first category are the environment pieces made by students who were intent on mixing the disciplines of sculpture and dance: Primavera Boman, who had trained in sculpture at St. Martin's and also as a dancer at the Graham School and LSCD, and Alan Beattie, a scientist who had studied art, design, and dance and had taught workshops at various London art schools integrating different media. The culmination of their work was the program *Five Situations,* shown at a sculpture forum at St. Martin's and at the Mermaid Theatre in 1968. Boman created her own sculptural environment, and Beattie used a neon-light structure devised by Stuart Brisley and Bill Culbert. They were joined in a third sculpture piece by one of Beattie's students, Peter Dockley. For both performances, the dancers used were from the LSCD, and the program stated the Contemporary Ballet Trust's interest in helping such projects.

These environment pieces presented the multiplicity of focus and independence of sound and movement that are reminiscent in concept of Cage, especially as the pieces were intended for an audience free to move within or around the events.[11] The action was fragmented and structured to promote a "flat" treatment of time. As did so much other new work of the period, these pieces rejected the traditional flowing or developmental types of progression and climax/release patterns of structure and encouraged the audience to become active and analytical. Cool examinations of form, they invited the viewer to adopt a self-consciously analytical stance and made an issue of revealing their own structures. Program notes insisted that the work was about form and ideas as opposed to emotional expression.

Beattie's collaboration with Brisley and Culbert, *Four Dancers, Four Colours, and Three Dimensions,* used a programmed neon-light sequence and a set of dance responses to the lights, each dancer moving to a particular color and with the dynamic quality that the color suggested to Beattie. Boman's *Momentum in Quadrille* had the dancers manipulating rectangular blocks "like a baby giant's construction kit."[12] These were a series of blocks hinged together and akin to the fundamental repetitive structures that U.S. minimalist sculptors favored. Dockley's *Four Sounds Four Structures* used four dancers, each in a different sculptural construction, investigating the particular characteristics of the structure—moving along its lines, complementing the planes suggested—in a sound environment that used the spatial dimensions of the performance area. Both Beattie and Dockley contributed to the *Explorations* series of Events/Happenings with which Howard opened The Place in 1969.

Likewise, Alston's work could be seen as modernist postmodern at that time. Interested in motion rather than meaning or expression, he followed Cunningham's precedent in maintaining independence between dance and music, allowing a measure of indeterminacy in some pieces, and recycling dance material for new contexts.[13] Thus the sections of *Nowhere Slowly* (1970) could be performed in any order, and the piece appeared with several different musical scores. For *Subject to Change* (1972, a Strider work), Alston mixed two solos, his own *Strider* (1971) and a solo *Blue* (1972) by the dancer Christopher Banner, who performed the piece. Banner first alternated chunks of material (taken in any order) from the two dances and later alternated isolated movements until he had exhausted the content of each solo. The music for this amalgam was subject to change as well; at an early performance it was played live on an electronic trumpet by composer Gordon Mumma (who often worked with Cunningham).

Alston gained much inspiration from reading, a key source being the *Dance Perspectives* issue "Time to Walk in Space" (1968),[14] which contains many photographs as well as articles on Cunningham's work. But he had also become acquainted with post-Cunningham American postmodern dance ideas of the 1960s. He had read a 1965 issue of the *Tulane Drama Review*[15] that contained articles by Yvonne Rainer and sculptor Robert Morris (on performance) and an interview with Anna Halprin, and also the material on American postmodern choreographers in Don McDonagh's *The Rise and Fall and Rise of Modern Dance* (1970).[16] During this period, Alston was allowed to teach a composition course at the LSCD according to postmodern principles. In 1972, Strider's opening publicity proclaimed its allegiance to the post-Cunningham choreographers: "If Cunningham brought movement per se to light, they re-examined it by setting it in new contexts. It is this kind of work, of which we aim to be a part."

More inclined toward Banes's second postmodern category are three women from the LSCD who later joined Strider: Diana Davies, who had been a lecturer in fine art; Jacky Lansley, formerly of the Royal Ballet; and Sally Potter, already experienced in performance art and filmmaking before she joined the LSCD. Theirs is theatrical work with meaning and a hint of the feminist stance that they were to develop in the mid-1970s and, unlike Alston, they did not look to the United States for their inspiration.[17] Much of their work subverted the conventions of dance in some way. Davies's *Band 7* (1973), for instance, mixed two nondancers with two highly trained dancers. In *Hundreds and Thousands* (1972), made collaboratively for Strider, the three women appeared in athletic garb, vigorously wielding clubs and lifting one another to the incongruous accompaniment of badly played saccharine waltz tunes and Tchaikovsky's "Dance of the Sugar Plum Fairy" from *The Nutcracker*.[18] Here the choreographers were using the technique of radical juxtaposition, which was common at the time. It is important too that these women also used as sources the homely and the familiar, what was "real" to them, in movement, props, costumes, and sound. In this respect they subscribed to the new, open, democratic model for art of the time.

Certainly, the outlooks of these three women extended well beyond traditional "technical" dance. While still students they formed Rescue Principle, making work that they later called performance art. Lansley and Potter continued in this vein as the duo Limited Dance Company (1974–75), performing in a variety of locations and using text and props as well as choreographed movement. Then Lansley went on to become a member of the Collective that ran X6 Dance Space, the center of New Dance, from 1976 to 1980. Potter established herself first and foremost as a filmmaker, moving from a formalist style (developed as a student at St. Martin's) to making work with a feminist content, as in the films *Thriller* (1979), *The Gold Diggers* (1983), and *Orlando* (1992). Davies won a Gulbenkian Foundation Dance Award in 1973 and joined the well-known performance art group Welfare State in 1974.

I will return to both Alston and Potter later to discuss in detail an example of their collaborative dance/film work, but with Banes's second postmodern category I have chosen first to focus on the group Moving Being, a mixed-media enterprise directed by Geoff Moore that was particularly important during this early period.

Moore came from an art school background, and he never had any formal training as a dancer or choreographer. Recognizing that we are "encased in bodies," he wanted to incorporate the particular physical intensity of dance in his work. Furthermore, he favored dance because "it is open enough to bear allusions."[19] In its first year, 1968–69, Moving Being presented several pure dance pieces, Howard gave Moore a rehearsal home at The Place, and he fell straightaway into dance culture, to be reviewed primarily by dance critics. However, pure dance pieces soon disappeared from the Moving Being repertory. Moore's main style was collage. The work mixed several media—film, slides, speech, recorded text, music, and sound effects, as well as dance—and bristled with references to contemporary issues and popular culture. Moving Being made an immediate impression, so much so that by May 1969 critic John Percival could proclaim that "almost single-handed, Geoff Moore has provided British ballet with its avant-garde."[20]

Similarly, in 1970, American theater director and writer Charles Marowitz reported from London in the *Village Voice* that Moving Being represented "the most committed attempt in England to refertilize the archaic notions of dance." Some of the work, he says, demonstrated a "defeatingly helter-skelter" randomness in the spirit of Cage and Cunningham, two major influences upon Moore; "too much can mean too little." At other times, he suggests, the various ideas collided in more interesting "smash-ups" with one another: signification became an issue.[21] The latter became the style of all of Moore's work: the radical juxtaposition of diverse elements sparking against each other, with the elements carefully selected and formally very controlled to encourage lively meaning resonance. In this respect, one is reminded of the ambiguities of many later postmodern works involving dance, which were, like the work of Moving Being, ready to use any other aspect of theater as well. In this kind of work, spectators are boldly invited to wrestle with many meaning possibilities and to bring their individual experience to the work; nothing seems certain, secure, or fully firmed up.

The early *Trio* (1969) illustrates these points.[22] The facts of the piece are as follows:

Two men and a woman in a white hospital gown in a V shape of light spots. They are still. Then they begin a sequence of minimal, often slow, motion. They move from one light spot to another during blackouts into new choreographed arrangements. (Accompanied by jangling harpsichord interruptions from Bach, these blackouts were punctuation devices or jolting mechanisms to renew the attention, like the formal alienation devices that Moore observed in the work of Bertolt Brecht and Jean-Luc Godard.)

Three texts: a portion from the opening sequence of Marcel Proust's *Remembrance of Things Past* (1913–27), when the author recounts his dreams of his great-uncle terrifying him, pulling his curls when he was a child, and his erotic dreams of women; the cult psychologist R. D. Laing's account of the dream state in *The Politics of Experience* (1967); a physiological account of sleeping patterns, rapid eye movements, increased heart rate, and so on.

Within the framework of sleep and dreams, various areas of meaning have been suggested in reviews and by Moore and his collaborators remembering the piece. The woman was seen fighting her childhood past, as the author's mistress, or as a victim, merely a figment of man's imagination. She acquired meaning from the texts. At one point she was suspended upside down between the two men, creating an image of being compromised. Necrophilia was also suggested. The woman seems to have gradually established her own identity as the dance movement developed, and the movement gradually became, according to Percival, less an illustration of the text and more a counterpoint to it.[23] Certainly, movement seemed to be a metaphor for liberation in many of Moore's pieces. It was also ready to be colored: he never intended movement as abstract experience. However, meanings are ambiguous; many readings are possible.

A telling statement of the period is that reviewers of Moore's early work usually attempted one or two quite specific interpretations of a piece or merely listed a number of the elements within the collage. They tended not to comment on the richness of the reverberations among images, on the many suggested meanings, or on the contradictory aspects of Moving Being's work. On the other hand, those involved in making and performing the works stress its ambiguities.

Moving Being left The Place for headquarters in Cardiff, Wales, in 1972. During the 1970s, Moore's inclinations shifted gradually toward text-based drama and away from dance.

The Richard Alston/Sally Potter collaboration *Combines* (1972) is one of the most extraordinary dance pieces from this period, and highly unusual too within the repertoire of LCDT. This fifty-minute work used a variety of media—dance, recorded music, props, film, and slides—and showed the formalist side of Potter's work, Potter as structuralist filmmaker.[24]

Alston has also mentioned the collage principle behind the work and the influence of Rauschenberg's combines (hence the title): their assemblage construction and their mixture of urban, everyday objects and painterly strokes as free-floating, independent entities. Likewise, the Alston/Potter *Combines* mixed the everyday and the vernacular— social dancing; 1950s songs sung by Mildred Bailey, Ella Fitzgerald, and Frances Langford; portraits of the dancers in 1940s street clothes; plain, pedestrian activity performed in boilersuits—next to stylized dancers dressed in leotards and the music of Schubert and Bach. The structure in time was a series of episodes, live dance alternating and sometimes overlapping with film or slides shown on one, two, or three screens simultaneously. Potter and Alston have both mentioned their interest in Gertrude Stein too, for her formal emphasis and suspension of time, repetition being an obvious device they borrowed from her.

The formalist influence of Stein links readily with another aspect of *Combines:* its intensely analytical aspect, as it foregrounds its own "works." Structures are laid bare, the conventions of the theater are drawn attention to, the backstage is presented (on film) as well as the onstage activity itself, and the dancers are shown as people in street clothes as well as performers. Potter and Alston shared these principles in their separate contributions, but it is interesting that Potter's ideas undoubtedly sprang from her background in structural film. This was an international film movement of the late 1960s and early 1970s, which, in Britain and other European countries, was often termed structural/ materialist film because of its emancipatory Marxist intentions. An important notion behind structural film was reflexivity, encouraging an apperceptive stance from the spectator. Viewers found themselves watching themselves in the act of watching the film. In order to achieve this effect, films exposed their own devices and conventions, such as the act of projection and the techniques of editing. Example devices were double screen projection, immediate repetition of sequences, and regular or rhythmic cutting.

It is important to consider structural film in this detail, because of its influence through Potter in the early days at The Place. While based there, she continued to make films—indeed, she made several films at The Place using fellow students and incorporating a dance element. Alston certainly felt that Potter's thinking gelled with his own.

Several characteristics of structural film are illustrated in Potter's first sequence for *Combines* (the only section of the film that Potter can now trace, and the earliest record of Alston choreography). This is a filmic manipulation of the solo *Nowhere Slowly*, which Alston had made

in 1970. In it he introduces large, technical contemporary dance movement and the plain performance manner and spatial freedoms of a Cunningham work. Alston has described the structure of the solo in terms
of "maelstroms" of on-the-spot activity and simple transitions.[25]

Potter filmed the solo twice, in a studio at The Place, performed by
two different dancers, Celeste Dandeker and Naomi Lapsezon, and
then projected the performances on two screens simultaneously. Thus
she brought attention to the act of projection by heightening viewers'
awareness of the boundaries of the screen. She also analyzed the dance.
At the beginning, twelve moments are fragmented from the entire
dance, with footage of the empty studio seen between the fragments.
The dancers appear and disappear. Later, when the solo is presented
as a whole, with all its transitions, some sections are repeated and shown,
analyzed, from different angles. Here, Potter interposes shots of dancers
putting on boilersuits backstage and shots of a stairway (the stairs at
The Place that lead up to the stage), and eventually we see shots of the
dancers ascending the same stairway. Such editing draws attention to
itself, especially as the "blinks" are synchronized across the two screens
simultaneously. It draws attention to itself even more strongly in the
passages when it is rhythmical; here, it cuts across the dance phrasing,
either as a regular visual pulse or as a metrical repeating rhythm:[26]

♩♩ or ♩♩♩♩.

There was the same analytical stance within the live parts of *Combines*. For instance, a dance for three women on and around a table
and chairs pushed gradually up the stage in a diagonal movement high-
lighted a process of change. The process measured by the length of
the diagonal, violent movement around the table gradually became very
slow, quiet motion, motion "cleaned" of emotional drive. A bicycle
dance to a Bach fugue involved stopping, backing up, and moving forward, underlining the fugal structure in the music. The performers'
learning process was incorporated in one section of the piece. A solo
for Siobhan Davies was repeated ten times and learned by the other
dancers in the moment of performance.

The structural, analytical aspects of *Combines* seem quite as important as its collage construction. Banes's term "analytic postmodern
dance," which she applies to a major area of work in the United States

happening at precisely the same time, surely must apply here. Similar in vein was Alston's earlier *Shiftwork* (1971), in which two women, one at a time, walked round a wardrobe, the first nine times, the second once, the first eight times, the second twice, and so on, while Alston paced a series of squares of ever-decreasing size in a corner downstage. Exaggerated formal simplicity gave a special prominence to the workings of the piece.

Critical reactions to *Combines* are telling. Although several critics found the piece interesting, they generally had a problem with its structure. They found it untidy and loose, clearly hoping for coherence, development, relationships, and connections.[27] But was coherence or development an issue in this kind of work? None of the critics noted the influence of Rauschenberg and what that implied conceptually. Nor did any of them comment on the analytical/structural aspects of the piece. Critics' reactions, even if positive, reflected the period and their own "schooling" in more organic, coherent forms of dance.

It is fascinating to speculate on how differently this strange corner of British dance history might have come down to us had it been recorded with an eye on the context of other arts. Conceptually, at least, this early radical work is lost from view until we look at the context of innovation in the other arts.

Now it seems that there is every reason to backdate the X6 idea of a New Dance to the work of the late 1960s and early 1970s and to admit its overlap with the American notion of postmodernism in dance. There is, after all, a thread linking the LSCD to X6 Dance Space through Strider. Before its demise in 1975, this group had embraced the theatricalism of Davies, Lansley, and Potter, the most abstract Cunningham-influenced work of Alston, and, from autumn 1973, the principles of release work and Contact Improvisation taught by the American Mary Fulkerson at Dartington College.

That this radicalism in British dance appeared so early might seem surprising, especially considering the very recent establishment of any strong contemporary dance tradition. Alongside the new Graham-derived tradition, there developed both analytic/formalist and meaning-based strands of postmodern work. Furthermore, although partly influenced by U.S. developments in postmodern dance, this radicalism appears to have been just as much prompted by developments at home in the other arts, especially by innovations in visual arts, film, and theater.

Notes

This essay expands upon issues raised in the author's "British Modern Dance: Early Radicalism," *Dance Research* 7, no. 2 (1989): 3–15. Further information on LSCD, Strider, the New Dance of the late 1970s, and Richard Alston is contained in the author's *Striding Out: Aspects of Contemporary and New Dance in Britain* (London: Dance Books, 1992).

1. In conversations with Robert Cohan (1 March 1990) and Janet Eager (12 March 1990) I learned that the new term was coined to distinguish the Graham-based dance from European modern dance (notes for a talk by Robin Howard in Eager's archive, n.d.) and from modern jazz and ballroom. Both terms seem to be in currency today.

2. Robert Hewison makes the point that "the Sixties did not really begin until about 1963, and that they do not fade away until 1975" in *Too Much: Art and Society in the Sixties, 1960–75* (London: Methuen, 1986), xiii.

3. Robin Howard, interview by the author, 13 April 1987.

4. Former students interviewed by the author between 1987 and 1989, including Richard Alston, Alan Beattie, Primavera Boman, Sally Cranfield, Diana Davies, Dennis Greenwood, Betsy Gregory, Henrietta Lyons, Jacky Lansley, and Sally Potter.

5. "Postmodern" is used here as it has been by Sally Banes, author of the seminal *Terpsichore in Sneakers*. She uses the term to encompass both that work which emphasizes the nature of the medium itself, "analytic postmodern dance," and the kind of work that is more prevalent now internationally and which directs itself outward toward meaning or signification. See Banes, *Terpsichore in Sneakers: Post-Modern Dance*, 2nd ed. (Middletown, Conn.: Wesleyan University Press, 1987), xx–xxxv.

6. For instance, Fergus Early, "Liberation Notes, Etc.," *New Dance* 40 (April–June 1987): 11; Jan Murray, *Dance Now: A Closer Look at the Art of Movement* (Harmondsworth, Middlesex: Penguin, 1979), 154–58.

7. Howard interview.

8. For "New Dance, A Celebratory Weekend" (12–13 July 1986, presented by Chisenhale Dance Space and the National Organization for Dance and Mime), the publicity leaflet proposed that "New Dance in Britain goes back . . . to the early seventies and even, in a few isolated instances to the late sixties."

9. Unlike the American situation, where postmodern choreographers insisted that their work be identified as dance and pressured critics and audiences to consider it as such.

10. Yvonne Rainer and Twyla Tharp also performed in London, in 1965 and 1967, respectively. However, since these visits predated the experimental movement in Britain, there is no evidence that they had a direct influence on the choreographers.

11. Information is taken from the following sources: Peter Dockley talks to *Dance and Dancers*, "Into Space," July 1968, 30; Primavera Boman and Dockley talking to *Dance and Dancers*, "Dance in Mixed-Media," March 1969, 39; and my interviews with Alan Beattie, 1 October 1987, and Boman, 22 August 1987.

12. John Percival, "Five Situations at the Mermaid Theatre," *Dance and Dancers*, October 1968, 41.

13. This account of Alston's works stems from my interview with him, 8 April 1987.

14. Selma Jeanne Cohen, ed., "Time to Walk in Space," *Dance Perspectives* 34 (Summer 1968).

15. *Tulane Drama Review* 10, no. 2 (1965).

16. Don McDonagh, *The Rise and Fall and Rise of Modern Dance* (New York: Outerbidge & Dienstfrey, 1970).

17. This account of the work of Diana Davies, Jacky Lansley, and Sally Potter is based on my interviews with Davies, 20 July 1987, Lansley, 24 April 1987, and Potter, 6 April 1987.

18. Early, "Liberation Notes, Etc.," 12.

19. Geoff Moore, interviews by the author, 20 April 1988, 22 June 1990.

20. John Percival, "Moving Being at Liverpool University," *Dance and Dancers*, May 1969, 43.

21. Charles Marowitz, "Moving Being: Anti-Dance," *Village Voice*, 27 August 1970. Marowitz had come to London in 1957 and, among other activities, worked with theater director Peter Brook. He became director of the Open Space Theatre in 1968.

22. Information about *Trio* stems from a variety of newspaper and magazine reviews, as well as my interviews with Geoff Moore (see note 19), Peter Mumford, technical director of Moving Being, 9 May 1990, and Pamela Moore, performer, 8 June 1990.

23. John Percival, "Moving Being," 43–44.

24. Information about the content of *Combines* and the ideas behind the piece stems from my interviews with Richard Alston, 9 April 1987, and Sally Potter, 21 January 1988.

25. Alston, in a lecture-demonstration at the Study of Dance Conference, University of Surrey, 11 April 1983.

26. Less "structural," however, is the drive toward a "climax" by the end of the film sequence as the pulse of editing accelerates. The climax is the sudden arrival of the boilersuited dancers live onstage.

27. See, for instance, Peter Williams, John Percival, and Noel Goodwin in *Dance and Dancers*, July 1972, 31–35; and James Monahan in *Dancing Times*, July 1972, 535.

10

Ballet Review's Beginnings

An Interview with Arlene Croce

Joan Acocella and Sally Banes

Editor's note: We conducted this interview with Arlene Croce, founder and first editor of *Ballet Review* (from 1965 to 1978), in the spirit of the freewheeling group interview about Judson Dance Theater that Croce and Don McDonagh held with James Waring, John Herbert McDowell, and Judith Dunn, which was published in *Ballet Review* volume 1, number 6 (1967), an issue devoted to documenting the Judson Dance Theater and related activities. Despite its name, *Ballet Review* did not limit itself to covering classical dance but was an entirely catholic publication that covered dance of all kinds (though primarily in New York), including experimental, or "downtown," dance. In order to convey the flavor of *Ballet Review*'s early years, we have tried to preserve here the style our interview deliberately shares with that earlier Judson one—its mixture of history and gossip, fact and speculation, biography and memory, seriousness and silliness. Our interview took the form of a long dinner conversation at Joan Acocella's apartment in New York City on 1 July 1991, during which we looked through and discussed the back issues of *Ballet Review*, beginning with the first issue. It has been edited considerably for publication here.

SB: I don't have all of the very first issue of *Ballet Review* here [volume 1, number 1 (1965)]. But I have part of the first issue—the first and second articles, including "Hughesiana," your piece on Allen Hughes, then the *New York Times* dance critic.

AC: He had been fired, but I didn't know it. I thought, "Allen Hughes is going to be our dance critic forever." So I wrote this. And then he wrote to me, and I felt guilty.

JA: But what could he say in response? What you basically said was that he didn't know anything.

AC: And he was a little upset by that. I didn't think he knew very much about ballet, but he did make a difference to the downtown people, because he took them seriously, and John Martin hadn't. John Martin, as I recall, hadn't even taken Merce Cunningham very seriously. So Hughes was a welcome change for those people. I still didn't think that made him a great metropolitan daily critic. But I had no idea that the man was on his way out. I didn't think I could hurt him, because the thing is, here I am, I'm nobody, and I attack the establishment. They are in power, and therefore they expect to be attacked. So I attacked them.

SB: And you feel you don't have power because they're the *Times* and you're *Ballet Review.* Issue number 1.

AC: Yes, I had a circulation of twelve!

JA: You know, something that's very much forgotten is where Balanchine's reputation stood at this time. When I read you in this issue, Balanchine was an embattled man.

AC: Oh, absolutely. You don't know what power [impresario] Sol Hurok had. He was the most important influence on the ballet scene. And the companies that Hurok brought over were the companies that were publicized, the dominant companies. Mostly, in those days, it was the Bolshoi or the Royal Ballet. At this moment, 1965, Rudolf Nureyev was the biggest news in ballet. Balanchine moved into Lincoln Center—it was nothing.

SB: But everyone was furious at Balanchine because he got a Ford Foundation grant, as you say in your article.

AC: Exactly. Furious, and then in moving to Lincoln Center he seems to have lost a large part of his City Center audience. So you have the fury of all the people who felt that the Ford Foundation had eliminated them. The "Balletrusse" phenomenon came back, first because of the Bolshoi and then because of Nureyev and the Hurok office, which got Nureyev on the cover of *Time* and *Newsweek,* I think in the same week. This was the great year of Nureyev's ascendancy.

  So it was as if all that work, all that building up of SAB [the School of American Ballet] and the New York City Ballet and the move to Lincoln Center, was all a move back to the starting line.

SB: It's interesting that you founded *Ballet Review* at this particular moment. You came out of the film world—you were an editor of *Film Culture*. Tell us how it started and why there was a need for *Ballet Review*.

AC: I felt that the time had come, that there should be a serious critical magazine about dance. I didn't think that any of the magazines on dance that existed at the time were seriously critical. I do remember, when I tried to find ways of funding this publication, writing to Lincoln Kirstein, and I said something that offended him. I don't know what it was that I said, but it must have been something to the effect of, "Well, we have *Dance Perspectives*, but . . ."

    Dance Perspectives had started, and it was setting itself up pretty high as a successor to *Dance Index*, and I didn't think it was very good. I don't know what I said to him, but he wrote me a nasty letter saying, "You just sit down and shut up and be grateful for Al Pischl." [Pischl was the founding editor of *Dance Perspectives*, a monograph series, which began publication in 1959. Kirstein, co-founder of the New York City Ballet, was a dance scholar and a founding editor of *Dance Index*, which lasted from 1942 to 1948. He died in 1996.—SB] But then about a year later, I went to the post office, opened my mail, and there was a check from Lincoln Kirstein!

JA: For how much?

AC: Oh, it was five hundred and something, enough to pay for a whole issue. I hadn't done a thing to deserve it, and I don't even know why it came. It just came out of the blue. That's Lincoln.

JA: But how did *Ballet Review* actually get started?

AC: It's awfully hard to remember. I know that I had the idea long before the thing happened. In fact, I am embarrassed to say how long. First I thought, "Now, why isn't there a serious critical dance magazine?" This thought was there quite some time before it occurred to me that maybe I should be the one to start it. The two things didn't come together somehow. One day I found a publication called *For Now*. It was Donald Phelps's personal literary review; he was a very good literary critic. And he had his own little publication. I thought, "This looks like it doesn't take fifty cents to publish, I can do this."

    So I called up Donald Phelps and said, "Who publishes this? Where do you get it printed? And how much does it cost?" He was very sweet. He told me, I found the printer on Fourteenth Street, and I went down there and started *Ballet Review*.

JA: How much did an issue cost?

AC: I think the first issues must have averaged about three hundred bucks a run.

SB: How many copies did you print?

AC: I can't remember. Not more than about three hundred copies, and a lot of them were sent out gratis.

SB: How did you distribute *Ballet Review* when it first came out?

AC: I just sent it out to everybody in the world who I thought should know that it existed.

SB: Were there bookstores where you would take a little stack of them to sell? The Kamin Bookshop?

AC: Yes, yes. The Kamin Bookshop. Maybe it wasn't even there by then, but I went to whatever the successor was. It was on Sixth Avenue, as I recall, in the fifties. You just rummaged around in the back, and you could find Diaghilev programs, amazing things. It was a wonderful place. Yes, and the Gotham Book Mart.

JA: How did you choose the people who would write for the magazine?

SB: Here it says David Vaughan and Robert Cornfield are the associates.

AC: David Vaughan wrote articles for *Sight and Sound* and film publications, like I did [Vaughan has also written dance criticism for many publications, and he is Merce Cunningham's archivist and the author of *Merce Cunningham: Fifty Years*—SB]. Bob Cornfield came because in some incredibly roundabout way, I met someone who knew him. Oh, now it's coming back to me. I thought one of the things that a serious dance publication should do would be to revive the career of Edwin Denby. That's right. I was going to get Edwin to write again. I didn't know why he stopped writing, I didn't even know him. But I thought, "Well, if he needs an outlet . . ." So I said to myself, "I will go to Edwin Denby and say, 'Edwin, I've got a place for you to write. Moreover, I think it is time you published a second collection. I will put it together for you.'" I didn't even know that someone was already doing it. So that's how I met Bob Cornfield, who was Edwin's agent; he was the one who was—

SB: Putting together the collection?

AC: Part of it anyway. I think Jackie Maskey had something to do with it too. *Dancers, Buildings, and People in the Streets* [a collection of Denby's reviews—SB] came out just about that same time. But I was sure I was the one who was going to do it for him. And I knew just the pieces I was going to put in it, too.

SB: One of the issues I love the very best is the Judson issue, where there is a long discussion in which you go through all the programs. Jimmy Waring and various other people are saying, "Oh, what is this?" And you talk about each thing as it comes up. Could we structure this conversation like that?

AC: Through David Vaughan I met Jimmy Waring, and through Jimmy, John Herbert McDowell [a composer who also showed dances at the Judson—SB], and I began to go to Judson myself to see things, but I was aware that it was just a little bit too late.

SB: But the Judson issue [volume 1, number 6 (1967)] was a keystone. It brought Judson to so many people's attention.

AC: We wanted to summarize it. No one had attempted to do that.

SB: And you did. In that issue there is also the Judson Dance Theater chronology, which is an important document.

AC: I went to Al Carmines [minister of Judson Memorial Church—SB] and said, "Where are the programs?" And he said, "Well, they're downstairs in the files." And I said, "May I look?" And he said, "Go ahead." I spent days in the files pulling them out. I think it is a complete chronology. I really did ransack the files, though there may be things left out.

SB: This material opened up a lot of people's eyes. The chronology, the discussion with Waring and McDowell, Jack Anderson's article on the Judson Poets Theater, Constance Poster's article on Meredith Monk and Kenneth King from the second generation, Jill Johnston's article. You had published Jill Johnston before that, on Martha Graham.

AC: Well, Jill was a very well known critic. At that time she was writing serious dance reviews in the *Village Voice*. And she was pretty much the voice of downtown dance. So you couldn't do an issue on Judson without her. I reprinted something of hers.

SB: Now let's go back to the origins. It was called *Ballet Review,* and yet, right from the start, you were interested in covering downtown dance, in covering experimental dance. I wonder, did you think of it as an experimental publication in some way? Even though the opening article is devoted to the crisis of ballet? Did you think of *Ballet Review* as an experiment in criticism?

AC: I thought of it as an experiment as a magazine, because I had no idea the first issue was going to be followed by a second issue, which would be followed by a third. I mean, you just brought out one issue. And then if people made it possible, you brought out a second. Then you brought out a third. It was just like that.

JA: Did you have another job at this time?

AC: Of course.

JA: What was it—were you working for the *National Review*?

AC: Yes. I had a steady job. I paid my rent.

JA: So you did this in your spare time?

AC: Yes. Everybody I know, pretty much, had a steady job. I certainly did

Ballet Review

vol. 1, no. 6

50¢

Cover of *Ballet Review* vol. 1, no. 6 (1967). The Judson Issue. Cover design by Arlene Croce. Courtesy of the Dance Division, The New York Public Library for the Performing Arts, Astor, Lenox and Tilden Foundations.

not pay people to write for *Ballet Review*. That was understood at the beginning. Nobody got paid a cent.

JA: Who was it who started paying? Francis [Mason—the current editor of *Ballet Review*, since 1980—SB]?

AC: No, actually, we managed to get enough grant money finally so I really could pay people to write. I'm very proud of that. The grants came from a division of what eventually became the New York State Arts Council. Paul Lepercq [a private investment banker—SB] gave us money. Some clever people, David and Shelley Singer, gave us a benefit. But that wasn't until much later. At first, everyone wrote for nothing.

SB: But you did use experimental formats. I am thinking about "A Foggy Day's Hard Night," in which you write that you overheard a conversation in the Crush Bar at the Royal Opera House in Covent Garden, in London, England. But it's an imaginary conversation. It is a dialogue between two critics—the British and the American. You don't think this is experimental?

AC: No, no.

SB: This is a standard form of dance criticism?

AC: Not dance criticism perhaps, but it was not an unusual thing to do. It was self-conscious.

SB: So that makes it not experimental? I think it is experimental. I think that this is exactly what people mean by experimental—that you have freedom, and you can do things that are unconventional.

AC: Well, yes, maybe I let myself go a little bit and said, "Now I'm my own editor, I'll say what I want and do it the way I want and this is amusing and I'll just do it!" But no, no, no, that form is certainly not unusual. I mean, Kenneth Tynan would do a question-and-answer type thing or assume two opposing personalities, and Kenneth Tynan wasn't the only one. Criticism was, in those days, a little more theatrical.

JA: Arlene, why didn't you collect some of these pieces? Why did you leave "Sylvia, Susan, and God" out of *Afterimages*?

AC: It was to get attention, it was pamphleteering. You don't expect people to want to read that.

JA: Well, Kirstein has collected some of his pamphleteering.

AC: That's right, this is in his tradition. But I'm not Lincoln Kirstein. That was just something that I wanted to say—here are all the reasons I can think of why this magazine is here. And it had to do *just* with that magazine. It didn't have to do with anything transcending that—just that magazine, that issue, that moment.

JA: There are a lot of things I've always been curious about. Did you ever think that you were going to try to build dance writers?

AC: One of my main purposes was to find people to turn into dance writers, whether they wanted to be dance writers or not. I can well remember the dilemma: should I get the dancers who can write, or should I get writers who can dance—or who at least *know* dance.

SB: Did you feel there were writers you discovered?

AC: I think these people would have found themselves anyway, I really do.

SB: But who were they?

AC: Well, Robert [Greskovic, now dance critic for the *Wall Street Journal* and author of *Ballet 101*—SB] is one.

JA: Tell us about his first piece.

AC: I was so thrilled with it, because he did what I asked him to do and so much more. I wanted him to write about the dancers of New York City Ballet. Just the ones he found interesting. And he said, "I can't write an article." I said, "I don't want an article, I want a list. Write 'Patricia McBride,' and write why you think she is interesting, and then write the next guy and why you think he's interesting, and that's all. And when you come to the end, stop." He did exactly that.

JA: Say what his marvelous line was about Jean-Pierre Bonnefous. Something like "Jean-Pierre Bonnefous holds his chin as if it were on a shelf."

AC: When he said that, I knew. My heart said, "This is wonderful." And he went on from there. He did similar kinds of pieces about other companies. We worked together very well, Robert and I. He's an editor's dream because he has the material, he has the substance. He comes at you with all kinds of stuff, and usually too much of it. Or he has three versions of the same thing. So all you do is sit down and say, "I like this way of saying it better than that way." And you shape it. Editing Robert Greskovic was a dream to me.

SB: Let's go down the list of some of these other writers.

JA: You picked up Charles France in the same ballet line where you picked up Robert.

AC: Yes, but Charles was not going to be a writer, he just had ideas, and he had a certain amount of skill at implementing them. I don't think that Charles was seriously destined to be a writer. But what he wrote for us was pretty good, I think.

SB: Who else was in the first issue? You wrote the first two articles, and then someone wrote about "Flamenco Dancing in the Pavilion of Spain, New York World's Fair, 1964."

AC: Yes, who was that? I know I started with a long list, the way you start any enterprise. Make a long list, like eighty-nine names, and you wind up getting four of them. That was the first issue: less than four, I had two articles by other writers. [There were five articles, three of which were by Croce.—SB]

JA: Did you ask the writers what they wanted to write, or did you make suggestions to them?

AC: Both.

JA: Were you a fan of dance writers? You said you had read David Vaughan. Did you have an idea of what you would like to read him on?

AC: I certainly did. David and I did not know each other. But I had read him in *Sight and Sound*. And one of his specialties was writing on dance, and so I thought, "Well, I have to have this guy; he lives here in New York." And one thing leads to another. It always does. So having found David, taken him to lunch, discussed the idea of writing, gotten five more names from him, I would take those five people to lunch and get more.

SB: Who were some of the people David suggested?

AC: Well, Jimmy Waring, for example. And then you go from there, and it all branches out.

SB: Here in the second issue we find R. P. Blackmur—"The Swan in Zurich."

AC: Oh, that was a reprint. I was obsessed by that article. It kept me awake nights.

SB: Where had you read it?

AC: In *Yale Review*, where it was first published. I knew Blackmur's work; I read his books at Barnard, especially *Language as Gesture*, which I think is a great book. And when this essay came out, I was upset by it, very upset and very fascinated.

JA: It brushes off ballet, as I recall.

AC: But it said things which nobody, in my experience, had said before about it.

SB: The next article is "The Royal Ballet: Family Circle," by David Vaughan.

AC: Well, he wanted to write about the Royal, and of course he should have.

SB: Then there is "A Foggy Day's Hard Night," your piece about the British reception of Balanchine.

AC: My first trip to London. Balanchine and the British had always had an odd relationship. I wanted to go and see what it was like firsthand. I found the audience so peculiar. We thought that this was ballet, and they thought that it was just American. Our ballet was not as good as theirs. Not as pure, not as serious. The thing they liked best was *Bugaku*. The British response to Balanchine has always made me laugh.

JA: What did you think of their ballet at that time?

AC: They had the most prestigious ballet in the world.

JA: Yes, I know, but what did you think of it?

AC: I thought it was in very good shape. I thought that Nureyev did bring something to the Royal Ballet, besides giving Fonteyn a second career. They had some marvelous ballerinas. They had a good male corps, they had a fine corps de ballet, they had Ashton, and Ashton was running it at this time. And I thought that it was a wonderful institution. It was not going to take the place in my heart of the New York City Ballet; there was no way in the world it could have done that. But they had a marvelous repertoire. They had style. When you saw that company, you saw into the heart of the English ballet. It was genuine.

JA: The kind of propriety and good taste that they valued in ballet, the fineness they sought, would have angered me if it was the high peak from which they looked down on American ballet.

AC: Well, I did get upset about the second production of their *Sleeping Beauty*. To me that was such a comedown from what they had had. They made all the wrong choices. And then they became very conscious of their position as the number one ballet company and became slightly self-parodistic.

JA: Is this the Peter Wright production? Oh, yes, I remember that piece. "Mr. Wright Is Mr. Wrong." [It was published in *Ballet Review* volume 3, number 4 (1970) and reprinted in Croce's *Afterimages.*—SB]

SB: Moving along—here is "'Don Quixote': Rehearsal and Performance," by Robert Cornfield, written in an epistolary form. Cornfield writes to a friend, "Edwin took me to a rehearsal of *Don Quixote* last night. The first performance is Thursday evening, tomorrow night, a special performance for which Balanchine will appear as the Don . . ." It's very informal—

AC: Yes, but after all, this wasn't going out to more than about—

JA: Twenty-seven people.

AC: To the people who wrote it and their friends. You have to understand. It had a teeny circulation. I let people do what they wanted to do.

JA: Arlene, you must have had to become so extroverted. It's hard for me to imagine you beating the bushes and taking all these people out to lunch.

AC: It was an agenda; I really did have to make an effort, because I'm pathologically introverted. But you do it or you don't do it. It wasn't that hard a thing to do, after all.

JA: I think editing is hard.

AC: No, no, editing is a release. It's peaceful to work on other people's work. I love it. I love to get other people's stuff in front of me. If it's there, if the goods are there, then it's just like polishing fine wood. It's a treasure. It's much better than having to write it yourself.

JA: Did you have certain things that you wanted to get said, and hire people to say them?

AC: I don't specifically remember particular issues. I do know that sometimes I felt, "I'm not going to get this piece unless I write it myself." And so I did find myself writing more than I planned. I thought I would just do the delightful work of editing, and I found that I would have to do more than that.

SB: I think that "Hughesiana" is important, because it begins one key thread throughout the life of the journal: you paid attention not only to writing intelligently about dance but also to being skeptical about dance criticism, to raising serious questions about criticism. It was a reflexive enterprise, because you were even writing sometimes about the critical writing within *Ballet Review* itself, as in the Cherry Heering "Outer Lobby" column, where there's criticism of an article published in an earlier issue of *Ballet Review*. [There was a series of articles in *Ballet Review*, usually of a fanciful sort, signed by an imaginary critic named after the Danish liqueur Cherry Heering.—SB] So it's a wonderful circle; there are people writing criticism of criticism, from "Hughesiana" to "A Foggy Day's Hard Night" to the interview with Edwin Denby and on forward.

AC: That's a reflection of me. It's like looking into the mirror and saying, "What sort of critic are we today?" "Oh, I like it this way." "I think I'll wear this."

SB: That kind of inquiry is crucial for the development of criticism, and no one else was doing that at the time.

AC: I didn't know that I was *doing* it, but as you say, it was reflexive. I would write one sort of piece or someone would write a piece and then I'd think, "Wait a minute," and then we would start fighting among ourselves. Gently, of course, but that was what we were there for.

SB: Were you Cherry Heering?

AC: David was Cherry Heering to begin with, and then sometimes it was me. He thought of the name Cherry Heering.

JA: Who was Elena Bivona [another byline that appears in the magazine—SB]?

AC: Oh, she was a real person. Many people ask about Elena Bivona. She was a New York City Ballet groupie. She went to practically every performance. I'd run into her in the lobby the way I would run into

Ted [Edward] Gorey. I thought, "I see these people every night. Why shouldn't they write for me?"

JA: After all, what do they do during the day that's so good they can't write for you? Now, Elena Bivona did the Bruce Lee article, didn't she?

AC: I think that she was beginning to lose interest in dance by that time.

SB: She was looking into paradance. Now here is volume 1, number 3. It has an Edward Gorey cover, with a ballerina holding a banner that reads, "Commencing in this issue, a story of the ballet by Edward Gorey." It's *The Gilded Bat,* part one of three parts. Was this before Edward Gorey was discovered by the general public?

AC: Oh no, Ted Gorey was well known; his works were well known. He was a famous person when I met him. But I don't think he had written anything on ballet.

SB: So you commissioned *The Gilded Bat?*

AC: Well, I commissioned a piece on ballet. What I thought I was going to get was what ultimately turned into another book he wrote, called *The Lavender Leotard.* I thought it was going to be that kind of satirical balletomania thing; instead he presented me with this. We went to lunch, and he opened up a great big portfolio and showed me this, and I turned the pages, and I knew it was a masterpiece. He gave it to me for not one cent, not one cent! Of course I made him do the three installments so that we wouldn't blow it all on one issue; that would be crazy. So we had to play it up to maximum height here—a cliffhanger. But it was something, obviously, that he'd had in mind to do, and that was his moment to do it. And he was marvelous—he supervised the production, got the plates ready, everything.

SB: "Grace and Spirit: Notes on Recent Dance Films," by David Vaughan. "Is There a Cure for Moon Reindeer?" That was about Birgit Cullberg, by you. And . . . oh! "Ben Hecht's Blue Rose," by Donald Phelps. The same Donald Phelps whose literary review originally inspired you?

AC: Yes, the same Donald Phelps. I took Donald to lunch.

SB: This is about a film by Ben Hecht, which is about—

AC: About ballet.

SB: "Often enough as I watched Ben Hecht's film *Specter of the Rose* . . ."

AC: It's a cult movie and a crazy movie, and if you have never seen it, you can't imagine what it's like.

SB: How did you become a dance maven, to begin with?

AC: Oh well, that's not interesting; you just go to the theater. And it happens, and that's it. It happens to everybody the same way.

SB: When did you start going to the New York City Ballet?

AC: In 1955. I moved to New York to go to school. And the first week that

Ballet Review

Editor: **Arlene Croce**   Associates: **David Vaughan, Robert Cornfield**

vol. 1, no. 3, 1966   **50¢ (3/6)**

Cover of *Ballet Review* vol. 1, no. 3 (1966). The first installment of *The Gilded Bat.*
Cover by Edward Gorey. Illustration reproduced courtesy of the Estate of Edward Gorey
and courtesy of the Dance Division, The New York Public Library for the Performing
Arts, Astor, Lenox and Tilden Foundations.

I was in New York, I went out on a blind date, and he took me. I knew
about the company. Very little, but I had talked to people who lived in
New York who told me about it. In fact, it was one of the first things
they did tell me about, along with Bloomingdale's. We went, and I still
remember the program; I remember being electrified by it. It was:
Swan Lake, with [Maria] Tallchief and [André] Eglevsky, followed by
Afternoon of a Faun, with Tanaquil Le Clercq and Francisco Moncion,
followed by a Balanchine piece that they dropped, called *A la Françaix,*
which had Todd Bolender in it. It was made for Eglevsky but it had
Todd Bolender in it at my performance. And the last ballet—how
about *Symphony in C?*

JA: *Symphony in C*—your jaw must have dropped. Or did it?

AC: Well, yes, it did, but I thought this was ballet. This wasn't Balanchine,
this wasn't anything special, this was just ballet, New York style. I just
thought this was the normal standard thing. Of course it's wonderful.
Of course your hair stands on end. The third movement has Jacques
d'Amboise throwing Janet Reed up into the flies. It was all simply
wonderful. And we came out invigorated, refreshed, thrilled. And I
never went back. I came to New York to go to school and study, and
I was not about to be wooed away from serious study by pleasure.
Pleasure! Going to the ballet. When I think of it now—what I missed
by not going to the ballet that year. Ballets that were retired, like
Roma, like *Opus 34,* like *Metamorphoses.* I could have seen them
all. But I thought, "Oh, I'll get to it, but first I must study, I must
work, I must get my degree." And I didn't go back to the ballet at all,
until I had left school. I did see Tanaquil Le Clercq's last season; for
that I am grateful. I caught her in *Concerto Barocco* and *Divertimento
No. 15.*

This is '56. Then, of course, I didn't miss the following season,
which was the season of *Agon* and the revival of *Apollo,* the great life-
changing season. But the New York City Ballet was known to people in
general as a place to go. My friends went there. We went there the way
we went to the newest interesting movie, or if there was anything to see
on the stage we went to that. The New York City Ballet was part of the
intellectual life of the city, and if you were serious intellectually, you
went. The Royal Ballet was also on the circuit, if you liked ballet. But
the New York City Ballet was on the circuit just because it was the
New York City Ballet, not because it was dance, but because it was part
of your life to be a New Yorker, to go to the New York City Ballet.

JA: Did any of those people go to [American] Ballet Theatre?

AC: I went, because I was interested in ballet. It was not au courant, they hadn't done anything interesting in years. It had all happened. You wanted to go back and maybe catch up on things that had already happened. It was not feeding you. Excitement, shocks—this was not happening at Ballet Theatre. It was happening every season at New York City Ballet.

JA: I'm curious about *Ballet Review*'s policy on interviews. Interviews can be a bad idea; they can fill space in a lazy, airy way.

AC: When I started the magazine I remember making a list of things I did not want, and one of them was interviews.

JA: But some of the best interviews with dancers I've ever read were in *Ballet Review*. One that jumps to my mind right now was a two-part interview with Alexandra Danilova. It was done by Charles [France].

SB: Speaking of interviews, I'm just plodding along and here is the first interview, an interview with Merce Cunningham.

AC: Well, Merce is Merce after all. And besides, it wasn't an interview; it was a questionnaire.

SB: Ah.

AC: I took a chance with him. I was terrified to approach him, so I wrote him a letter and I put it in the mail. I didn't expect that he would answer the questions, but he did.

SB: And this turned into an entire issue on Cunningham [volume 1, number 4 (1966)]. The other articles include "McLuhan and the Dance," by Carolyn Brown. There is an interesting short article by Sumio Kam'bayashi on "The Old West and the New East in Cunningham's Dance," which is on Buddhism and Cunningham, and "Something New, Simple, and Fundamental," by William Poster, which is a review of the recent Cunningham season. It is a special theme issue.

AC: You can only do theme issues if you have a lot of time. I had a lot of time by default, because the articles never came in, and we never had deadlines. So I had plenty of time to dream up or put together theme issues. You see, it was my way of pretending that the issue that finally arrived on your subscription was the one that I was thinking of putting out in the first place. And I was really only improvising around one or two articles that *had* come in.

SB: You were often talking about the ballet world. How far away was the world of Cunningham?

AC: Now, don't forget, David [Vaughan] was on the masthead. It was not far at all.

SB: Was David already working as Cunningham's archivist?

AC: Yes, I think so. Maybe it was because of David that Merce answered my questionnaire.

SB: You, yourself, went to see all different kinds of dance.

AC: I didn't care about everything, but I went to see everything at this point. I thought I should know. I really went down to Judson, as I say, too late. I went down there because I thought, here are some interesting people with ideas. I should get to know somebody with ideas; God knows, there are plenty of balletomanes with no ideas. Maybe some of these people downtown have something to say. It was all in search of people who thought about dance, that was the main thing. I didn't really care what they said, as long as it wasn't stupid. I would have been ready to publish an anti-Balanchine article. If it wasn't a dumb article I would have been happy to. Nobody wrote one, but . . .

JA: Did you ever publish an article that you completely disagreed with?

AC: No, but I did publish articles that I didn't completely agree with, and that was when I began running the standard little line that said, "Editors don't necessarily endorse this."

SB: In this issue, volume 1, number 5 (1966), there is something new. Don McDonagh is a contributor, and he's written about the economics of dance: "Money for Dance: Who Gets It and How." And there's an editorial, entitled "Strike!" People are writing about the finances of the dance world.

AC: Social issues.

SB: Right, not the artistic side, but the practical side, the political side. Did this have to do with fact that the ABT [American Ballet Theatre] dancers were threatening a strike?

AC: Maybe that was an era when such a thing as a dancers' strike could be contemplated. I don't remember that that had been part of the scene until then. It was a new event. So we took note of it. Don was a big addition to *Ballet Review*. I must give him a great deal of credit. He's the one who organized us, more or less, as an ongoing institution. He got us the post office indicia that allows you to print and do bulk mail. And he and Jenny McDonagh both backed us. Gave us a place to sort or read the mail, and in his basement we would gather and have mailing parties every issue.

JA: When did you start publishing letters to the editor?

SB: Oh, here is "Correspondence," as early as volume 1, number 4. Let's see what it says. I remember that somewhere there is a letter from Jimmy Waring, criticizing an article by Jimmy Waring.

JA: David Vaughan does the same thing. I copied it from him once.

SB: Here is "British Critics," a letter from Mary Clarke, criticizing something—see, already in London they were protesting what you were doing. "To the editor, 'Protest, Protest, Protest!' Clive Barnes was *not* 'until a few months ago' the dance critic on nearly all our serious journals." And then David Vaughan responds, "I am so sorry that Miss Clarke took seriously what was intended to be a *jeu d'esprit*."

AC: I must say that's a good line that applies to the entire publication. That puts it in a nutshell. I never dreamed it would get so far. I mean really, it is crazy. In my mind it was a social good deed, but at the same time I knew it was half-cocked.

SB: In this same issue is your first obituary, and then in the next issue, another. These are two interesting obituaries. The first is of Frank O'Hara. And the second is of Edward Gordon Craig. And, appropriately, Craig's obituary is in the same issue as your review of a book about Irma Duncan's life with Isadora Duncan. Gordon Craig and Isadora Duncan. There is the end of a life and its associations—the end of an era.

AC: I wouldn't have known about Gordon Craig if I haven't read about him in Lincoln Kirstein. Although he wrote in a negative fashion, it was enough to make me look up the Craig writings. I also think David liked Craig, so that we knew who he was and what he stood for. So he only died that year.

JA: It's so strange. He must have been a hundred years old.

SB: It says he was ninety-six.

JA: The idea of Craig's living into the time of *Ballet Review* is very odd, when you think of when Isadora died.

SB: And Frank O'Hara, the poet, died in an accident the same year as Craig. You wrote, "He did agree to review books for us now and then, and was to have gotten around to his first contribution—well, any day now."

AC: Right. He was a very sweet man, and very sweet to me, for no reason at all. Didn't know me.

JA: He was a pal of Denby's, wasn't he? And of Bob Cornfield's?

AC: That's right. Someone suggested that I look him up, talk to him about writers. I didn't talk to him about writing, I talked to him about writers. And that's the only real contact that I had with him, about one hour. We were in his apartment, a very nice chat, a very nice man, and the next thing I knew he was dead.

JA: You said earlier that you had hoped to get Denby writing again.

SB: Why had he stopped?

AC: Well, if you want my honest opinion now, it's that he just simply reached the end of his interest. I think that he'd done what he felt he could do, with all honesty and with all his heart behind it, and then I think he felt that things had changed at the New York City Ballet, or that he'd said enough of what he really believed about Balanchine and then after that it would have seemed repetition. I think every dance critic reaches that point. I think he just covered the moment that was real to him. And then once that had happened there was no need for him to go on writing. And there was no place for him to go on writing, and he didn't want to write anymore for the newspapers. That was my idea, not his, that there was no place for him to write. But I don't think that was the reason. The interesting thing is he continued to go and see everything, and I think as a writer he just lost interest. Maybe not as an observer.

JA: Did you ever get anything from him?

AC: Well, we got interviews from him. He was very sweet about that. That's when I became reconciled to the idea of interviews. If you could interview an Edwin—and Edwin talked the way he wrote; it was all very clear and direct and full of stuff—what better? I was thrilled with those interviews because he really broke the silence for us.

SB: "A Conversation with Edwin Denby, Part 1." Volume 2, number 5 (1969). It is relevant to the anthology on experimental dance in the sixties for which we are doing this interview that this appears in an issue with an article by Twyla Tharp, "Group Activities." There is also an article by you, "The Avant Garde on Broadway." An article by Jack Anderson on Yvonne Rainer. The famous Elena Bivona on Paul Taylor. George Dorris on Satie.

This article by Twyla Tharp is a score for a dance. Were you the first publication that paid attention to her?

AC: I don't know. I remember very well the first concert of hers I saw down at Judson. I got excited about Twyla. I got interested in her way of operating as a choreographer and her method—those charts that she made. And I remember I asked if I could publish one of them, and she said, "Sure," and she sent me one, but it was in orange ink and we couldn't print it. So I had to send it back to her, and I said, "Sorry, we can't publish this," and she did the whole thing over in black. I thought that was fantastic, wonderful. Twyla was a great discovery.

SB: I think it was in '71 that you published an entire Twyla Tharp issue [volume 4, number 1]. "Twyla Tharp's Red Hot Peppers," "Twyla Tharp: Questions and Answers."

AC: Oh, yes, yes, yes. That is a lot later, by then she was famous. Yes. Twyla was one of the Judson people at first. They used to always link them—Meredith Monk, Yvonne Rainer, Twyla Tharp.

SB: Let's go to this article by you in this very same issue. This would have been 1969. There was a season on Broadway where these downtown people were being presented: Rainer, Tharp, Monk. At the Billy Rose Theater.

AC: Yes, there was an avant-garde season on Broadway.

SB: Tell us about it.

AC: It was business. *New York Times* leisure section news.

SB: And here is an article by Jack Anderson on Yvonne Rainer.

AC: By the way, by this time *Ballet Review* is not just people funneling material to Croce, but they're talking together. We have parties at Don McDonagh's house, and some of the ideas come out of conversation. So there is a certain amount of discussion about ideas, not that I ever formalized it in any way. But people had begun to be a little loose and free, and so things opened up in that way.

JA: One of the things that *Ballet Review* did for me was to tell me about the context of ballet. For example, the interview that Dale [Harris] and David [Vaughan] did with Bill [P. W.] Manchester, where they talked about Anatole Chujoy's *Dance Encyclopedia*. Suddenly I began to understand balletomania, how people who just love dance and go to it all the time finally wind up writing about it, and how encyclopedias get written. The world *around* dance: the fans, the scholars, the collecting of knowledge. Bill Manchester talked about Arnold Haskell, and she said that yes, he really was just a fan in many ways. But then she talked about his virtues, and it was the first time that I learned to respect balletomania and to think how much the balletomanes had contributed. That was a wonderful thing about *Ballet Review*, that it had all kinds— dancers, professors, groupies.

SB: In volume 2, number 1, you began the Reviewers' Ratings.

JA: Why did you start the report cards?

SB: Now, let me just say for the record who was doing that. Jack Anderson, Arlene Croce. Edwin Denby was doing Reviewers' Ratings! Yes, he was! He gave an A+ to *Rubies;* that was his best grade.

AC: Oh, he was being kind to us kids.

JA: You got something out of him.

SB: Leighton Kerner, the music critic. Robert Kotlowitz.

JA: Who was he?

AC: He was an editor of *Harper's* at the time, and he was a great dance fan and had written about the New York City Ballet. Then he went to Channel 13. He's a novelist. He left Channel 13 a few years ago. Anyway, he was a New York intellectual who gravitated to the ballet. You know. You ran into these people.

SB: Jack Kroll of *Newsweek*. William Livingstone.

AC: Of *Hi-Fi and Stereo Review,* yes.

SB: Don McDonagh. Constance Poster.

AC: She was a dancer. A dancer and a writer. She was married to a poet, William Poster. She worked down at Judson, and she danced with Judith Dunn. She was a very interesting woman.

SB: David Vaughan. And James Waring. So these were the first reviewers.

AC: They were the first. I will tell you—and I am ashamed to say it, since this isn't by far the most memorable feature of *Ballet Review*—that the Reviewers' Ratings had no function other than to take up a page in the issue. Because you see, the way the magazine was put together—you took a sheet of legal-size paper and folded it in half, which gave you four pages. So the whole issue was put together at the end. Now, you could fill the pages up at the beginning because you had copy for the beginning, but what about the end, where you would find you would maybe have as many as three blank pages? That's when I invented Reviewers' Ratings. They were charts. You could put them in or you could leave them out. They could be long or they could be short. Perfect solution. You can't imagine how crushing it was to me to discover that that was the first thing people turned to in every issue.

SB: In volume 2, number 2, James Waring grades his own ballets. Everybody hates Balanchine's *Slaughter on Tenth Avenue.*

AC: That's right.

JA: When you look back on the issues, which obviously you haven't in a while, how do you feel? Are you proud of them?

AC: I think they stand for their moment. That's the best we could do at that moment. It's just certain people with certain ideas; obviously some of them were terribly mistaken. But it's what we were trying to do within a certain range of aspiration at that moment. That's all they are. They're neither good nor bad. I don't have any opinion about them at all.

SB: This is the special issue on Martha Graham [volume 2, number 4 (1968)]: "Martha Graham: An Irresponsible Story: The Head of Her Father," by Jill Johnston, and "Tell Me, Doctor," by Arlene Croce. "A Chat with Martha Graham," by Don McDonagh. Why a special issue?

AC: Why not? I don't think there was an occasion.

SB: Now here's another interesting new feature of *Ballet Review:* competitions. This competition is on "tired old classics, brought up to date. Submit a libretto for a contemporary version of *Swan Lake, The Nutcracker, Giselle, Coppélia, The Firebird,* et cetera." But "suitable for viewing by mature audiences."

JA: This was another way to fill up space, right?

AC: Yes, right.

JA: Did you find that some people hated you? People still speak to me today of what they call the *Ballet Review* "club."

AC: Club?! I let in everybody. Everybody who wanted to come in the front door came right in and sat down and could write. There was no club. It's ridiculous.

JA: Another thing I'm curious to know—did you ever get any reactions from Clive Barnes? This is the mid-sixties. Clive is coming down hard on New York City Ballet. Clive would probably think of himself as the top voice in town on dance, and here are you guys.

AC: I attacked Clive.

JA: Yes. So didn't you get any reaction from him?

AC: Sure. He said "Look, here is five dollars; lay off."

JA: It meant he had subscribed.

AC: Yes. We all attacked each other. There is no consensus in *Ballet Review*, is there?

SB: No.

AC: You could drive someone crazy if you said, "What do these people have in common?" I don't think you could find it, could you? Well, I never thought there was a consensus, and I steered away from it. I wanted people to write what they wanted to write, so long as it was intelligent and of interest to more than three people. I was not striving for an ideological consensus—it was fruitless. Even if I had wanted to—even if I had wanted to have some kind of marching army here—there was no way to get it; New York was not like that in the sixties. It was impossible—there were lots of people who were interested in dance, and they had lots of things to say. If you wanted to publish a magazine, then you asked people to write about what was interesting to them.

SB: So you got things ranging from Judson to Isadora Duncan, from Fredrick Ashton to Merce Cunningham to August Bournonville.

AC: By then, you see, I'd learned my lesson about who should write. I decided that the people who should write were the writers. It was much better to get writers to discuss dance than to try to get dancers to discuss dance. Occasionally you would get a Carolyn Brown, or a Twyla would be a dazzling interview.

JA: Annabelle Gamson.

AC: Annabelle, yes. But these people were exceptions. For the most part, the people who really wrote were writers, whether they knew it or not.

SB: Who's Steven Smoliar?

AC: He's somebody who went to a lot of Merce Cunningham, and I think that's where I met him. A very bright guy. I think he was from MIT.

He was interesting. And he contributed. For some of these people, it just might have been the only dance piece they ever wrote in their lives.

JA: I think it was the only one Annabelle Gamson ever wrote. She said it practically cost her her life. I think you had asked her for it something like two years before she did it. And then she only did it because she was in the hospital and didn't have anything else to do. To me, a way in which *Ballet Review* seems experimental is not so much funny formats or pictorial novels or question-and-answer or whatever, but that sense of this being what these people have on their minds at this moment. David Vaughan submitting a piece on the first European *Sleeping Beauty*, at La Scala; no one knew about that before. It is like "This is July 1967. This is what we think this month; these are the thoughts we're having." That's what people used to value the *Village Voice* for, too.

SB: Here is a cover by Gorey.

AC: That's a brilliant cover, yes.

SB: It's volume 4, number 1 (1971), and the caption is "La Déesse Éclectique."

AC: It is a portrait of Ballet Theatre.

SB: She has three pairs of legs—one barefoot, one with toe shoes, and one with heeled shoes. And she has three pairs of arms; one pair belongs to a marionette. One hand holds a hatchet.

AC: Did we have an accompanying article on Ballet Theatre?

SB: "Ballet Theatre: Taking a Chance on Love," by Dale Harris. Now we're getting into the seventies, but I consider '71 still part of the sixties. "Twyla Tharp: Questions and Answers," "Twyla Tharp's Red Hot Peppers" by you, "Revolution in Connecticut" by Don McDonagh.

AC: About the American Dance Festival.

SB: He mentions Doris Humphrey, Twyla Tharp's *Medley*, and James Cunningham.

AC: James Cunningham had a moment. He was considered a very bright, larky, crazy, unpredictable, and then to me, ultimately rather frivolous and uninteresting choreographer, but he excited a lot of people for a considerable period at that time. Sometimes I felt that events carried the magazine and that I was just paddling along in its wake, that these things should be there because people wanted them and talked about them and were interested in them. It wasn't so much that I was. For a long time, things got into the magazine because I was interested in having them there. But then after a while I wasn't. That's when I began to think that perhaps I wasn't that interested in having a

Ballet Review

volume 4, number 1   **price 75 cents**

Cover of *Ballet Review* vol. 4, no. 1 (1971). "La Déesse Éclectique." Cover by Edward Gorey. Illustration reproduced courtesy of the Estate of Edward Gorey and courtesy of the Dance Division, The New York Public Library for the Performing Arts, Astor, Lenox and Tilden Foundations.

magazine. But you go through the transitional period of thinking, "Well, so what if I am the editor? So many other people are interested in the subject, it should be in the magazine."

SB: Don McDonagh was reviewing the season. If it didn't interest you, well, it was still the current season.

AC: I always think a magazine is as good as its editor. Ultimately, a magazine achieves a profile through the interests of the editor. At the beginning things were there because either I was interested in them or I could be interested in them. After a while, it wasn't like that.

SB: Because your taste changed?

AC: No, because the magazine got to have a life of its own, even on its lousy little scale. There was no money behind it. God knows, we could just barely fund each issue as it came on, but still enough people knew about it and were interested in it and would contribute to it. But ultimately, it just got swept up and had its own impetus.

SB: Didn't that reflect the way the dance world was changing at that time? It was the early seventies, wasn't it? The beginning of the dance boom?

JA: When did you start writing the Astaire book? What's the relationship between the Astaire book and *Ballet Review*?

AC: The Astaire book started with an article I wrote in *Ballet Review*.

JA: "Notes on La Belle, La Perfectly Swell, Romance."

AC: My infatuation with Fred and Ginger started in a series of their films that were shown in 1964 at Daniel Talbot's New Yorker Theater. He ran a retrospective, and he was the first person in my New York experience to do this. He showed every Astaire-Rogers film. Up 'til then I'd only seen about two. I went every night, and I became an addict. I couldn't keep away from the place.

JA: There were no videotapes then. You were completely dependent on what the movie theaters would show.

AC: He showed those films, and I couldn't think about anything else. It was my second great epiphany. It was very important for me. It meant that there was such a thing as American classicism that was there for Balanchine to ratify. I was in a dreamworld, I was so excited by it all. I think I really wanted to write that article, and that that very well might have been the reason I started the magazine, just to get it into print.

JA: That's a good enough reason, God knows. The Astaire book was published in '72. How did you manage? Were you still working for *National Review* at that time?

AC: No, I'd left it long since.

SB: How were you supporting yourself?

AC: I applied for a Guggenheim in something like 1970, and it didn't come through. People encouraged me to try again, I waited another year, and I won the Guggenheim my second time around, and it was with the Guggenheim that I wrote that book. I had another job. I worked as an editor for a publication called *Book World*. Terribly unhappy experience, awful. I must have gone somewhere from there. Oh, I know, it was the *New Yorker*. That was really fascinating, how that happened. That was when Bob Gottlieb came into my life. I published the Fred and Ginger book in '72. And a few months after that, I had a call from Bob Gottlieb. He said, "I love your Fred and Ginger book. Now, I think you should do another book. A dance book." I had left *Book World*. I was laid off. I had no job; I was desperate. I had also lost my apartment. So out of the blue came this call from Bob Gottlieb. I only knew him as the editor who did not lunch; I didn't know anything else about him.

SB: He didn't lunch?

AC: He was famous in New York as the editor who did not lunch. But he said, "Come to see me. I've got an idea for a book." He wanted me to write about modern dance. I said, "I'm not your person." And he said, "Yes, you are. Why don't you just look into it?" I said, "If you give me a little stipend, maybe. I will go to the library and see what I can find." And I started to go through the St. Denis collection—the letters, everything. It was in the midst of that that I had another call, from William Shawn at the *New Yorker*. Shawn said, "Come to see me." I didn't know what he wanted. He just said, "Come to see me."

We talked, and he said, "I'm thinking of having a dance column. Would you write it? We're starting in the fall." This was in May, and I thought, "I'll never live until the fall, I just can't do this." So I went back to him and I said, "I'd like to do it, but on the condition that you allow me to start submitting articles to you now. You don't have to publish them, I just want to see whether they are what you want, and whether I can do them." I had never written about dance for a deadline. I took months to write an article for *Ballet Review*!

We had a Bolshoi season coming up in June, I covered it, and I sent him the piece. He published it. We still did *Ballet Review*. Then *Ballet Review* went into another phase; Marcel Dekker bought it. They thought that they would add it to their string of journals, and they undertook to pay the bills. I was the happiest person in the world.

SB: It immediately became more expensive.

AC: Yes, because I insisted on paying authors. That was the beginning of *Ballet Review* as it is now.

JA: When did you let go of it, '78?

AC: Yes.

JA: How did you choose Bob Cornfield as your successor?

AC: Oh, poor dear, he just said he would. I needed someone to take it off my shoulders; I couldn't do it anymore. He did it for about a year or so. He was a damn good editor, he knew even more people than I knew, and he was able to do a few good issues. But he couldn't give it a lot of love. You have to think about it all the time. Every issue that you see represents about four times as much thinking and wondering and analyzing and substituting.

SB: Backing up to 1968, volume 2, number 4, in "Correspondence" there is a letter from Sergei Alexandrovitch, through a letter from Zora Astor Zash, and you say, "The following communication, together with its enclosure, is reprinted in its entirety exactly as received, in plain wrapper bearing, curiously enough, a London postmark." Did you know that this long polemic was from Kenneth King?

AC: I knew it was from Kenneth King. I thought Kenneth was an important person at that moment. I liked his dancing. People knew who he was, and they knew about his masquerades.

SB: In volume 4, number 5 (1973), we have "Notes on Music and Dance" by Steve Reich. This is always quoted: "For a long time during the 1960s one would go to the dance concert where no one danced followed by the party where everyone danced." What about the Bruce Lee stuff?

AC: Elena had fallen madly in love with Bruce Lee—so we pretended it was a dance subject.

SB: Well, this is what I mean by experimental. You could talk about the World's Fair; you could talk about Bruce Lee kung fu films.

What was the shape of the dance world at this time? Was there a sense of a changing of generations? Was there a pantheon of masters? Where were they headed?

AC: All of them, in their different ways, were approaching crises: Martha, Merce, George. We had no idea. When I look back on the sixties and seventies, for those who were making dance, life was in crisis. We took their work very much for granted.

JA: In the sixties and seventies, what did you think of Graham? Did you still have a lot of respect for her work?

AC: Yes. I thought of Graham as a great, great artist who had come to the end of her creativity, and who was trying to invent substitutes for it (and there were none). I look back on the entire range of Graham's creativity, and I see that she had done this many times before. But now the effort was exacerbated by the fact that she herself was no longer able to perform. That was the horrible part of that particular period for Graham. We didn't think about what Graham was going through in those days. The younger generation had written her off. Isn't that the strange thing? That a person who has shaped so much of the dance scene in your lifetime comes to the end of her life as a force, and no one is there to see her when it happens. You are all looking away, you're all looking at something else. Those seasons take place by themselves, you don't even go. Or you may go, but you don't really think about them. This terrible tragedy is taking place behind the scenes, and people don't register it.

People didn't register what was going on at the New York City Ballet in the sixties, that there was a crisis that had reared up between Balanchine and his dancers over what was to be the style of the company. I think what took place in those years is still being felt today in the way the company dances. The misunderstandings. That was a very critical stage.

I don't know that whatever we thought we could do about it would have made any difference at all. This is entirely up to those people— the dancers. It's their world. But I'm saying that the separation between the dancers' world and the world that we observe is very great. Even though we thought about it seriously, we weren't really doing a serious job here. Ultimately we were entertaining ourselves.

JA: We make the distinction between being a critic and being an insider. You were not an insider.

SB: But *Ballet Review* does have a certain tone of having insider status, a tone of knowingness, of understanding. Maybe the humor contributed to that.

JA: Also, you had people on the inside write for you. I do think that's important.

AC: I guess the dancers were satisfied that we were reasonably attuned to their situation, but when you look back now on the major events of the sixties and seventies, I think we had no idea of what was happening.

SB: You weren't a newspaper, reporting what was happening in terms of daily changes in staff. You did document those sizable changes, and maybe that's why you had your issue on Graham during her swan song. You chose to turn the spotlight on her just at a certain moment, and you did the same thing with Twyla Tharp at the beginning of her career.

AC: It was done out of respect. We respected these people enormously, but at the same time I don't think we knew anything about what it was really like.

SB: Maybe at the time, even in retrospect, you felt that. But to us, you had your finger on a crucial pulse, because these are important documents of their time. You say, "Oh, I came to Judson too late." But you brought out that Judson issue just at a moment when many people were looking back, saying, "What was the Judson after all? And why has it been so influential and important?" To me it has always been a crucial document. I still refer to it constantly.

AC: It served a little purpose. A lot of those issues served a little purpose. But when you think of what was really happening in the lives of the people who were making this dance, does this magazine matter? I don't think so.

JA: Don't be so skeptical. I know that for your readers and for people who were gradually thinking that they might write about dance, it was enough to have fresh minds applying themselves to dance, telling us what was going on that was new and saying intelligently why it was interesting.

AC: If only we'd been more serious.

SB: What would have happened?

AC: You'd have a much clearer picture of the reality of things. I'll tell you something. I started dumb and I ended dumb. I didn't know what the hell was going on any more when I gave it up than when I started.

SB: Well, then, you just lucked out.

AC: Yes, maybe that's quite true.

11

PAST*Forward* Choreographers' Statements

Editor's note: In 1990, the dancer and producer Mikhail Barysh-nikov, renowned as a virtuoso ballet dancer, founded the White Oak Dance Project, a small modern and postmodern dance repertory company. In 2000, with David Gordon, he organized PAST*Forward,* a project for White Oak that features both recon-structed dances from the 1960s and new works by several chore-ographers—Trisha Brown, Lucinda Childs, Simone Forti, David Gordon, Deborah Hay, Steve Paxton, and Yvonne Rainer—most of whom were members of the Judson Dance Theater. The PAST*Forward* choreographers' statements provide a look at the past by some of the artists who created it.

Trisha Brown

A questionnaire on career guidance in my high school informed me
that I should become a music librarian. I thought, quoi? Now, however,
I get it. My formal training at Mills College and summer American
Dance Festival courses with Louis Horst, the preeminent composition
teacher in dance, set me up to love structure forever. John Cage, in a
sublime performance of his lecture "Indeterminacy" (1960), coupled
with improvisation à la Anna Halprin, gave me space to fly, and I have
been ordering my esprit around ever since. Bob Dunn's class provided
the setting and support for his recombination of form and content (Judith Dunn joined later as coteacher).

The mounting of the PAST*Forward* project by the questing catalyst
Mr. Baryshnikov is an enlightened endeavor indeed. I gave him *Homemade,* a dance made in 1965 in which I used my memory as a score. I
gave myself the instruction to enact and distill a series of meaningful
memories, preferably those that have an impact on identity. Each
"memory-unit" is "lived," not performed, and the series is enacted without transitions. The dance was then filmed by Robert Whitman and
performed at Judson Church with a movie projector mounted on my
back and the film of the dance projected on the availing surrounds, more
or less in unison with the actual dance.

For Misha's version, I gave him the identical instruction "to enact
important memories," and his material was integrated into the original
dance. This new dance, a combination of both our memories, was then
filmed by Babette Mangolte.

I urge the audiences in attendance to imagine a nontheatrical setting
while viewing this seminal work by a collective of very young, highly
individual dance artists. Think raw, found, intimate, haphazard. Think
of a projected film wheeling around on the white walls and ceilings of
a church. It was unusual for a dancer under thirty-five to present a concert of his or her own work in those days, and the emerging artist was not
a category of concern beyond the artistic community we were primarily
addressing. The National Endowment for the Arts was not to be established until 1965. Pre-money, pre-theater, and abundant time. Time to
explore, fail, get it right, and, in my case, find the motor for a lifetime
of dance.

In my early conversations with Misha I requested that my current

Mikhail Baryshnikov in *Homemade*, choreographed by Trisha Brown. Photo © 2000 Stephanie Berger.

work also be included in the project, since I am not one who likes to go back. I can't go back. It isn't there anymore. Not the context and not the ratio of what the world does and does not know about dance.

Correction: I was able to find an excerpt from *Foray Forêt* (1990) to represent a more recent choreography to contribute to the PAST*Forward* project. *Foray* was the first piece in a new cycle of work called "back to zero." It follows the "valiant" series, dances focused on powerful movement, and is the transition piece between two cycles of work. I find transition pieces very interesting because, as I shift from known vocabulary to the unknown, you can see the wheels grinding. The excerpt you will see appears early in the choreography and is on its way toward the "subconscious" vocabulary of "back to zero."

The overarching subject of *Foray* is perception. In the original production, the music of John Philip Sousa was played by a live marching band maneuvering around the exterior of the theater on a path predetermined by me. The music therefore simultaneously accompanies two choreographies: one visible on the stage before the audience (*Foray*), and the other an aural deduction by the listener of a spatial pattern circling and passing in the distance. Add to this the mind working its way back in time through memories of other marching bands and their occasions of pomp and parade. The dance asks the question, "What do *you* see?"

Lucinda Childs

Nothing is necessarily extraneous to dance, including the professionally trained dancer's susceptibility to the influence of the movement of
nonprofessionals. The Judson Dance Theater concerned itself with this
idea. While some of the choreographers adhered to chance methodology
and task-oriented rule games to extend the range of movement outside
the traditional guidelines, I was among others who developed some different methods.

I used commonplace materials to explore movement activity outside
dance movement. Although the dances were composed in a unified idiom of action, I was more interested in a cumulative trend of activity
that did not follow along one isolated scheme. I therefore chose to create
sections within dances that focused attention on activity from different
points of view. *Carnation* (1964) has three sections: first, preparation
(for the moment); second, alternative options; third, follow-through or
completion.

My involvement with objects was subordinated to formal concerns
with respect to time and space in order to arrive at a tension equivalent
to any highly structured choreographic form while consisting solely of
nondance movements. This was a difficult and perplexing period as I
struggled to establish a plausible aesthetic expression in the midst of
contradictory influences. The making of each work felt like a rigorous
exercise in problem solving in which I was operating under an extraordinary self-imposed handicap. I was like someone religiously determined
to make an omelette with anything but an egg.

Concerto (1993) is based in the minimalist aesthetic using the music
of Henryk Gorecki. I continued to build phrases from simple movements, but the traditional dance vocabulary began to emerge. This vocabulary is essentially reinterpreted by me and my dancers in terms of
the dynamic that we use. Each phrase has accents in it, but the accents
are much less extreme than those I associate with other techniques. The
dancers are either moving continuously or absolutely still. When they
are moving continuously they maintain a vertical balance as they pass
through one position to go on to the next. The turns have no prepara-
tions, and the momentum of each phrase is never broken until they stop.
One sees in fleeting moments a typical dance position such as arabesque,
passé, tendu plié, but the dancers are only momentarily arrested in these

positions, or they merely pass through the end point of a position in the process of going on to the next one. Similarly, the arms are never fixed in one position or another but are used for control in executing changes of direction.

I have great admiration for the White Oak Dance Project company and their extraordinary ability to assimilate these two ambitious works into the repertory for PAST*Forward.*

Simone Forti

When I first got to New York as a very young dancer, I worked for a while in a nursery school. One day we had taken the kids to the park, and one of the boys climbed up on a boulder that had a rather sheer drop on one side. He had a crushed aluminum can on a long string, and he asked us to all sit facing the sheer side of the boulder. He slowly let the can down the rock face, jiggled and bounced it on sharp ledges, held it still, gave it sudden jerks, and kept everyone mesmerized for many minutes. It was a brilliant performance that has stayed with me to this day. But I couldn't really tell you if it was dance, or theater, or music, or what it was.

I remember the 1960s and 1970s as a time when visual artists, dancers, musicians, poets, and others were very much talking to each other. As a young dancer I was being influenced by what was modern in music and in painting. Robert Rauschenberg was combining objects, cloths, print, anything he found in the street, even using his bed as part of a painting, with a wonderful sense of composition. John Cage was arranging all kinds of sounds by chance. And introducing a lot of silences in his music, to bring a new kind of attention to listening to all sound. You could say it was an atmosphere of "anything goes." But that "anything" had to come from a clear source of longing or inspiration.

In the summer of 1960 I had a job as a camp counselor. We were going to take the kids on a hike, not for any real rock climbing but for some pretty serious clambering. I was in a difficult period of transition in my life just then, and I was very much looking forward to being in touch with the rocks and to the sheer effort of the climb. But I got sick and they went without me. The next spring I was invited to do my first evening of my own work. The idea for *Huddle* came to me very naturally. The performers join together as one solid form, like a small mountain, and take turns climbing over the top. I still find it very satisfying to do. Or to see.

Scramble, the other one of my pieces currently being presented in the PAST*Forward* program, came ten years later. It too has its origin in daily life. I was in Los Angeles learning to drive. I found the freeways amazing. How could it be that we could all so intuitively be changing lanes, weaving and blending in the flow in the traffic? This piece plays

The White Oak Dance Project in *Huddle,* choreographed by Simone Forti. Photo ©
2000 Stephanie Berger.

with the dynamic of several people darting and slaloming and scram-
bling through the spaces between each other.

Both of these pieces have a plain kind of beauty. The performers
are just doing what they need to do to climb or to sustain each other
climbing. Or they're just running and dodging in and out between each
other. Their movement is unadorned, the way a plain wooden bowl is
unadorned. And it's beautiful the way a plain wooden bowl is beautiful.

Huddle was first performed in the spring of 1961 in a New York loft.
At the time I was very interested in the work of a group of Japanese
painters and sculptors, the Gutai group, who had started to extend their
artwork into actions, or performances. For instance, Saburo Murakami
had done a piece in which he walked through many layers of paper
stretched across wooden frames. I was moved by the simplicity and
eventfulness of this very singular action. Another artist who very much
interested me at that time is the early photographer Eadweard Muy-
bridge. He had made some stop-action sequences of people performing
tasks such as chopping a block of wood. I was moved by this framing
of a moment of action and by the beauty of the ordinary body just doing
something. I saw *Huddle* both as action and as sculpture, with room for
people to walk around and look at it close up or from further away. My
intention was to have the onlookers be able to focus on the performers

just as they are, moving calmly and quite directly to accomplish the task at hand, and to have the onlookers enjoy the beauty of this singular form, the huddle.

Since then, *Huddle* has been performed in various kinds of situations. In 1978 it was performed as part of a longer piece, in a shallow fountain in the sculpture garden of the Museum of Modern Art. In 1982 it was performed in the sculpture garden of the Stedelijk Museum in Amsterdam, beside a reflecting pool in view of its outdoor café tables. When *Huddle* was done in an Avant Garde Festival at the World Trade Center Plaza, as the huddlers finished they each gathered volunteers from the crowd of onlookers and got several more huddles going.

David Gordon

I've written, directed, and choreographed plays in the last ten years, and I've directed and choreographed plays other people wrote. I've met up with dramaturgical questions and advice about "inciting incidents"— the actions that set characters and circumstances in motion. "Characters" are people, and "people and circumstances in motion" seems a good enough definition of a career in dance. Here's a casual list of some of the "inciting incidents" of my career.

Meeting and studying with Augusta Irving (high school English teacher), who kept within board of education guidelines by only unrecommending certain outside reading: "Under no circumstances must you read *Catcher in the Rye.*" She smiles as I jot down the title.

Meeting and studying with Ad Reinhardt (teacher in the art department at Brooklyn College), whose final exam begins with three questions: What is Art? What is is? What is what?

Meeting Barbara Kastle (fellow art student with live guppies in her fishbowl earrings) and following her to the modern dance club, where (before ever taking class) I'm a dancing troll in *Peer Gynt,* and meeting Judy Weinberg (Anitra), who takes me to watch the last audition for the witchboy in *Dark of the Moon.* "You there," the professor-director calls out, "the boy in the back, come up here and read for this part." Without ever taking class, I get the part.

Meeting James Waring in Washington Square Park in New York City. He assures me I'm a dancer, so I join his company and meet downtown dance/art/music makers, including Merce Cunningham and John Cage.

Meeting Valda Setterfield (the first day she arrives in New York from England), who starts to dance with Jimmy and marries me.

Taking Jimmy's composition classes.

Taking the Dunn/Dunn composition classes.

Becoming a father two days before the first Judson performances.

Getting booed for the first time at the Judson for the fifth piece I ever made.

Retiring as a choreographer and beginning to dance with Yvonne Rainer.

Meeting the Sato brothers, who open six stores named Azuma in New York. (I support my family and my dance career as a window dresser for eighteen years.) I learn that a store window is a proscenium stage and vice versa.

Becoming a member of the improvisational company Grand Union. I learn to think on my feet while performing (which is a lot like thinking on your feet while choreographing and/or directing).

Allowing myself to be persuaded, by Trisha Brown, to leave my charming Greenwich Village top-floor apartment (in an ivy-covered brownstone) to buy a loft in Soho (twenty-five years ago) with living space and a studio. I can roll out of bed and start dancing—that is, if I can stand up.

Meeting Misha Baryshnikov, who keeps giving me jobs I don't know how to do.

Staying married to one person for forty years.

Deborah Hay

When Misha asked me how I would like to participate in the PAST-*Forward* project, I thought of this paragraph from my new book, *My Body, The Buddhist* (Middletown, Conn.: Wesleyan University Press, 2000):

My interest has narrowed. I want to work with experienced performers who are interested in exploring the more subtle boundaries of visible performance consciousness, work which, understandably, has limited interest for untrained performers. I want to choreograph exacting movement content that contains no end to discovery, where milliseconds of stunning recognition take place within a strict choreography in time and space. Where soundless rhythms drive the dance.

White Oak Dance Project has commissioned the following two new dance works, described here by film historian Rino Pizzi:

Single Duet, immersed in the sonorities of Morton Feldman's *Piano for Four Hands* (1958), explores a hypothetical space where classical ballet training encounters the iconoclasm of the sixties. Lightly moving against the grain of a choreographic design dominated by stillness, Baryshnikov and Hay engage in a dance that seems to contemplate and reject at the same time the audience's expectations for symbolic gestures.

A choreography for six dancers, with a score composed by Alvin Lucier, *Whizz* explores with formal solutions the great range of possible aesthetic understandings of movement, dissolving in the process the assumed differences between learned and not learned action, behavioral and performed responsiveness, and even the boundary between audience and dancer.

I asked composer Alvin Lucier if he would create the music for *Whizz*. He sent three of his CDs, which I listened to at home, but I found that I didn't think any of the pieces would work. I called to ask if he could make changes to one of his compositions, and as the request came out I knew I was stepping on sacred ground. Alvin was understanding and suggested I find another composer. However, I was unwilling to let go of my aesthetic choice to work with Alvin. In the studio a few days later I again listened to *Clocker,* but this time it was as I danced *Whizz*. The parallels were very satisfying, and I called Alvin to tell him. He then made a shortened and special version of *Clocker* for *Whizz*.

In Conversation with Deborah Hay, August 2000

Q: When thinking back to the sixties and seventies, what interested you about making art and seeing artmaking? What interests you now? Is there a "then and now" for you when it comes to creating work? If so, could you describe it?

HAY: I don't think about making art and/or seeing artmaking. It is about my primary need for space to ask questions that do not require answers but instead stimulate vividly experiential inquiry.

In the sixties I was not conscious of a personal aesthetic. It was probably there, but I had relatively little awareness of it. Now my aesthetic is clear to me and it has become something I continually challenge. What is that aesthetic? Less is more.

I am at a time in my work where practically all the conditions I construct to determine both the choreography and performance of my dances are impossible to achieve, therefore, I am free from meeting goals that draw me away from my attention to dancing. For example, what if the past and the future are condensed within my perception of each moment of the dance? This deepens my experience without embellishing my performance or the choreography. This is what I mean by "less is more."

Q: When you think about the title PAST*Forward*, what comes to mind?
HAY: The past and the future in the present.

Steve Paxton

Flat was first performed in a composition workshop held in the basement gymnasium of Judson Memorial Church in 1964. I showed up
dressed in a suit. I watched a few other works, and when asked if anyone
else had something to show, I walked into the space with my chair. It
was the early middle of my ten-year obsession with ordinary movement.
It is difficult to reasonably justify this obsession, because to do so requires something like an appeal to the mystical, that area which is by
definition beyond words . . . yet I and several of my colleagues were
enamored of the concept; and although we spoke of it, I cannot recall
any conversation where we managed to really pin down the allure of
the ordinary.

Having written that, it seems obvious that ordinary movement would
have no allure. Allure was embedded in the mirrored technique classes,
the accepted glamour of the dance world of the times. Ordinary movement was barely noticed activity embedded in one's environment (here,
reference to the mystical, the parable about fish being unconscious of
water).

It is the job of dance students to bring the unconscious movement
of their bodies into the realm of consciousness; to form not only the
movements of their bodies but the source of the movements (in the
mind) into an array useful for patterning into the customary choreographies of their culture. For the student and the culture it is a precious
legacy, both the steps and their patterning and the way we learn them.
Cultural legacies, however, can be confining.

My inquiry was not so much about escaping the legacy of dance
as discovering the source of it. Where was something pre-legacy, pre-
cultural, pre-artistic? Where was ancient movement? This was the fascinating question for me of those days, and it remains my interest. The
answer, of course, was right under my nose. I placed the chair in the
space and began to stand.

Satisfyin Lover was first performed at the University of Utah, in
1967, where during a teaching residency I had met forty-two people
whom I asked to be in it. I was by this time more comfortable with my
obsession, and *Satisfyin Lover* and a companion work, *State,* were to
be the most essential of my essays in ordinary movement. In *State,* the
forty-two people stood still. In *Satisfyin Lover,* they walked, stood, and

one sat down in a chair. Apparently foolproof in their simplicity, I regarded them as failures. I did not foresee that the instruction to "walk naturally" would be impossible with the self-consciousness brought about by the instruction, let alone performing it in front of an audience.

I saw the resolution of this annoying paradox in an early work by Lucinda Childs, who placed the audience inside a building across the street from the performance space. She and the artist James Byars, dressed unexceptionally in shabby black raincoats, made gestures toward a display window, gestures timed to coincide with an audiotape of Childs's voice describing the building they faced. The phone connection identified the pair as performers: presumably conscious of that, and to some degree self-conscious.

By chance another man in a black raincoat walked by, and he stopped for a moment at the window. In the moment when I wondered if she had arranged this or not, my world was illuminated. Nothing changed, except my attitude. People on the street continued to walk. But now, I doubted them. Were they "real"? Of course they were?! . . . A distant siren went ooooh. The whole city joined the duet Childs made. This was the moment I had been looking for. (Thank you.)

My own failures showed me a few things. There was something about the play of consciousness/self-consciousness in front of an audience, and in the audience. There was something about the chair . . .

Now, thirty years later, I see chairs as an evil; and to the play of consciousnesses, I strive to better describe the interior place where performance occurs.

However preordained the choreographic concept may be, there remains a salutary aspect of the unpredictable, of-the-moment, that is improvisational, appreciated by virtue of being within a stable form.

And there was something about the human body . . .

Yvonne Rainer

The White Oak tour of PAST*Forward* is an undisguised blessing no
less than a most curious and unique cultural phenomenon. It is easier
to discuss the former. Misha's invitation to contribute to the repertory
of the 2000 tour was extended to me at a point at which I was trying
to decide where to go as a filmmaker increasingly exasperated with the
unreasonable economic and physical demands of film production after
a twenty-five-year immersion. To return to dance (after a twenty-five-
year absence) promised much pleasure, but also relief from being chief
cook and bottle-washer of my artisanal practice.

This particular opportunity to make a dance rather than a film was
accompanied by unprecedented circumstances of production and presentation. As an independent, somewhat underground filmmaker I had
been forced to assume the multiple roles of fund-raiser, writer, producer, director, occasional actor, editor, and postproduction supervisor.
Now, under the aegis of White Oak, I could concentrate on the complex-
ities of making—pure and simple—without my accustomed temporal
and budgetary constraints.

As for the "cultural phenomenon"—or more to the point, the "Misha
phenomenon"—that's another story. More people will see my choreography during this brief tour than ever saw my entire oeuvre from
1960 to 1975. And I'm sure this applies equally to the work of many
of my colleagues from the same period. Baryshnikov's presence and ce-
lebrity draw not only numbers, however, but accord a legitimacy and
seriousness that were originally brought to bear on our work by only
the most dedicated and persistent cognoscenti. The importance of the
tour thus lies in the attempt to retrieve an elusive zeitgeist, as well
as making the work available—and intelligible—in venues and to audiences that would never have housed it or been exposed to it to begin
with.

There are those who will carp on the question of "authenticity," protesting that the original performers were less polished, therefore more
like "ordinary" folks, in keeping with the ethos of the period. But there
is no way to replicate with any exactitude either the postmodern dancer's
physical "set" of the sixties—marked as much by training as by refusal
of that training—or the revelatory moment in which the bare feet, leo-

The White Oak Dance Project in *After Many a Summer Dies the Swan,* choreographed by Yvonne Rainer. Photo © 2000 Stephanie Berger.

tards, and tights of traditional modern dance were replaced by street clothes and sneakers. (Not to mention that notions of "ordinary" clothing as costume have been radically changed by mass marketers like the Gap.)

But questions of performance and appearance cannot be divorced from those of audience reception and expectation. For all of Misha's generous and adventurous validation, we cannot promise the present-day audience the same thrills of discovery that awaited a few of us (all too few of us, I should add) back then. We cannot promise the same intimations of possibility, the same epiphanies of shock and surprise. The same sense of triumphal entry through the palace gates of high culture, forced open to allow our rabble of poets, painters, composers, musicians, dancers, and friends to walk, run, drag, scream, fling, eat, or just sit still before the thirsting gaze of a new polyglot audience. We can't promise any of that, because that moment has passed and that audience has aged, as we have, and dispersed.

All White Oak can offer is a tentative and fragile sense of connection to that moment—changed as the historical and cultural circumstances may be—through this prism of reconstructions and new work by the same choreographers still going strong.

Trio A, 1966

(Excerpts from Yvonne Rainer, *Work, 1961–73* [Halifax and New York: The Press of the Nova Scotia College of Art and Design and New York University Press, 1974])

Trio A was first performed at Judson Church, January 10, 1966, as *The Mind is a Muscle, Part 1.* My memories of rehearsing it for that particular performance have merged with other rehearsal memories, some very recent. At that time it was performed by Steve Paxton, David Gordon, and me. I remember showing it to David for the first time; he expressed doubts about being able to execute it in the proper style. Now I say anyone can master the style, or just about anyone.

When I first began teaching *Trio A* to anyone who wanted to learn it—skilled, unskilled, professional, fat, old, sick, amateur—and gave tacit permission to anyone who wanted to teach it to teach it, I envisioned myself as a postmodern dance evangelist bringing movement to the masses, watching with Will Rogers–like benignity the slow, inevitable evisceration of my elitist creation. Well, I finally met a *Trio A* I didn't like. It was fifth generation, and I couldn't believe my eyes.

Contributors
Index

Contributors

Joan Acocella is the dance critic of the *New Yorker*. She is the author of the critical biography *Mark Morris* and the editor of the recent, unexpurgated *Diary of Vaslav Nijinsky*. She has also written books on literature and psychology. She was a Guggenheim fellow in 1993–94 and is a fellow of the New York Institute for the Humanities.

Sally Banes is professor of theatre and dance at the University of Wisconsin–Madison and past president of the Society for Dance History Scholars and the Dance Critics Association. Her books include: *Terpsichore in Sneakers, Democracy's Body, Greenwich Village 1963, Subversive Expectations,* and *Dancing Women,* among others. Banes is also a former editor of *Dance Research Journal* and the producer/director of the video documentary *The Last Conversation: Eisenstein's Carmen Ballet*. As a journalist, she has written for the *Chicago Reader, Soho Weekly News, Village Voice, Hartford Courant,* and *Dance Magazine*.

Mikhail Baryshnikov was born in Riga, Latvia, of Russian parents. He began studying ballet in Riga and after a few years was accepted by the Vaganova School in Leningrad, where he studied under the renowned teacher Alexander Pushkin. At eighteen, he entered the Kirov Ballet as a soloist and remained with the company from 1968 to 1974, when he left Russia. From 1974 to 1979, he danced with ballet and modern companies around the world. He was a principal dancer with the New York City Ballet from 1979 to 1980, and from 1980 until 1989 he was artistic director of American Ballet Theatre. In 1990, with Mark Morris, Baryshnikov founded the White Oak Dance Project. He is a 1997 Bessie Award recipient and received both the Kennedy Center Honor and the National Medal of Arts in 2000.

As a member of the Judson Dance Theater in the 1960s, **Trisha Brown** changed modern dance forever, pushing the limits of what could be considered appropriate movement for choreography. Since founding her own company in 1970, Brown has created repertory including the Robert Rauschenberg/Laurie Anderson collaboration *Set and Reset; Newark,* made in collaboration with Donald Judd, *For M.G.: The Movie,* and *M.O.* Her first opera production, Monteverdi's *Orfeo,* won the Grand Prix in 1999. Brown is currently at work on a staged version of Frank Schubert's *Winterreise* for baritone and three dancers. Brown has received five NEA fellowships and two Guggenheim Fellowships and was the first female choreographer to receive the MacArthur Foundation Fellowship. In 1988 she was named chevalier dans l'Ordre des Arts et des Lettres by the government of France, and in January 2000 she was elevated to the level of officier. She was a 1994 recipient of the Samuel H. Scripps American Dance Festival Award and, at the invitation of President Bill Clinton, served on the National Council on the Arts from 1994 to 1997. In 1999 Brown received the New York State Governor's Arts Award. She has received numerous honorary doctorates and is an Honorary Member of the American Academy of Arts and Letters.

Noël Carroll is professor of philosophy in the Department of Philosophy at the University of Wisconsin–Madison. He is the author of ten books, most recently: *Philosophy of Mass Art, The Philosophy of Art: A Contemporary Introduction,* and *Beyond Aesthetics.* Carroll is a past president of the American Society for Aesthetics. He has contributed dance criticism to the *Chicago Reader, Soho Weekly News, Village Voice,* and *Dance Magazine.*

Lucinda Childs began her career as choreographer and performer in 1963 as an original member of the Judson Dance Theater in New York. After forming her own dance company in 1973, Childs collaborated with Robert Wilson and Philip Glass on the opera *Einstein on the Beach,* participating as leading performer and choreographer. Childs also performed opposite Wilson in his play *I Was Sitting on My Patio This Guy Appeared I Thought I Was Hallucinating* (1977) and appeared in Wilson's productions of *La Maladie de la Mort* (1996) by Marguerite Duras and *White Raven* with Philip Glass (2001). She has collaborated with a number of composers and designers, including John Adams and Frank Gehry, on a series of large-scale productions. The first of these, *Dance,* choreographed in 1979 with music by Philip Glass and film/decor by Sol LeWitt, was awarded a Guggenheim Fellowship. Childs's choreography has been commissioned by a number of major ballet companies including the Paris Opéra Ballet, Pacific Northwest Ballet, Berlin Opera Ballet, Lyon Opéra Ballet, Rambert Dance Company, Bayerisches Staatsballett, Les Ballets de Monte

Carlo, and Baryshnikov's White Oak Dance Project. She has also choreographed several operas, including Verdi's *Macbeth* for the Scottish Opera and has directed operas such as Mozart's *Zaïde* for La Monnaie in Brussels and Gluck's *Orfeo and Euridice* for the Scottish Opera. In 1996, Childs was appointed to the rank of officier dans l'Ordre des Arts et des Lettres in France.

Simone Forti's roots are in improvisation, which she originally studied with Anna Halprin in the 1950s, and in the John Cage–influenced work of the Judson Church choreographers in 1960s New York. From her early minimalist dance constructions through her studies of dance behavior of animals, land portraits, and improvisational dance-narrative news animations, she has created idioms for exploring the "natural world."

David Gordon performed in the companies of James Waring and Yvonne Rainer, showed dances at the Living Theatre and participated in the original Judson Church performances, and was a founding member of a 1970s improvisational group, the Grand Union. He started the Pick Up Performance Company in 1971. Gordon has received numerous commissions from companies such as American Ballet Theatre, Dance Theatre of Harlem, Extemporary Dance Theatre of London, Group de Recherche Choreographique de l'Opéra de Paris and the White Oak Dance Project. He has made work for television, which has appeared on PBS nationally and on Channel 4 and the BBC in England. Gordon has been commissioned by the Guthrie Theater, American Conservatory Theater, Mark Taper Forum, and American Repertory Theatre. For his work in dance and theater, Gordon has won two Obie Awards, two Dramalogue Awards, and three Bessie Awards.

Andrea Harris holds an MFA in modern dance and is presently a Ph.D. candidate in theatre and dance research at the University of Wisconsin–Madison. She has been a company member of Li Chiao-Ping Dance and Contemporary Dance/Fort Worth and performed with the Martha Graham Dance Company in New York City and the Spoleto Festival of the Arts in the United States and Italy. Andrea has been part of the dance faculties at Texas Christian University, the Universidad de las Americas (Pueblo, Mexico), Sam Houston State University, and the University of Oklahoma.

Deborah Hay tours extensively as a solo performer and teacher. She has been the recipient of numerous fellowships from the National Endowment for the Arts, plus Guggenheim, McKnight, and Rockefeller Foundation Bellagio Fellowships. Her writings appear in the *Drama Review, Contact Quarterly, Movement Research Journal,* and the *Performing Arts Journal.* She has written three books including *Lamb at the Altar: The Story of a Dance,* and *My Body, The Buddhist.* Her choreography experiments with the nature of experience, perception, and attention in dance. Mikhail Baryshnikov said that working with Hay "has deepened my understanding of what we do as dancers." In 2002 the Austin Critics Table selected her as one of the first group of artists to be inducted into the Austin Arts Hall of Fame. She has lived in Austin since 1976.

Jill Johnston was a critic, columnist, and contributor for the *Village Voice* from 1959 to 1980. She wrote reviews for *Art News* from 1959 to 1965, reviewed books for the *New York Times Sunday Book Review* from 1985 to 1995, and has been a contributor to *Art in America* since 1985. Johnston has published ten books, including *Marmalade Me, Gullibles Travels, Mother Bound, Paper Daughter,* and *Jasper Johns: Privileged Information.* Her forthcoming book is titled *Carillon: A Tale of English Secrets, American Money, and the Making of Big Bells.* Johnston has also lectured extensively in America and Europe.

Stephanie Jordan is Research Professor in Dance at Roehampton University of Surrey in London where she directs the Centre for Dance Research and has overall responsibility for the doctoral programme in dance. A former dancer, musician, and dance critic, she now publishes and presents at conferences internationally. Examples of her publications are her two books *Striding Out: Aspects of Contemporary and New Dance in Britain* (1992) and *Moving Music: Dialogues with Music in Twentieth-Century Ballet* (2000), both published by Dance Books. For the latter, she was awarded the 2001 Special Citation of the Dance Perspectives Foundation, New York. Stephanie's next writing project is a book on Stravinsky and dance, which will examine recent settings of his work.

Deborah Jowitt began to dance professionally in 1953, to show her own choreography in 1962, and to write a regular dance column for the *Village Voice* in 1967. Her articles on dance have been published in two collections: *Dance Beat* (1977) and *The Dance in Mind* (1985), as well as in numerous journals. Her third book, *Time and the Dancing Image,* won the de la Torre Bueno Prize for 1988. In 1997 she edited *Meredith Monk.* She is currently working on a critical biography of Jerome Robbins. In addition to lecturing and giving workshops both in the United States and abroad, she teaches in the dance department of New York University's Tisch School of the Arts.

Steve Paxton began his training as a gymnast and has studied a variety of dance forms (Graham, Limón, and ballet) as well as Aikido, yoga, and Tai Chi Chuan. He performed with the Merce Cunningham Dance Company from

1960 to 1964 and was one of the founders of the Judson Dance Theater in the 1960s, the Grand Union in the 1970s, and Touchdown Dance in the 1980s. In 1972, he instigated Contact Improvisation, which continues today as an international network of dancers who convene to practice and who publish news and research in the dance and improvisation journal, *Contact Quarterly* for which Paxton is a contributing editor. He has published numerous articles in *Contact Quarterly* on subjects including dance for the physically disabled, dance for the visually disabled, dance analysis, and Contact Improvisation technique and theory. Paxton received Bessie Awards for choreography in 1987 and 1999 and grants from the NEA, the Rockefeller Foundation, Contemporary Performance Arts Foundation, and Change, Inc. In 1994, he received the Vermont Governor's Award for Excellence in the Arts and a Guggenheim Fellowship in 1995. Paxton teaches, performs, and choreographs in Europe and the United States and lives in Vermont.

Wendy Perron began dancing at an early age, studying both modern dance and ballet intensively. She danced with many choreographers in the early 1970s, including Sara Rudner, Kathryn Posin, and Twyla Tharp, and from 1975 to 1978 she was a member of the Trisha Brown Company. She began showing her own choreography in downtown New York in 1970 and later formed the Wendy Perron Dance Company, which performed from 1983 to 1984. Her work has been seen on public television, and she is one of eight choreographers featured in the documentary film *Retracing Steps: American Dance Since Postmodernism*. She has taught modern dance technique, choreography, improvisation, criticism, and dance history at Bennington College, Princeton University, Rutgers University, New York University, Movement Research, and the Trisha Brown studio. While on the faculty of Bennington, she founded the Bennington College Judson Project and continues to lecture internationally on Judson Dance Theater. In the early 1990s she was associate director of Jacob's Pillow Dance Festival and also curated programs at Judson Memorial Church. She writes widely on dance for such publications as the *New York Times, Village Voice,* and *Dance Magazine,* where she is currently the New York editor.

Yvonne Rainer was born in San Francisco in 1934. She trained as a modern dancer in New York from 1957 and began to choreograph her own work in 1960. She was one of the founders of the Judson Dance Theater in 1962, the genesis of a movement that proved to be a vital force in modern dance in the following decades. Some of her better known dances and theater pieces are *Terrrain* (1963), *The Mind is a Muscle* (1968), *Continuous Project—Altered Daily* (1969–70), *This is the story of a woman who . . .* (1973), and *After Many a Summer Dies the Swan* (2000). Since 1972 Rainer has completed seven feature-length films, beginning with *Lives of Performers* and more recently *Privilege* (1990, winner of the Filmmakers' Trophy at the 1991 Sundance Film Festival, Park City, Utah, and the Geyer Werke Prize at the 1991 International Documentary Film Festival in Munich), and *MURDER and murder* (1996, winner of the Teddy Award at the 1997 Berlin Film Festival and Special Jury Award at the 1999 Miami Lesbian and Gay Film Festival). Her films have been shown at major international film festivals. Her most recent book is titled *A Woman Who . . . : Essays, Interviews, Scripts* (1999). In 2002 the Rosenwald-Wolf Gallery in Philadelphia mounted a Rainer exhibition consisting of video installations, film screenings, and dance memorabilia.

Janice Ross is a dance historian and critic who has teaches in the Department of Drama and School of Education at Stanford University. For ten years, she was the staff dance critic for the *Oakland Tribune* and her articles on dance have appeared in the *New York Times* and the *Los Angeles Times*, among other publications. She is the author of *Moving Lessons: Margaret H'Doubler and the Beginning of Dance in American Education,* and she is also the recipient of a 2001 Guggenheim Fellowship.

Leslie Satin is a choreographer, dancer, and writer who lives and works in New York City. She teaches at New York University and SUNY/Empire State College, and recently was a Visiting Associate Professor at Bard College. She is also on the Editorial Board of *Women & Performance: A Journal of Feminist Theory.* Her writing has appeared in *Moving Words: Re-writing Dance, Performing Arts Journal, Theatre Journal, Dance Research Journal, Women & Performance,* and elsewhere. Since 1999, she has been creating and performing a series of dance-and-text pieces about travel, called *Foreign Currencies.*

Gus Solomons jr has danced in the companies of Pearl Lang, Donald McKayle, Martha Graham, and Merce Cunningham, created the leading role in Donald Byrd's *Harlem Nutcracker,* and currently performs with Carmen de Lavallade and Dudley Williams in the repertory trio PARADIGM. Solomons teaches dance at NYU/Tisch School of the Arts; he has also taught internationally, in Argentina, Russia, Austria, and France. He has written about dance for the *Village Voice, Ballet Review,* and the *Chronicle for Higher Education.* He writes regularly for *Dance Magazine.* Solomons holds a degree in architecture from M.I.T. and loves pockets, puzzles, and structures. In 2000 he won a Bessie for Sustained Achievement in Choreography, and in 2001 he was awarded the first annual Robert A. Muh Award from his alma mater as a distinguished artist alumnus. He also bicycles everywhere.

Index

Nature, 11–12, 45
Needlebrain Lloyd and the Systems Kid (Monk), 125, 130–32
Neels, Sandra, 110, 138–39
Nelson, Lisa, 143, 148
Neville, Phoebe, 106, 113, 118; choreography by, 126, 135n. 6; performances by, 114, 116, 124
New Art, The (Battcock), 119
New Dance, in Britain, 152, 157, 162, 163n. 8
New Dance (Humphrey), 144
New Dance (magazine), 152
New England Dance Theater, 63
New Kind of Love, A (Waring), 64
New Left, 33, 49n. 23; background of leaders of, 43–44; goals of, 34, 47, 48; guerilla theater of, 38–40; politics and culture, 27–28; values of, 40, 43, 46
New York Avant-Garde Festival (1965), 126
New York City Ballet, 166–67, 172, 176–78, 185, 190–91
New York Magazine, 147
New York Poets Theater, 58
New York Times, 58, 165–66
New York University. *See* Loeb Student Center, New York University
New Yorker, 189
Newman, Rosalind, 154
Newspaper Event (Schneemann), 6
Nichols, Nichelle, 105
Nijinsky, Vaslav, 65
No. 3 (Hay), 94
North, Alfred, 123, 128, 135n. 17
Norwalk, Jeff, 116
"Notes on 'Camp'" (Sontag), 67
"Notes on La Belle, La Perfectly Swell, Romance" (in *Ballet Review*), 186
"Notes on Music and Dance" (in *Ballet Review*), 190
Noverre, Jean-Georges, 90–91
Nowhere Slowly (Alston), 156, 160–61
Nudity, 128; in Mace/Lace spoof, 39, 44–45; in *Parades and Changes,* 25–27, 44–45
Nureyev, Rudolf, 166, 174

Obscenity, 26–27
O'Hara, Frank, 57, 181
"Old West and the New East in Cunningham's Dance, The" (in *Ballet Review*), 179

Oldenburg, Claes, 6–7, 20n. 22, 134n. 2
One Hundreds, The (Tharp), 145
One of No Way, The (Perron), *147*
Open Theater, 153
Opera, 134
Opus 34, 178
Ordinary, the: as art, 60, 88–89; blurring boundaries of art and, 82, 96; in *Combines,* 159–60; defamiliarization of, 5–17; valued by avant-garde, 3–4, 18. *See also* Movement, ordinary
Ordinary Dance (Rainer), 13
Originale (Stockhausen), 103
Orlando (Potter), 157
Oukrainsky, Serge, 65–66

PA RT (Paxton and Nelson), 143
Pageants, by Monk, 130–33
Painting, 61, 88, 118–19
Parades and Changes (Halprin), *26,* 33, 38, 43; challenging logic and narrative, 35–36; nudity in, 25–27, 45
Parties, Johnston's performances at, 100
Passloff, Aileen, 59–61, 63, 68, 69, 126
Pasquale, Liz, 146
PAST*Forward,* choreographers of, 193–210
Pastorale (Waring), 64
Pausé, Raoul, 55, 65
Pavley, Andreas, 65–66
Paxton, Steve, 96, 103, 134n. 2, 148; choreography by, 6, 12, 143; Contact Improvisation movement by, 17; in PAST*Forward,* 193, 206–7; performances by, 103, 210; use of ordinary movements, 18, 82, 93–94
Paz, Octavio, 76n. 16
"Peasant poets," 9
People: dancers as ordinary, 25–26; heroism of, 8–9
Perception, 196; influences on, 4–5, 10; Monk's use of, 127–28, 130, 133
Percival, John, 158–59
Perez, Rudy, 139–40
Performance art, 147, 152–53, 157
Peripateia (Waring), 60
Perls, Frederick (Fritz), 44, 47
Permissiveness, in dance, 29, 99, 113
Perrault, John, 128
Perron, Wendy, *147, 149;* background of, 143–47; and ballet *vs.* modern dance, 139–40, 144; at Bennington College,